MW00622533

ENLIGHTENMENT!

The Yoga Sutras of Patañjali

A New Translation and Commentary

by MSI

Printed and bound in the United States of America.
Second Printing
SFA Publications
130 Biodome Drive
Waynesville, NC 28786

ISBN #0-931783-17-8
Library of Congress Catalog Card Number: #95-061425

Dedicated to:
Iśa Iśvaram.
Your constant guidance and inspiration
made this text possible.

"Vitam Impendre Vero:
Consecrate life to Truth."
--Juvenal

CONTENTS

INTRODUCTION

The Yoga Sutras of Mahāṛṣi[1] Patañjali are the most concise formulation in history of the mechanics of the growth of consciousness from the Waking State to the highest degree of human consciousness, Unified Consciousness. They present a systematic and complete understanding of the psychological, emotional and physical transformations that occur as an individual develops full enlightenment. This process of development is called Ascension, or rising beyond the boundaries of ignorance. This text is thus the fullest formulation in the history of the world of the pre-Christian roots of Ascension.

Mahāṛṣi Patañjali was also known as *Govinda Yogindra*, "The Light-Filled King of the Yogis." He was commonly considered to be the Teacher of the first Śankaracharya, who revitalized the knowledge of Ascension some five centuries before the birth of Christ. Mahāṛṣi Patañjali was a fully conscious human being. *Mahāṛṣi* literally means "great sage." A *ṛṣi,* a sage, is an individual who has Ascended to the first stage of enlightenment, Perpetual Consciousness, which is characterized by recognition that the inner Self is Infinite, not limited by space, time or causation, one with the omnipresent One, the Creator of All that Is.

A Mahāṛṣi is an individual who has Ascended to Unified Consciousness, in which the inner experience of Infinite Awareness is also experienced outside, as the essential Reality of everyone and everything. Patañjali was

---

[1] -- There are fifty letters in the Sanskrit alphabet. There has not been great consistency in transliteration to English. For example, ṛ is often written ri; ṣ and ś are often written sh. So Mahāṛṣi is often spelled Maharishi.

established in this ultimate level of human consciousness. His text of Yoga was designed to help anyone rise to this state of human perfection.

Sutras are very short and concise statements. *Sutra* literally means "thread." The Yoga Sutras are the threads that together constitute the tapestry of Yoga. *Yoga* comes from the root, *yug,* which means to join together. So the Yoga Sutras are the threads that join together. Yoga is the science of joining together the individual lower self with the universal higher Self, the indivisible spark of God that resides within everyone.

Yoga is not a belief system or a religion nor even a philosophy -- it is an extremely practical methodology for systematically expanding the conscious mind. Said another way, Yoga is *the* Science for overcoming the self-destructive and limiting beliefs and internal programs that keep individual life bound to the experiences of the Waking State of Consciousness -- the state in which life is alternately happy and sad, loving and hating, healthy and sick -- in short, dual. Yoga provides a systematic ladder for climbing beyond the often painful experiences of the Waking State of duality into the state of non-changing Unified Consciousness, a.k.a. full enlightenment.

This is not a mystical or even a difficult or complicated process. Those who have thought that Yoga was difficult and/or complicated were doubtlessly basing their thinking on their personal experience, but that level of experiencing is not the whole story of human life, as this text will make clear. Perfection is within every human. Given this fact, it is surprising that so very many have failed to realize this.

Part of the problem stems from faulty translations of the texts that can serve in the development of consciousness. The Yoga Sutras are a prime example. Properly understood, they provide a straight and broad path for realization of the highest degree of human consciousness. Improperly understood, they are at best useless and at worst quite damaging.

Indian society is today caught deep in a quagmire of mistaken belief about the mechanics of realizing enlightenment. The custodians of the system of Yoga have so poorly managed its essential teachings that practically no one in the world anymore understands that Divine Union is perfectly easy to attain. The typical interpretation of the path to enlightenment is through renunciation, or giving up of the world. Expansion to Infinity by giving up! Nothing could be more ludicrous, given a true perception and understanding of higher consciousness.

Without full enlightenment, the attempt to understand, translate or teach the Yoga Sutras is doomed to inevitable and inglorious failure. The reason for this is only partly found in the vast dissimilarity between Sanskrit and our Western languages -- even the commentators on the sutras who wrote in Sanskrit did a woefully poor job of understanding Patañjali's meaning. The root cause of the perennial failure of the translators and commentators has to be traced to the dissimilarity of the translators' and commentators' level of consciousness with that of Patañjali. Even those commentators who were experiencing a low level of enlightenment did not much succeed in unravelling the knots of Patañjali's meaning. The greatest of the authors and commentators of antiquity was Vyasa. But the commentary attributed to him is deficient in several significant respects. It must be that Vyasa did not actually write it and someone borrowed his name for it, or else one of his later followers tried to embellish it and instead ruined it.

The prime problem area of all the commentaries is in the interpretation of key verses that make the practice of Yoga seem complicated or difficult or suitable only for those that are renunciates -- those that have dedicated their entire lives to being monks or nuns. With this as the standard interpretation of this system of mental development, small wonder that Yoga has been considered valueless by many in the West! Who wants to give up all enjoyment of life to realize enlightenment? Give up enjoyment to realize Infinite bliss? It even sounds absurd! Fortunately, it *is* absurd. It is not necessary; it is actually easier to continue with a regular, balanced life in the world and add the effortless and natural techniques to Ascend from the Waking State and accomplish Union. The mind is quickly absorbed by the experience of the Infinite when it has the use of valid techniques for the growth of consciousness; it is *never* a laborious, difficult or slow process.

As the growth of consciousness proceeds, every area of life develops -- heart, mind, body, environment. Yoga, properly understood, is not a system of giving up life. It is a system of adding to life.

When the world hears and understands this Teaching, all the age-old problems which have seemed so intractable for centuries will melt away with graceful and perfect solutions. There is no problem, mental, emotional, physical, societal, or environmental that can withstand the wholly beneficial power of Infinite Mind. When the world hears and understands this Teaching, world peace will be assured for all ages to come. When the world hears and understands this Teaching, global health, happiness and progress will be achieved for all future time. May this day come soon!

-- MSI

Dedicated on MahāŚivarātri, 1995

FIRST QUARTER: ASCENDANT CONSCIOUSNESS

YOGA is the Science of Union. The union of what with what? The union of the Waking State of Consciousness with its most expanded state. This fully developed state is called enlightenment. There are four stages of this development of higher consciousness; these are discussed in the four quarters of the Yoga Sutras.

The first stage is called Ascendant Consciousness. Ascendant Consciousness is the experience of the conscious mind settling down into its own essential nature. The self of the Waking State, with its myriad of contradictory and self-defeating thoughts and beliefs, is only a shadow of the Self that lies within. The Self within is quite literally indescribable (Christianity has done as well as possible by calling it, "The peace which passeth understanding"[2]) for it lies forever beyond the power of any words to describe, beyond the ability of the mind even to contemplate. It can, however, be experienced -- this is the purpose of the Yoga Sutras, of Yoga in general, and specifically of the First Quarter of the text. The experience of this transcendental Union is the topic of the first fifty-one sutras.

The First Quarter of the Yoga Sutras describes Ascendant Consciousness. Ascendant Consciousness is called Satori in Japan, Samadhi in India, often "the Fourth" in the ancient literature, the One or the Absolute or the Transcendent or the Infinite or Unbounded Awareness or Pure Consciousness in English. This experience is a fourth major state of consciousness, distinct subjectively and physiologically from Waking, Sleeping and Dreaming. In this text, we typically call it Ascendant Consciousness, for it lies beyond the

---

[2]-- "The peace of God, which passeth understanding..." PHILIPPIANS 4:7. Cf. JOHN 14:27.

normal experience of the Waking State. The name is irrelevant, the experience is everything.

To qualify as a distinct state of consciousness (unlike an altered state of consciousness, such as one produced by hypnosis or biofeedback), the physiological correlates must be significantly distinct and so must the subjective experience. The Ascendant State of Consciousness is characterized by expanded awareness and deeper rest than that of sleep -- the mind requires less energy to experience consciousness without thought; this causes the body to settle down to deep relaxation. In that silence and rest, stress dissolves.

The experience of the Ascendant is not enlightenment, but it is required to grow into enlightenment. The Second Quarter of the Yoga Sutras defines the first stage of enlightenment, Perpetual Consciousness; the Third Quarter deals with the second stage, Exalted Consciousness; and the Fourth Quarter describes the ultimate fulfillment of human evolution, Unified Consciousness.

The Yoga Sutras have been misinterpreted as the means to walk down the path to enlightenment. They are not. They are a description of the nature of enlightenment. Patañjali included no actual techniques of Ascension or Yoga in this text. His descriptions of the mechanics of enlightenment are so brilliant and clear, however, that many of the sutras have been widely misunderstood as actually being the techniques themselves. One purpose of this translation and commentary is to correct such unfortunate misunderstandings. Attempting to move ahead in consciousness by taking the Yoga Sutras as techniques for Ascension is impossible -- that would be rather like attempting to build a working electrical system and wire a house by reading a text on the nature of electricity.

Pada I. Sutra 1

अथ योगानुशासनम् ॥१॥

Atha yoga anūśāsanam

Now, the Teaching of Yoga.

The typical experience of the adult human mind is that awareness is rarely in the present moment. Scientists have estimated that the average adult thinks some 50,000 thoughts every day; these are almost without exception concerned with the past or the future or the distant. There is little or no experience of life as it is Now and Here. When we do rarely for an instant slip beyond the continuous barrier of our unending thought streams, we find that life suddenly becomes vastly different from our typical Waking State experience. Instead of being caught by regret for the past or worry for the future, we are free to experience life as it is *right now*, free from self-defeating beliefs and judgments, free from the limitations imposed by past experience, established in peace and joy.

Therefore the Science of Yoga begins and ends in the present moment. Everything to be understood about the transformation of life from suffering to permanent happiness, from failure to success, from ignorance to enlightenment is to be found in the present instant of time. Life in freedom is the result of learning to turn from the imperious demands of our past experience. Nothing can be done for the past, it is over; nothing can be done for the future, for it never comes; all that can be done is to make the present Ideal. Then the future will take care of itself. Perfection of the present instant is at once the goal and the means of the Science of Union.

In this, the very first sutra, Patañjali describes the entire process of the growth of consciousness from bondage and suffering to enlightenment. With the grace of a consummate artist, he opens his sutras in a wholly traditional manner that nevertheless contains in seed form the entire story of the 195 sutras that follow. All the rest are a commentary on the first three words: Now, Teaching, Yoga. But Patañjali is generous. In case anyone fails to catch this (and we have to assume, since no other commentator has mentioned the magnificence of the teaching in this first sutra, that very few if any have caught this), he will elaborate in detail.

The first word, **Atha**, is built up of **A** + **th** + **a**. "A" is the representation of the Universal sound of creation, the cosmic hum, the Alpha and the Omega of the West. It contains in the fullness of its silent vibration the totality of all that is at this moment of time. "Th" is derived from **Dha**, which means "bestow" or "give" or "compassion." The Universal wholeness of "A" with compassion gives the totality of the Universe. And to what is it given? Back to "A" again! The Wholeness gives itself to Wholeness, over and over again, eternally. The Eternal Now is recreated from within its own Self. Atha therefore describes the essence of the Ascendant: it is universally expansive, it is ever new, it is eternally the same. "A" is fullness; it moves from fullness to fullness by passing through fullness; it recreates itself perfectly in itself. The Universal Force for Good of the cosmos manifests itself in the Universal Force for Good in the individual. The Universe is contained within and furthermore is given to every spark of individuality. And all of this is contained, continually new and ever-new, in the present instant of time, in the Now. All of this and much, much more is hidden within the vibratory matrix of Patañjali's first word, Atha.

"The Teaching of" translates **anūśāsanam. Anū** means "again" -- this is the repeated sequence of experiencing the Now over and over again until it becomes permanent. A wise Teacher repeats the lessons with great patience and compassion until the student fully understands. Yoga or Ascending is a process of gradually refining the perceiving mind and senses until consciousness fully remembers its Infinite status. Anūśāsanam can also be translated as "rules, royal decree or governor" -- the role of the Eternal Now is to be forever in charge of the life, of the process of the growth of consciousness, of Yoga, of the creation of Ascendant Consciousness.

By deriving the word a different way (from śām instead of from śās), this first sutra could be translated, "The attitude of repeated Praise creates Union with the Now." Praise is one of the fundamental tools of Ascension. Another valid translation is, "Sitting in stillness again and again creates Union with the Now." Stillness, śām, can also be translated, "quietness, tranquillity, cessation." When the mind stills its noisy activity, consciousness experiences the Now, which is eternal peace. All activity ceases in that silence. By repeating this experience over and over, the mind becomes habituated to the Silence and stays there permanently, even in the midst of the most dynamic activity.

Which is the correct translation? They all are! The glory of this discourse is that so many equally valid meanings can be found in a single series of vibrations. The Yoga Sutras are a perfect expression of a fully enlightened mind. Anyone who desires to free life from suffering need only follow through on this wonderful, magical Teaching. All secrets of space and time are open to those who sincerely ask; there are no limits to the human other than those we artificially impose.

Life is meant for freedom, joy and continual progress. How is this to be accomplished? By freeing our experiencing machinery from bondage to past experience. Union with the universal Higher Self is easy to accomplish; it is only necessary to turn the mind away from the noise of the internal programming and experience the perpetual peace of the present instant, already present within.

Pada I. Sutra 2

योगश्चित्तवृत्तिनिरोधः ॥२॥

Yogaś chitta vṛtti nirodhaḥ

Yoga (Union) is consciousness with its movements still.

This sutra can also be translated, "Stilling the movements of the mind leads to Union," and "Union leads to the stilling of the movements of the mind." Yoga or Union is both the path and the goal. How to still the mind is described in sutra I.12.

When the surface of the lake is still, it reflects the full moon above it perfectly. When the water is troubled, the one moon appears as many. Consciousness in the human identifies with what it sees. If the mind is filled with the incessant hammering of innumerable thought streams, it is impossible for the mind to experience its peaceful nature. Yet let the chattering of internal noise still for even a moment, and the individual mind naturally slips into what the psychologist Abraham Maslow described as the peak experience. This is a radically different style of functioning of the nervous system; it is characterized by internal silence, clarity, joy and perfect fluidity of effective, life-supporting action.

If we carefully analyze the preconditions of the peak experience, we find that it naturally occurs in moments of intense absorption -- the "jogger's high," the "zone" of many athletes, the mystical union experienced by painters, composers, artists at the moment when, through intense enjoyment or focus, all the subsidiary, random, chaotic movements of the mind still and consciousness experiences itself, one without a second.

Transformation of consciousness is natural. What is unnatural is to continue with the mind hammering out its 50,000 thoughts a day, most of them the same as yesterday's, many of them self-contradictory. The body attempts to respond to these constant thought streams -- the neuropeptides the brains cells release to communicate with each other are read by every cell of the body, in every organ, throughout every system. What happens when so much activity runs ceaselessly through the machine of the body? What would happen to any machine that never shuts down periodically for maintenance? If you were always running your car without changing the oil, what would happen to it? Yet this is what we do to our bodies. Small wonder they start falling apart and rarely reach the century mark! The mind is never still in the Waking State.

When the constant chattering of the internal dialogue is stilled, Union with the higher Self is natural, for this is the normal state of the nervous system. It is the constant activity which is abnormal. Simply because the typical human only rarely experiences inner peace does not mean that the frenetic chaos of the Waking State mind is meant to endure forever.

When the surface of the mind is cluttered with noise, it is difficult or impossible to experience Union. With the surface of the pond broken into countless wavelets, it is impossible to tell exactly what is being reflected. So the requirement for Union is simple -- allow the mind to become still. How is this to be accomplished? Not through force or effort, which only raises the physiological rate and tires the mind.

Force or effort is often included in the typical translation of this sutra -- it is commonly said that Union is the result of repressing or restraining the movements of the mind. This thinking betrays an unfamiliarity with the natural condition of the mind. The natural condition of the mind *is* silence. If you drop a handful of pebbles into a still pool, the surface erupts in chaos. If you continually barrage consciousness with the movements of thought, it will be impossible to see what consciousness really is. But let the movements still --

even for an instant! -- and consciousness recognizes its Union with its higher Self, the omnipresent spark of Eternity that exists inside everyone, everywhere, always.

It must be emphasized that this sutra does not tell *how* to still the movements of consciousness. Nor does it suggest that strenuous effort is required. It is precisely the misinterpretation of sutras such as this one that has led to the demise of the effectiveness of the Science of Yoga. If we wish the mind to still, introduction of strain or effort will not serve us. On the contrary, by trying to force the mind to calmness, we will raise the physiological rate and tire the mind. Have you ever studied hard for a test? It is tiring work. Stimulants such as caffeine will succeed for only so long -- eventually the mind will be exhausted and impose stillness -- but it will be the stillness of sleep, not the stillness of expanded consciousness.

What *is* required to still the mind is an object of attention that charms the mind, thereby allowing it to settle down to more and more universal and silent levels of functioning. This object could take any number of possible forms, but the one universal requirement of the practice of Ascension must be that it is increasingly effortless. If it is desirable to still the mind, it is necessary to begin from where the mind is, active in the midst of motion.

Systematically quieting down the mind is the purpose of the Science of Yoga. It is not only natural, it is extremely easy. There are only three requirements. There must be 1) **a functioning nervous system**, capable of thought. There must also be 2) **a suitable vehicle** for the mind to follow in this process of stilling, a vehicle which naturally and effortlessly pulls the mind inward to ever deeper levels of silence, until even the faintest level of activity is Ascended and the conscious mind experiences its true form, the higher Self. And there also needs to be 3) **competent guidance** to ensure the necessary feedback that verifies the correctness of the practice. Thus it is extremely difficult for tapes or books to teach techniques validly, for the third requirement is missing. Even if the prospective student is proceeding completely correctly, how would he or she ever know without verification from a qualified instructor?

What happens if the movements of thought do still?

Pada I. Sutra 3

तदा द्रष्टुः स्वरूपेवस्थानम् ॥३॥

Tadā draṣṭuḥ svarūpe avasthānam

Then the Seer rests in the True Form of the Self.

The "Seer," **Draṣṭuḥ**, is the Knower, the Experiencer.

The "True Form of the Self," **svarūpa**, is the Ascendant Self. Other literally correct translations of svarūpa are, "True Nature of the Self," "True Condition of the Self," "True Character of the Self."

When the surface of the lake is agitated, the bottom cannot be seen. Immeasurable treasure could lie there, but it will remain undiscovered until the day the water stills. When the mind becomes quiet, consciousness naturally experiences union with its fundamental reality, the True Form of the Self, Ascendant Consciousness.

In the Waking State, we identify with our thoughts and do not experience consciousness as it is. And yet were it possible, by any means, to still the random, chaotic thoughts until there was no more motion in the mind (and assuming we did not fall asleep in the process), then we would directly see what consciousness *is.*

Stilling the chaos of the limited ego's individuality and perceiving the Reality lying within is the goal of Ascension, of Yoga, of every valid meditation; indeed, this is the goal of every true prayer. What is this experience like?

Hard to describe in words is the experience of Ascendant Pure Consciousness -- consciousness seeing itself, devoid of any thought. The reason it is hard to describe is that *any* words impose limits, and consciousness without thought moving is unlimited. The experience is that consciousness is without form, Unbounded, unrestricted by any of the familiar limitations of Waking State experience. Without the familiar conditions of thought, the first tastes of this experience can be so novel that the individual may not be quite sure exactly what just happened. When one Ascends the Waking State, thought stills and the conscious Experiencer, the Seer, is left without thought, experiencing consciousness without any movement of consciousness. This is the ultimate of subtlety; it takes the average person repeated experience of consciousness without thought moving to recognize exactly what this Ascendant Consciousness truly is.

An analogy might serve to clarify this. Consider a movie. Image after image flashes across the screen, giving the experience of continuity. The screen is not seen because the mind is focussing on the moving pictures. But were the film to break and the projector light remain on, the screen would suddenly become visible. This can be very surprising, if the involvement with the movie is very intense at the time.

This is like the experience of Pure Consciousness without thought. When the thoughts still, consciousness experiences itself without boundaries. Merely turning off the projector is analogous to sleep, for the movie is not experienced and neither is the screen.

Pure Consciousness, Ascendant Consciousness, the True Self, Absolute Awareness -- all these are synonymous terms. This is the True Form of the Self. The Self when it experiences transformation or change becomes the self with a small "s," a.k.a. the ego. The limitations accepted by the Self create the sense of I-ness. "I am so many feet tall, so many feet wide; I live here, this is my house; this is my past, these are my beliefs" -- these are the limiting thoughts that restrict the True Form of the Self into the narrow boundaries of experience. When these boundaries melt back into silence, the Self experiences its essential nature, which is Unbounded, unlimited by space, time or causation.

Ascendant Consciousness thus means consciousness devoid of thoughts. It is omnipresent, never-changing, Infinite, Eternal.

It may sound surprising on first hearing that our True Nature is Infinite, but that is only because of our life-long habit of identifying with the boundaries of experience. This has led us to consider the changing display of our thoughts to be the real us. Yet only still the mind -- even for an instant! -- and a whole new vista of unlimited potentiality is revealed. And that vista soothes and heals. The Seer *rests* there. "Dwells, stands, abides, remains, is stable, is established" -- these are all acceptable translations of **avasthānam**, here rendered "rests." Ultimately soothing, eternally peaceful -- this is resting in the Self, the experience of the Seer experiencing the Ascendant Self. That is the permanent and real state of the Self -- the movements are temporary and illusory.

The remainder of the first chapter is devoted to explaining exactly what Ascendant Consciousness is and what it is not.

Pada I. Sutra 4

वृत्तिसारूप्यमितरत्र ॥४॥

Vṛtti sārūpyam itaratra.

At other times, the Seer identifies with the movements.

The mind is like a mirror -- it reflects whatever is put before it. If the Seer is identifying with the movements, Reality is not experienced: the True Form of the Self is the awareness of the silent, Absolute Eternity of the present moment. When the mind moves, when it is out of the perfect serenity and silence of the Ascendant, then the Seer sees the movements and believes the movements are the reality.

This is the structure of identification, the root of the Waking State of Consciousness. The Seer sees only what the mind presents to it. If the mind is chaotically active, the Self loses sight of its silent nature and identifies with the activity. It is not that the Self *becomes* the perceived object, that is impossible. The Self can never truly be out of itself. But it *is* possible for the individual to *believe* that he or she is out of the Self. This happens whenever the mind is not still. At these times, the Self thinks that it is limited by space, time and causation. This is the root cause of all human suffering, mental, emotional and physical. This will become clearer as we proceed.

Patañjali is playing with the word, **rūpa** (form) in the third and fourth sutras. In the third sutra, he gives us **Sva + rūpa**: the form of the Self. Here we have **Sa + rūpa**: the form that resembles. The Self can never truly *be* the movements in the mind, but it can resemble them and think it is them. Sva without "v" = sa. What is this element of v? That which supports or sustains everything. The Infinite is the one support of everything that is. Without true perception of that, one experiences only the shadow of reality.

Vṛtti, translated "movement," is also found in the second and fifth sutras and a total of seven more times throughout the Yoga Sutras. Vṛtti is an extremely rich word -- it also means "whirlpool, rushing, gush, mode of life, course of conduct, behavior, addiction to, devotion to, subsistence, circle, appearance, transformation into." Thus it stands for all the play and display of the ceaseless activity of the mind, cycling around and around endlessly never seeing the Self, caught, seemingly forever, by the internal programs of belief, judgment and experience. Dragged downward into illusion, the mind falls, victim of its own beliefs in separation and judgments of duality. What it sees, it thinks it becomes.

Pada I. Sutra 5

वृत्तयः पञ्चतय्यः क्लिष्टाक्लिष्टाः ॥५॥

Vṛttayaḥ pañchatayyaḥ kliṣṭākliṣṭāḥ

The movements are of five kinds and are destructive or creative.

These five kinds will be listed in the next sutra and analyzed in the following five. Destructive movements of consciousness are those which increase the bondage of the Seer. Ignorance increases as a result of these; they lead to greater unhappiness, ill health and lack of success in every area of human concern.

Creative movements of consciousness are those which lead to the liberation of the Seer. These thoughts improve health, happiness, and increase success in every area of human life. Liberating thoughts gently remind the forgetful self that it is the Self.

Sanskrit is a wonderful language. **Kliṣṭāḥ**, here translated "destructive," also means "painful, tormenting, annoying, afflicting, damaging, wearing out, distressing, obscuring and forcing." Creative thoughts are thus not painful; they are comforting, soothing, supporting, healing, renewing, pacifying, clarifying and effortless.

When the mind is filled with destructive, painful, hard thoughts, awareness becomes coarser, more crude, and the nervous system and the body respond by producing unhappiness and ill health. When creative, not-painful thoughts fill the mind, awareness becomes subtler, more refined, and the nervous system and the body respond by creating happiness, health and youth. The quality of our thoughts is thus directly responsible for the state of our well-being, our progress and our longevity.

No illness springs into being overnight. Wrong thoughts must continue for a long time before the body's magnificent immune system fails.

This should (or at least can) bring great hope to the suffering of the world. It is perhaps difficult to cure a disease after it has taken hold of the mind and body. But it is absurdly easy to cure in advance, before the disease roots itself firmly in our being. Change the mind and the effects will change.[3] How difficult to pull up a mighty oak. How simple to pinch off an acorn's sprout.

This is skill in action. If you desire a glorious future, transform the present. There is actually no other choice. What control we have over our environment is strictly limited. But we do have complete control over how we use our own minds. We may have completely forgotten this fact; we may feel we are victims of forces, external and internal, that are quite beyond our control. But it is not so. For example, we have found in the teaching of Ascension that it is absurdly easy to reverse even life-long habits of painful, damaging, forced, dark thinking. The response is immediate and obvious. The lines of deep care start vanishing as the face starts glowing with its own internal radiance. Within a few short days, happiness, peace and health become the normal experience. It is not difficult to change the mind; it is only necessary to learn a new way of thinking -- thoughts that are liberating, joyful, light and easy -- in short, creative.

---

[3] -- It is interesting to note that another meaning of John the Baptist's word, "repent" in the Greek was "change your mind." Change the mind and the direction of your life will change.

Pada I. Sutra 6

प्रमणाविपर्ययविकल्पनिद्रास्मृतयः ॥६॥

Pramaṇa viparyaya vikalpa nidrā smṛtayaḥ

{These five kinds of movements are:}

Upward thoughts, downward thoughts, dreaming, sleep and memory.

These five will be elaborated in the next five sutras.

"Upward thoughts," **pramaṇa**, also mean "great, filling, fulfilling, true, satisfying, and nourishing beliefs, wishes, desires, perceptions and observations." Thus this kind of movement of consciousness leads directly to positivity, to health, to expansion of consciousness, to all that is great and worthwhile in the mind.

"Downward thoughts," on the other hand, mean all that is destructive. **Viparyaya** can also be translated as "inverted, opposed, perverse, altered, changed for the worse, disfigured, calamitous, unfortunate, wrong and erroneous thinking." Thus downward thoughts lead to all that is damaging in life, to greater bondage, to increased ignorance and destruction.

These two kinds of movements together constitute the thoughts of the Waking State of Consciousness. Downward thoughts include all the self-destructive beliefs, habits and judgments that make life difficult, that lead to failure of all kinds -- mental, emotional and physical. Upward thoughts include those thoughts that lead to liberation. Any thought that is directed upward -- toward Truth, Beauty, Love, Light, God -- is under this category.

Of the nearly Infinite number of possible upward-rising thoughts, a small handful can be considered to be truly liberating from the confines of the Waking State ego. In our experience, there are approximately 108 of these Great Thoughts (**Mahāvākyas** in Sanskrit) that lead directly to enlightenment. Of these 108, we commonly teach only twenty-seven, because these twenty-seven are the most universal, effective and easiest to use, given proper guidance.[4]

"Dreams," **vikalpa**, include all illusions and fantasies. See Sutra I.9.

"Sleep," **nidrā**, will be discussed in I.10.

The fifth type of movement of consciousness, flawless memory, is the most important of the five. Flawed memory, the usual experience of the Waking State, falls under the category of downward thoughts. Nothing is remembered perfectly in the Waking State, for nothing is experienced perfectly, as it really is. Rather, the previous impressions of experience and belief color every experience, every thought, so nothing is or even can be seen exactly as it is. Cognition of the True Form of the Self is a function of flawless memory, and therefore so is seeing life exactly as it is. More of this in the commentary to Sutra 11.

Nothing is remembered perfectly in the Waking State because nothing is experienced perfectly. ॐ

---

[4]--Without proper guidance, any technique will be likely to fail, for there will be no feedback to verify whether or not the aspirant is using the technique correctly.

Pada I. Sutra 7

प्रत्यक्षानुमानागमाः प्रमाणानि ॥७॥

Pratyakṣa anumāna āgamāḥ pramāṇāni

Upward thoughts result from clear perception, logical deduction and direct cognition.

Clear perception includes direct and immediate experience. It implies that the windows of the senses have been cleansed, that previous experience and belief are not coloring the reality seen as it is Now. The typical experience of the Waking State is that the past is never quiescent -- every experience is shaped and colored by memories of previous experiences. These operate on such a subtle level inside that it is rare to be aware of their existence. Yet, if for even the briefest of moments, we can slip beyond the limitations of our past and see life as it truly is right Now, we find that every moment is filled with glory, wonder, love, life and joy.

Clear perception and valid inference or logical deduction are impossible in the absence of the third characteristic of correct understanding: direct cognition. Direct cognition means those thoughts that rise without distortion from the Source of Thought. The Source of Thought is the unlimited reservoir of creativity, intelligence and bliss that lies within each of us. In the Waking State, this reservoir is far beyond normal experience, for only the most surface or manifest level of thought is perceived. So thoughts are appreciated only when they have moved through the nervous system and reached the conscious thinking level, the 10% thinking level, the surface of the mind.

Most thoughts making their way to the surface of the mind have been distorted by stress. They are no longer particularly filled with clarity, intelligence, happiness, love or energy. Previous life experiences and the beliefs based on those experiences twist and maim the original intention and purity of the thoughts arising from their Source in Universal Intelligence. The actions resulting from these diminished thoughts are necessarily flawed, mutually contradictory and weak; they inevitably lead to lack of progress and ever-increasing difficulty in life.

But those fortunate thoughts that arise purely and without distortion from the Source remain surcharged with energy, intelligence and bliss; they, being unflawed, never contradict each other (or the Universe) and therefore result in greater harmony, happiness and success in every area of life.

Direct cognition thus also includes those thoughts that have been expressed by the enlightened, for one quality of enlightenment is the ability to think and therefore speak without distortion from the Source.[5] Every valid scriptural statement falls under this category. Of course, the trouble in recognizing which of the world's scriptures are direct expressions undistorted from the Source is that it takes a mind that is incapable of being distorted to verify the reality of the written words. Thus following any book blindly in the hopes of improving life is about as intelligent as trying to learn to fly by reading a novel about airplanes. But for those whose mental instruments do in fact translate thought without distortion from the Source, reading or hearing the expressions of other such minds is a constant thrill of delight. It is never a matter of competition. A truly enlightened follower of any faith will see only the Beauty in all other religions.

---

[5] -- Compare this with Christ telling his disciples not to worry about what to say when they spoke his Teaching, for the Holy Spirit would give them all the words they needed: "Take no thought how or what ye shall speak: for it shall be given you in that same hour what ye shall speak. For it is not ye that speak, but the Spirit of your Father which speaketh in you." -- MATTHEW 10:19&20. Cf. MARK 13:11; LUKE 12:11&12, 21:15; EXODUS 4:10-12; ISAIAH 50:4; JEREMIAH 1:9.

Pada I. Sutra 8

विपर्ययो मिथ्याज्ञानमतद्रूपप्रतिष्ठम् ॥८॥

Viparyayo mithyā jñānam atad rūpa pratiṣṭham

Downward thoughts consist of apparent knowledge only; they are not a stable form of the Ascendant.

"Apparent," **mithyā**, can also be translated "wrong, incorrect, false, unreal, purposeless, fruitless, vain, temporary." It has phenomenal existence only. It is believed to be true today and false tomorrow. Thus apparent knowledge is marked by inconstancy. It is the realm of belief rather than direct experience, the hallmark of upward thoughts. Apparent knowledge is like a mirage -- it seems tangible, but there is no substance to it. Because it is not rooted in the Ascendant, the Source, it is not stable. Like a leaf at the mercy of the wind, it blows wherever the prejudices of the past impel it. It changes with the mood. It can mimic true love or happiness, but the merest change of circumstances transforms love to hate, happiness to sadness, health to disease, life to death. Thus downward thoughts are constantly changing, never stable.

Downward thoughts lead to greater bondage. Following through on distorted thoughts creates distorted actions which lead to distorted results. Since changeable knowledge is not directly linked to the pure or True Form of the Ascendant, and since it has been colored or distorted by previous impressions of experience, it no longer serves the purpose of Evolution. Instead of being a wave of happiness, love, energy and intelligence, thought becomes a wave of confusion and fear. This leads to action that reinforces the limiting experience that originally distorted the thought. Distortion feeds itself; distortion creates further distortion.

For example, a young person smokes a cigarette for some reason -- peer pressure, rebellion, experimentation are common causes -- and this experience makes an impression in the mind and a corresponding stress in the nervous system. The energy of thought always begins purely at the Ascendant, so every thought is initially imbued with the intention of greater happiness, health, love and progress. But if the rising thought stream collides with a stress in the nervous system, it will lose the purity of its original intention. This causes the thought to take on the characteristics of the limitation, of the deforming stress; in this example, the thought transmutes into the desire to smoke another cigarette.

This is the fate of most of the thoughts experienced in the Waking State. Because there is so much stress in the average nervous system, it is very rare to have a pure thought of direct cognition or a clear perception or a valid logical deduction about *anything.* Therefore life continues in difficulty and suffering. Breaking any self-destructive habit is extraordinarily difficult if the conscious mind habitually operates on a level that is more gross or manifest than the stresses and impressions of previous experience that are distorting thought and causing the damaging habit. The only solution is to rise beyond the source of the distortion and learn to pick up the thought in its direct, pure and distortion-free state.

Pada I. Sutra 9

शब्दज्ञानानुपाती वस्तुशून्यो विकल्पः ॥९॥

Śabda jñāna anupātī vastu śūnyo vikalpaḥ

Dreams follow the echo of experience; they are void of Reality.

Experience in the Waking State overloads the nervous system and creates stresses in the body. With the rest of sleep, these stresses start to dissolve; their movement creates the illusion of reality in the mind. In other words, the source of most dreams is the reverberation of previous experience. Attempting to derive meaning from the symbols contained in dreams is therefore largely a waste of time. Much more can be accomplished in the Waking State, given the appropriate tools and guidance, than can be accomplished by analyzing dreams. They are like the shards of the broken pottery of Waking State experience: difficult to piece back together, hard to manipulate effectively, time-consuming and of questionable value in the end. Time is precious. Why analyze illusions when so much of Reality remains to be understood? Enlightenment comes more quickly by studying Reality than by studying fantasy. There is wonder enough in the waking world to keep anyone enthralled indefinitely. As fascinating and instructional as dreams can certainly be, Evolution comes most quickly by focussing on transformation of the Waking State.

None of this should be taken to mean that direct cognition cannot occur in the dream state. It can occur in any state. Lucid dreaming does not fall under this definition of dreaming. Truth and Beauty can be found anywhere at any time. But it is not from studying dreams that direct cognition most easily flows.

Pada I. Sutra 10

अभावप्रत्ययालम्बना वृत्तिर्निद्रा ॥१०॥

Abhāva pratyaya alambanā vṛttir nidrā

Sleep is the movement that adheres to the thought of nothing.

Patañjali reintroduces **vṛtti**, "movement," here to reinforce his explanation that sleep is not a state of mind completely without thought. The mind completely without thought, it must be reemphasized, experiences Ascendant Consciousness (see I.3, commentary). When the stress of the day's activity becomes too great for the body to continue functioning effectively, when the fatigue toxins have accumulated too much for the body to deal with them efficiently, sleep comes to restore the balance. The EEG records that brain waves continue during sleep, they are registering a thought of non-existence or nothingness. A thought of nothing is not the experience of Nothing!

"Nothing," **abhāva**, literally means "not Being." **Bhāva** is Being, a common and useful word for the Ascendant. "Thought," **pratyaya**, also means "belief, faith, conviction, cause, idea." And "adheres to," **alambanā**, also means "supporting" or "foundation." So sleep is the movement of consciousness of non-being that supports the beliefs and causes the ideas of the Waking State. This means that the thought of nothingness underlies all the movements of the mind. Being remains forever Ascendant to the reality of the world; it remains forever beyond thought and experience. What then underlies and supports all the movements of consciousness? Not Being. Nothingness. This is a very abstract understanding of this sutra, and one that probably makes little sense to the Waking State, for one of the primary beliefs of the Waking State is that its thoughts and perceptions of the external world are undeniably real. Thus someone falls ill because of a wandering bacteria or virus; one ages; one suffers; one dies.

There is another way of experiencing Reality, one that begins with the premise that the underlying support of all thoughts and external perceptions is, in fact, nothing. If this concept can be understood, not intellectually, but as a direct and living experience, then the ability to redirect the world in any desired manner can be effortlessly accomplished. The transformation of consciousness that makes this a reality is the subject of this work.

Pada I. Sutra 11

अनुभूतविषयासंप्रमोषः स्मृतिः ॥११॥

Anubhūta viṣaya asaṃpramoṣaḥ smṛtiḥ

Memory is the absence of loss of the experience of objects.

Objects are rarely experienced exactly as they are. Previous impressions of experience collide with current sensory data to distort or color all images. The mind's natural function, to experience clearly and remember perfectly, is obscured when the nervous system is stressed. The experience will be improperly stored if it is not clearly cognized. This is the typical experience of the Waking State -- partial or complete loss of the experience almost immediately. The less is lost, the more is remembered.

Patañjali writes this sutra in the negative (absence of loss) to imply that memory is the natural state of the mind when it is functioning properly. When the experiences are not lost, memory is automatic. This means that when stress does not cloud the nervous system, eidetic memory is the normal state of human life. Flawless memory is our birthright; anything less is not using the machinery as it was designed.

"Loss," **pramoṣaḥ**, can also be rendered "theft" or "stealing away." Our experiences are stolen away; the memory fails. Who or what steals away the experience? Stress is the physical answer; conditioned responses, beliefs and judgments are the mental answers. The nervous system is trained to eliminate experience. The vast majority of sensory and mental input is filtered out before it reaches the conscious mind by the Hypothalamus and the Reticular Activating System in the brain stem. This of course serves a useful purpose -- it keeps the mind from being overwhelmed by excessive data -- but it also has the unfortunate effect of keeping the mind locked away from knowing anything as it truly is, right now. And this keeps the boundaries of the Waking State firmly in place.

When memory is purified, then no experience of anything is lost -- nothing is ever forgotten. The great teacher Śankaracharya, who revived the full philosophy of enlightenment about 2,500 years ago, once read through a lengthy manuscript one of his disciples had laboriously created over the period of several months. Shortly thereafter, the manuscript was destroyed in a fire. The disciple was understandably devastated. But fortunately, Śankaracharya had read it. From having seen it that one time, he quoted it back word for word. Such is the perfect memory of the fully enlightened.

When memory is perfect, the ability to remember the Absolute continually naturally develops. Having experienced it clearly once, flawless memory maintains the connection, for the experience is not stolen away. Everything continues always. Our perception of time is an illusion. Once experienced, always experienced -- this is the Teaching of this sutra. No experience is ever lost -- it continues forever in the subtle recording medium, which is called **akaśa**. Akaśa is omnipresent and infinitely flexible. It retains the imprint of all thoughts, of all experiences, of all sensations, of all feelings.

Everything that has ever happened to us is recorded by our nervous system. As the stress decreases, these experiences become available for review. It is a common experience in the practice of Ascension for a memory to float through about something that happened years before. This is caused by the inhibiting stress dissolving -- now the part of the nervous system formerly occupied by the stress is freed again for use.

Memory is the purest and simplest of the movements of consciousness; it exists best when the mind is not obscured by limiting beliefs and judgments. If the mind is troubled by noise, experiences and memory are quickly overshadowed.

Pada I. Sutra 12

अभ्यासवैराग्याभ्यां तन्निरोधः ॥१२॥

Abhyāsa vairāgyābhyāṃ tannirodhaḥ

By approach and detachment, the movements still.

Approach will be further defined in sutras 13 and 14; detachment will be explained in Sutras 15 and 16. Approach and detachment are two sides of the same coin. If you are walking from Paris to Rome, every step closer to Italy takes you one step further from the beaches of Normandy.

Approach means Ascending, the practice of expanding the mind to the Ascendant. As one moves effortlessly inward to more and ever more expanded levels of awareness, one is also quite naturally withdrawing from the outer world, the more contracted and bound levels of experience. By habituating the mind to this march toward increasing inner stillness and peace, the structure and meaning of life naturally begins to change.

In other words, it is not necessary to renounce with force or effort the destructive behavior patterns of the mind or the outer world. This sutra is not recommending a reclusive life of renunciation, even though this is how it is typically interpreted. Giving up the limited and limiting boundaries of the

Waking State is not painful or difficult, *as long as* this withdrawal is accompanied by approach, by expansion. Without the experience of Ascending, no amount of renunciation will accomplish anything at all. If thought is given up without inward movement to the Ascendant, the individual will experience nothing -- which is commonly called sleep -- not Ascendant Consciousness. On the other hand, by Ascending, one naturally gives up the boundaries of relative experience, just as one naturally removes clothes that have been outgrown, or just as a bud is lost when the flower blooms. This is not painful or difficult! This is a movement of purest ecstasy, a joyful movement toward Truth and Beauty. Only if we are looking out the rear window of the car do we notice where we have been, receding quickly in the distance. But why bother? It is so much more exciting and satisfying to look ahead!

The recluses have done a great disservice to this sublime teaching for more than 2,000 years. Ascendant Consciousness does not come from forcing the mind away from desires! The Fourth State of Consciousness is not the result of straining to restrain the movements of the mind! Such misinterpretations of these sutras have been a devastating blow to the simplicity and grandeur of the Science of Union. Who wants to grow closer to God if it means giving up everything you love and enjoy? This is not the path to enlightenment!

It is true that desires change with the expansion of consciousness -- desires are constantly changing anyway. That which was enjoyable as a child is not so as an adult.[6] But the path to freedom does not come from attempting to

---

[6]-- "When I was a child, I spake as a child, I understood as a child, I thought as a child: but when I became a man, I put away childish things." -- I CORINTHIANS 13:11.

force down or restrain desires! That only serves to strengthen them, for they build on the negative energy of suppression and take deeper hold of the mind.

Thus the recluse in his cave may or may not be more enlightened than the householder in his home -- it depends entirely on the internal experience, not at all on the outer lifestyle. The monk may, in fact, be much more bound to the Waking State, for by forcefully repressing his natural desires, he may have strengthened them to the point that he dwells on them *all the time* in his mind. The householder, on the other hand, by having natural channels for acting out desires, may have gradually risen to a much broader and more comprehensive viewpoint in which he or she rarely or never is bothered by vagrant thoughts or desires. The outer manifestation is nothing, the inner experience is everything.

The custodians of Yoga have betrayed this Science by their intense and rigid vows and unnatural restrictive practices as the precondition for Ascendant Union. Because of their faulty understanding, Yoga has not been producing enlightened individuals. Because of their faulty understanding, the most direct path to liberation from self-destructive beliefs and internal programs has fallen into chaos and uselessness.

Fortunately, the Truth cannot remain buried forever. It only takes an objective mind to see and understand exactly what Mahāṛṣi Patañjali meant. With this correct understanding, it should prove extremely simple to revive this ancient Teaching for the good of all humanity.

There is a wonderful old movie by Orson Wells, called **Citizen Kane**, that illustrates this principle of the effect of repressing desires quite well. Kane, a newspaper publisher, lived a life of fabulous wealth, romance, power, happiness, loneliness, health and illness. What was his last thought at the moment of death? Something of the great adventure of his life? Something of romance, or of one of the earth-shattering tragedies of his variegated life? One of his greatest achievements; perhaps, one of his monumental accomplishments?

No, his last thought was of his snowsled, Rosebud, which he had been forced to abandon when he inherited his fortune. Forceful renunciation is not freedom, nor does repression lead to liberation. On the contrary, it leads to greater boundaries. Unfulfilled and repressed desire does not magically disappear; it lurks just beneath the surface of the mind, seeking always its chance to escape and manifest confusion once more.

Pada I. Sutra 13

तत्र स्थितौ यत्नोभ्यासः ॥१३॥

Tatra sthitau yatno abhyāsaḥ

Of these, approach is the endeavor to reach stability.

What is the ultimate stability? The Self experiencing its own essential nature. There and there only does the flow of changes cease. "Stability," **sthitau**, can also be translated "steady adherance" or "duration" -- the aim of approach is not just to touch the Ascendant once but to stay there permanently.

"Endeavor to reach," **yatnaḥ**, can also be translated, "seeking union with," or "devoting oneself to." So approach seeks to unite the Waking State of Consciousness with its root in the unchanging Ascendant. How does this occur? By devoting oneself whole-heartedly to the practice, one arrives quickly at the goal.

The Waking State is characterized by movement, by continual change -- often in the twinkling of an eye, love transforms to hate, peace to chaos, happiness to misery, health to sickness. The weary soul seeks calmness and peace everywhere and finds it nowhere. But there is one movement of the mind that leads to permanence, to stability, to duration -- and that is the movement which leads to silence. Approach is the essence of Ascension. Without this built-in desire in every human heart, it would be difficult or impossible to move to enlightenment, for there would be no impelling force driving the expansion of consciousness. But because the desire to approach stability is built into everyone as our own nature, it is not only quite possible, it is completely natural and effortless to move into higher consciousness.

Again it must be emphasized that "endeavor to reach" or "seeking union with" or "devoting oneself to" do not imply arduous effort. If you sincerely desire something, you do not have to force yourself to go and get it. The action to fulfill the desire is the natural by-product of the desire itself. Trying to force yourself to do what you naturally want to do is not only a waste of time, it is potentially mentally deranging.

And yet devotion is not a passive state, it is ardent, zealous. Simply waiting and hoping for expansion of consciousness accomplishes nothing, nor does simply saying, "I am in Unified Consciousness," without having the requisite experience to support the statement. And endeavor is certainly not doing nothing. The mind does not reach the Ascendant by attempting to blank out thought or experience. Expansion follows in the wake of the practice of approach. The next sutra clarifies these distinctions.

Pada I. Sutra 14

स तु दीर्घकालनैरन्तर्यसत्कारासेवितो दृढभूमिः ॥१४॥

Sa tu dīrgha kāla nairantarya satkāra āsevito dṛḍha bhūmiḥ

But this becomes firmly established when it is continuously applied for a long time without interruption and with devotion.

"Established," **bhūmiḥ**, literally translated is "grounded." The Ascendant is the root or the ground of all other states of consciousness, of all other experiences, of everything there is. If one is connected to this ground, all of life works together for good. If one is not connected to this, one is at the mercy of all the vagaries of human experience, like a ship at sea without an anchor.

"Continuously applied," **āsevito**, can also be translated "service," "worship" or "addiction." First, addiction: in order to structure enlightenment, one must be persistent. Where one's treasure is, there is one's heart[7]. Most in our modern world cherish primarily the things of this world. We will work ourselves quite literally to death for our homes, cars and bank accounts, but aside from an occasional visit to church on Sunday, how much attention does the average individual put on the realization of the Divine? It is virtually nil.

There is an old tale that illustrates this point. A disciple asked his master as they were crossing a river, "Sir, how much zeal do I need to gain enlightenment?" Without the slightest warning, his Teacher leaped on him and pushed him under the water. The disciple struggled vainly to be free from his

---

[7] -- "Lay not up for yourselves treasure upon earth, where moth and rust doth corrupt, and where thieves break through and steal: But lay up for yourselves treasures in heaven, where neither moth nor rust doth corrupt, and where thieves do not break through nor steal: For where your treasure is, there will your heart be also." -- MATTHEW 6:19-21 Cf. LUKE 12:33,34

master's iron grip. Just as he thought his lungs would surely burst, his Teacher pulled him up and answered, "When you have as much desire for the Ascendant as you just now had for air."

One must intensely desire the goal, else one will be distracted by the cares of the world and be irregular in the practice. After learning a valid technique for expansion, regularity is everything. The body contains numerous circadian rhythms; it is only by matching the flow of life with the inflowing of consciousness from the Absolute that Ascendant Consciousness is quickly made permanent.

Second, worship: this translation underscores the word devotion in the sutra. A worshipful attitude is useful -- this is a holy quest, this learning to recognize the temple of God's Light in our human hearts. If we wish to see Divinity in all things, it is necessary to begin to culture the all-important tendency of worship. What is it that we are approaching? It is the omnipresent Source of all that is. This attitude naturally cultures the requisite humility, so vital to progress.

Third, service: the quickest road to approach lies in making every action a service to humanity. The more the life is committed to growth of consciousness not just for its own sake but to heal the suffering, illness and despair of everyone in creation, the more we will be continuously dedicated to the practice. The more we recognize that hundreds or thousands are waiting behind us in line, waiting for us to become part of the solution rather than part of the problem, the more inspired we will naturally become to help solve the difficulties of the world, rather than continue creating them.

"Devotion," **satkāra**, can also be translated "earnest action." It is necessary to be serious in our practice to reach the goal. It also means "the maker of Eternity," for this quality more than any other creates our awareness of the Absolute. It can also be read as "praise." Of the movements of the mind, praise is the most active and the easiest to use in culturing Ascension, which is exactly why the Praise Ascension Attitude is the first technique we teach. If we appreciate life instead of condemn it, if we seek the good instead of the bad in everything, our life is impelled into approach at a faster and faster pace. Quickly the entire structure of our existence transforms around us as we effortlessly rise into full human consciousness.[8]

Satkāra, devotion, also means, "kind treatment," "hospitable reception" and "favor." This is not a difficult path, this is a gentle and benevolent movement of life toward Life, of love toward Love, of happiness toward Joy. All good comes to those who follow this path; by seeking first the Kingdom of Heaven, all else is added.

---

[8] -- The repeated reference to Praise in the Bible shows the profound understanding of the Christian and Jewish founding fathers for this fundamental characteristic of the growth to enlightenment.

Pada I. Sutra 15

दृष्टानुश्रविकविषयवितृष्णास्य वशीकारसंज्ञा वैराग्यम् ॥१५॥

Dṛṣṭa anuśravika viṣaya vitṛṣṇasya vaśīkāra saṃjña vairāgyam

Detachment is the mastery of consciousness that cuts asunder the taste for the seen, the heard and the experienced.

"Mastery," **vaśīkāra**, in this sutra is the by-product of the devotion -- **satkāra** -- of the last sutra. Both words come from the same root, **kāra**, which literally means "the maker" or "the doer". In the satkāra of the last sutra, the doer (kāra) was directed toward Sat, the Eternal, the Real, the Ascendant. Here, in vaśīkāra, the doer is directed toward self-mastery. **Vaśī** means "ruling" or "self-control." How is the ego to be mastered? By praise, devotion and earnest action, action toward the Real, the Ascendant. Detachment is thus not a technique in itself; any who would attempt to grow in Ascendant Consciousness by cutting away the objects of sensual enjoyment and experience will fail, for the taste for them will persist.[9]

Taste here means addictive or compulsive attachment. If one is continually, without ceasing, praising or devoted to the Ascendant, the taste for relative experience naturally decreases and ceases to bind the mind. What is it that is so very sticky about habitual self-destructive internal programs? They are continually being reinforced by repeated experience. How does one break free from the pull of the past? Only by releasing consciousness from the fetters of the Waking State. By experiencing the Ascendant, the binding influence of the past falls away.

---

[9] -- Compare this with II.59 of the **Bhagavad Gita**: "The objects of sense turn away from those who abstain from them, but the taste for them remains. But even the taste ends when the Ultimate is seen."

This sutra does not mean that those who are growing in consciousness are becoming less involved in the world. Quite the contrary result is the response from Ascending. When one is freed from the binding influence of desire, one can focus without distraction and choose naturally for what one *really* wants. When desire is not undermined by addictive or compulsive behavior, it naturally flows in concordance with the forces of evolution -- this leads to fulfillment in every area of human concern. It is when the individual acts from addiction that life is caught by the boundaries of ignorance. Thus detachment reestablishes the doer in his or her correct relationship with the world -- that of the master, rather than that of a slave. We are born to steer the ship of our life safely to our goal; we are not born to founder on the shoals or reefs of outrageous experience.

Pada I. Sutra 16

तत्परं पुरूषख्यातेर्गुणवैतृष्णयम् ॥१६॥

Tat paraṃ purūṣa khyāter guṇavaitṛṣṇyam

The supreme detachment occurs when awareness of the Ascendant cuts asunder all attachment to even the fundamental forces of nature, the guṇas.

The three fundamental forces of nature, the guṇas, are responsible for the creation, maintenance and destruction of everything in the Universe. This sutra says that by arriving at the goal, the Ascendant, all attachment for the relative is severed. This has three different levels: 1) in the experience of the Fourth State of Consciousness, Ascendant Consciousness; 2) in the experience of Perpetual Consciousness, the first stage of enlightenment; and 3) in the experience of Unified Consciousness, Absolute Oneness, the highest degree of enlightenment.

Supreme detachment occurs in Ascendant Consciousness, because the individual awareness is completely absorbed in the Absolute. There is no potential for attachment to the guṇas, because there is no experience of anything other than the Infinite Silence of the Ascendant. But this experience is temporary; coming out from this state, one again is caught by the binding influence of action.

When, by repeated experience of the Ascendant, the stress in the central nervous system is sufficiently dissolved that one does not lose the awareness of the Ascendant even in the midst of dynamic activity, one has established Perpetual Consciousness, the first level of enlightenment. In this state, one completely and permanently retains the awareness of the Ascendant and therefore is completely separate from the field of activity. One is permanently withdrawn from the guṇas of nature. Life continues very much as before on the outside, but the individual is separate on the inside from attachment to action or desire.

This can be visualized by thinking of a boat on the surface of the ocean. If it has no anchor, it is tossed about by the waves and is carried away by the wind. But if it is anchored to the silent depths, it will not be swamped by the storms or run aground by the tides. Perpetual Consciousness is a state of being permanently anchored to inner silence and stability; the changes of the outer world cannot ruin or even damage life.

But the supreme value of detachment occurs in Unified Consciousness, when even the outermost field of activity is also experienced as being Infinite. The Absolute is not just lived inside, it is lived on the outside as well. In this state, there is no attachment, no desire, no taste for anything of the relative Universe, for everything of the relative Universe, even the most fundamental forces, the laws of Nature and their moving power, everything everywhere always is experienced as being nothing other than the Ascendant. In this state, there is no potential to be attached to anything of lesser value on the inside or the outside. This state of Unified Consciousness is called Absolute Freedom, for one is permanently freed from all previous beliefs, experiences and limitations. Life is experienced in its full, Infinite value on both the inside and the outside.

Pada I. Sutra 17

वितर्कविचारानन्दास्मितारूपानुगमात् संप्रज्ञातः ॥१७॥

Vitarka vichāra ānanda asmita rūpa anugamāt samprajñātaḥ

These are the stages that develop Ascendant Consciousness: Surface, Meaning, Feeling and Knowing.

These are not four distinct practices, they are the four degrees of increasing subtlety in Ascension. These four will be explained in greater detail in sutras 42 to 50.

The range of Surface is from contemplation to inward-directed Ascension. Contemplation means, "thinking about." In this stage of development of consciousness, one begins to question the why of individual existence. By repeatedly experiencing self-destructive internal programs and the tenacity of life-damaging habits, one starts to be disenchanted by life in the Waking State and begins to seek alternatives. When this stage develops, one is no longer content with receiving answers from external authority figures. The desire comes to know the Truth directly, without having it filtered through other human nervous systems of the present or the past. The questing soul begins to seek ever more deeply for meaning beneath the surface of experience and belief.

In time, sincere contemplation leads to the conclusion that the answers to life's fundamental questions will never be had from the outside, nor even by thinking *about* the nature of Reality. The hunger grows ever more strongly to experience Reality directly, not just think about it. This then naturally leads to the desire to move inward more deeply, to quest vertically rather than horizontally for True Knowledge. And this then will in time lead to the practice of an inward-directed technique of Ascension.

Any valid technique of Ascension takes the awareness from the surface of the mind to more expanded levels of experience. With a true Ascension, the thought used as a vehicle for the inward march of the mind automatically becomes subtler and subtler. Thus any valid technique always rises beyond or Ascends its own structure. Contemplation is very like walking on the surface of the land; Ascending is like floating into the Heavens.

As one leaves the surface, there are several distinct transformations of the process that lie within. In other words, contained within the vehicle for Ascending are increasing levels of subtlety. The first of these Patañjali calls Meaning. Meaning does *not* mean thinking *about* the meaning -- that is still just contemplation and keeps the mind restricted to the surface. Meaning is the spontaneous experience of the full range of the meaning of the vehicle used for Ascending; this full range is automatically experienced as the mind is pulled inward.

If the vehicle for Ascending were the word, "Mother," for example, the Meaning aspect would be what Mother means -- not just a dictionary definition, but the full composite of every thought, experience, belief and judgment one has ever had about mothers, might have had, or even wished to have had. This is obviously not a matter of contemplation; it is a matter of direct experience.

The next level of subtlety is Feeling. One learns what the vehicle for Ascending *feels* like in this level of increasing abstraction. In our example, what is the full range of the feelings associated with Mother? Again, this experience does not come from thinking about Mother or attempting to mood-make what Mother feels like; it comes automatically by opening oneself to that level of experience.

Feeling is much subtler than Meaning. A child could intellectually understand that Mother is at home, but unless the feeling is there, there will be a subtle level of anxiety that will affect the comfort of play. But let the *feeling* be there, "My Mother is at home"; the child's courage is boundless.

Or a scientist might *understand* a theory, but her support for it will depend on whether or not she *feels* it is right. A scientist, dedicated to objective knowledge, has no business being effected by feelings -- but who cannot be?

Already built into every valid vehicle for Ascending are the Meaning and Feeling levels. All true Ascension techniques are manifestations of the purest feeling level of life -- pure bliss. So the fullest development of this stage of meditation is accompanied by the form of bliss. Joy spontaneously wells up ever more forcefully inside; the increasing happiness of the inward movement of mind takes over and impels one more and more quickly toward the Ascendant. No effort is required for this to occur: the natural tendency of the mind to enjoy fuels this inward march into more refined or expanded levels of awareness as one becomes familiar with Feeling.

In meditations that attempt to Ascend using meaningless sounds, "blacking out" often occurs at this stage, for it is extremely difficult for the mind to remain awake and alert if the Meaning and Feeling levels are cut off from the vehicle for Ascending. This is why the teaching of many Eastern meditations is less effective in the West -- in India, everyone knows the meaning of the mantras taught as the vehicles for meditating, so the subtle Meaning and Feeling levels are naturally engaged throughout the practice. As one Ascends, one remains awake if one knows something about the vehicle being used.

Correctly practiced, Ascension naturally refines further into pure Knowing -- the direct cognition of the *full* meaning of the vehicle for Ascension. (This will be explained further in the commentary on the 48th sutra.) This fourth stage is accompanied by the clear experience of the individual Self.

In the Waking State, there is little or no understanding of who one really is. Past limiting beliefs, judgments and habits are so deeply ingrained that there is almost no perception of the true grandeur and dignity of the individual -- that pure spark of crystallized Divinity in human form. Most of the opinions about the Self have been gathered from others -- parents, siblings, teachers, ministers, friends, doctors, society. These opinions cripple freedom of choice, independence of thought and the expression of creativity.

So after the experience of pure bliss impels the meditator inward comes the experience of the pure "I-ness" of the individual. This is not yet Ascendant Consciousness (Ascendant Consciousness will be described in the next two sutras), but it is only one step removed from it. From there, it is a small jump to the full use of the enlightened intellect, the smallest crossing from the experience of pure individuality to the experience of pure Ascendant Consciousness.

It must be stated again and again that this inward march of the mind does not consist of four different practices. One properly chosen vehicle will take the awareness from the surface of the mind to the silent depths in the ocean of Infinity. This practice is difficult to describe in words, but extremely easy to learn and practice. All that is needed is appropriate guidance from a qualified Teacher -- one who has walked down this path sufficient times to teach others how to do the same thing.

There are those born into higher consciousness, or who fall into it very early on in life. They often consider themselves avatars, with good reason -- they have realized that they are an indivisible spark of God. But such people are rarely if ever Teachers, for they know nothing of the path for others to follow to reach the goal of enlightenment. In other words, to properly Teach others, it is not sufficient to *be* enlightened -- it is also required to know exactly *how* you became enlightened in order to be able to help others to become enlightened. Simply smiling at those in the Waking State with love or demonstrating the powers of your own enlightenment may be a very nice blessing to them, but what they *need* is a path to remember who they are -- how to move from the boundaries of ignorance to the Unbounded Ocean of Infinite Bliss.

Pada I. Sutra 18

विरामप्रत्ययाभ्यासपूर्वः संस्कारशेषोन्यः ॥१८॥

Virāma pratyaya abhyāsa pūrvah saṃskāra śeṣo'nyaḥ

When thoughts cease because of approach, all other impressions become dormant.

Approach is defined in the commentaries on Sutras 12, 13 and 14.

The impressions (saṃskāra) referred to are the internal programs -- the beliefs, memories of experience, judgments, stresses and habits -- that structure and maintain the individuality. Thus when thought has completely stilled and the individual experiences Ascendant Consciousness, even the sense of "I-ness" melts into universality. It is not that the impulses of individuality are gone when the conscious mind experiences the Ascendant; rather, they wait in a dormant or resting state. As soon as awareness returns from the Absolute, individual existence wakes up again due to previous impressions. The individual remembers individuality, experiences bliss, and then gradually moves outward, back to the surface level of thinking -- this is the reverse of the inward direction of the previous sutra.

Diving into the Ascendant coats one with bliss, intelligence, creativity and energy. This naturally changes the dominance of impressions -- it re-orders them, lessens the significance of painful ones and increases the significance of joyful ones. This inspires the individual to repeat the experience of Ascending. Thus Ascension creates an automatic feedback loop of Self-referral.

Śeṣa, here translated, "dormant," has deep Cosmic significance. What maintains individuality from one lifetime to the next? Śeṣa -- with death, all manifest appearances still -- this is true if the death is of an individual or a

Universe. What maintains the integrity of the individual after death? Śeṣa. This is represented in allegorical imagery by God in the form of Narayana, floating on the megacosmic serpent Śeṣa on the Universal waters. When the Universe implodes, the individual souls therein return to dormancy in Śeṣa. When God again creates time and space, these individual impulses return to occupy the new Universe, picking up in their evolution from wherever they happened to have left off when the Universe ended.

The point is that "impressions become dormant" does not say they are destroyed -- they sleep or rest to manifest again when the impulse of individuality stirs again.

Pada I. Sutra 19

भवप्रत्ययो विदेहप्रकृतिलयानाम् ॥१९॥

Bhava pratyayo videha prakṛti layānām

When thought aligns with Being, the body ceases and the mind is absorbed in Nature.

This explains the state of stilled thoughts of the second sutra as well as the ceased thoughts of the previous sutra. It reiterates the fact that stilling or ceasing of thoughts is not an experience of nothing, of a void, it is the experience of Pure Infinite Being.

Being is another name for the Ascendant. When thought is experiencing Absolute, Unbounded Being, awareness of the body ceases -- it is gone. (If there is still some faint mental activity, there can be the experience of feeling bodiless, or of floating in space, or feeling that the body is huge.) When the awareness is experiencing the Ascendant, there is little or no demand placed on the body from the mind; respiration falls and the heart slows. In the state of complete Ascendance, the body's activity stills completely. When this occurs, the mental processes are absorbed in their ultimate source, Nature.

When the impressions return to dormancy, as described in the previous sutra, the mind is also stilled -- it is absorbed by its maker, Nature. This also further explains the sixteenth sutra -- when the mental processes have returned to their Source, all attachment to the primary motive forces of Nature, the guṇas, naturally ceases as well.

The body and mind are stilled, yet awareness continues. Thus is Ascendant Consciousness beyond the limits of the body and mind, forever free from the false impositions of the ego, the past, belief, judgment and habit.

A second meaning of this sutra is that when the mind is reabsorbed in Nature and the body ceases to bind, all thought naturally manifests purely from the Ascendant. This is therefore a clear description of Perpetual Consciousness. A third meaning is that in Unified Consciousness, all awareness of the body is completely converted to awareness of the Ascendant. This is true ceasing of the body, true bodilessness, for there is no longer even the faintest attachment to the physical structure of the body. The mind continues to function, but solely as a fluctuation of Nature -- there is nothing left of the isolated, limited individuality, nothing left of stress or failure -- all that is, is universal in experience, mind and body and soul.

It is the magnificence of Patañjali's perfect command of Sanskrit that allows him to express such disparate thoughts with the same words. He displays extraordinary beauty with utter grace and simplicity.

Pada I. Sutra 20

श्रद्धावीर्यस्मृतिसमाधिप्रज्ञापूर्वक इतरेषाम् ॥२०॥

Śraddhā vīrya smṛti samādhi prajñā pūrvaka itareṣām

Ordinarily, stabilizing the intellect in Ascendant Consciousness is preceded by faith, effort and memory.

Normally, something must happen to inspire individual life to move toward enlightenment, but it can happen that one spontaneously slips into the experience of the Ascendant. Technically, nothing is *required,* for the Ascendant underlies and permeates all consciousness, everywhere, always; therefore anyone can at any time experience it. This is why Patañjali uses the word, "ordinarily." There are no absolute rules about the path to enlightenment; there are always exceptions. But for the majority, the pull of the former beliefs, habits, judgments, stresses and deep-rooted internal programs is so very great that simply falling into the Ascendant by accident is rare. It may occur spontaneously and temporarily once or twice in an average lifetime, but for most, the intensity of the belief in the past is too great to make the experience permanent.

Other translations of "stabilizing," iṣām, are "mastering," "entitling one to" and "capable of." To master the experience, to be entitled to its permanence, to even be capable of sustaining it, some work is typically required.

"Faith," śraddhā, extends the word Devotion of the fourteenth sutra. Faith implies devoted action to higher power, for devotion can be directed to anything. One can be intensely devoted to a dog, but it is unlikely that such devotion will quickly lead the mind to the Ascendant. The concept of faith will be further developed in the 23rd and 24th sutras.

"Effort," vīrya, further amplifies "continuous application" (also of the fourteenth sutra) and will be further explained in the following two sutras.

Here effort does not mean straining during the practice of Ascension -- again, it must be made absolutely clear that any effort during Ascension, even the slightest, only serves to keep the awareness on the gross and tires the mind. What effort here means is the requisite energy to take the time away from the busy demands of the world, find a comfortable chair, sit down in it, close the eyes and Ascend. This need not continue for more than fifteen or twenty minutes two or three times a day for the wonderful results of contacting the Ascendant to begin to manifest. This much effort *is* required, as is enough faith for one to take the time to Ascend regularly.

Having developed sufficient faith to believe it is possible to erase the old internal programs (which is exactly enough faith to inspire one to take the effort to rearrange the schedule for a few short breaks in the day), the only other requirement for developing the level of the intellect that can maintain Ascendant Consciousness is memory (see the commentary on the sixth and eleventh sutras). Memory is the best movement of the mind, for it is the only one that has the capability of clearly reflecting the Reality of the Ascendant. If one moves effortlessly to the Ascendant even once and perfectly remembers the path, one can again move there effortlessly at will. Further, if one clearly remembers exactly what the experience of Ascendant Consciousness is, one is but a hair's breadth removed from Perpetual Consciousness. The crystalline structure of consciousness being perfectly clear, the Infinite light of the Supreme reflects flawlessly in it.

None of this is complicated or difficult. Faith in progress is naturally and inevitably reinforced as one begins to experience growth as a result of correctly practiced Ascension. The desire to find the time to Ascend naturally develops as one experiences more and more clearly the marvelous improvements in health, happiness and every area of human life as a result of

Ascending. And memory naturally blossoms and becomes flawless as repeated experience of the Ascendant dissolves more and more of the limiting stresses from the central nervous system, thereby opening an ever-broader and clearer channel to the full and permanent experience of Ascendant Consciousness.

Pada I. Sutra 21

तीव्रसंवेगानामासन्नः ॥२१॥

Tīvra saṃvegānām āsannaḥ

To the intensely vehement, soon.

"Soon," āsannaḥ, can also be translated, "near." There is no distance to be traversed to realize the Self; therefore any attempt to do so will be amply and immediately rewarded. It does not have to take a frightfully long time to experience Ascendant Consciousness. If the tools are functional, it takes only the passionate zeal to wield them to quickly reach the goal.

Patañjali here describes only those who have useful tools. No amount of effort will enable an aspirant to reach the Ascendant without a ladder to climb out of the field of boundaries. But with the appropriate vehicle, the ride quickly accelerates the more one strives to attain the goal. And once more, let us be abundantly clear: vehemence is not the path to the goal, it is the necessary energy to race down the path. Ascension is effortless, but how dedicated one is to doing it and how committed one is to understanding it can dramatically reduce the time required to experience the Absolute and then maintain it in daily activity. This is further explained in the next sutra.

Pada I. Sutra 22

मृदुमध्याधिमात्रत्वात्ततोपि विशेषः ॥२२॥

Mṛdu madhya adhimātratvāt tato api viśeṣaḥ

Subtlety and inward focus must also join that intensity to create extraordinary and wonderful results.

From the previous sutra, one might infer that the only requirement for the evolution of consciousness was fanaticism. This sutra clarifies that misconception. Subtlety, mṛdu, (which can also be translated, "gentleness," "tenderness," "mildness" or "delicateness") is also required to reach the goal of Ascendant Consciousness. Sleeping on beds of nails is not required. Mortification of the flesh is not required. Any sort of mental, emotional or physical abuse is not required. Moderation is recommended for those who seek enlightenment. And that moderation should be applied in moving inward, to subtler and subtler levels of experience.

Where, then, is the appropriate placement for zeal? It must be a zeal for ever-subtler levels of reality, zeal for inward development, not for striving to reform the world. Often, those interested in converting others to their beliefs are doing so to mask to themselves the fact that they hardly believe what they are teaching. Zeal for the goal, yes; but that is directed inward. The focus of attention must be delicately and gently applied in an inward direction. Zeal is what inspires one to do it. Any other interpretation of this verse distorts Mahāṛṣi Patañjali's teaching at best and at worst transforms it into meaninglessness.

Pada I. Sutra 23

ईश्वरप्रणिधानाद्वा ॥२३॥

Īśvara praṇidhānād vā

Or by surrender to the Supreme Being.

Intensity of zeal is one way to quickly grow into Ascendant Consciousness (see the commentary on the 21st Sutra), but it is not the only way -- the 20th sutra mentioned three, including faith. This is the emotional approach to the Absolute; it comes from the level of the heart. If one can sincerely surrender one's self-created fantasies of limitation, fear, sickness, unhappiness and death to the Supreme Being, consciousness naturally expands to the Ascendant. Since the Supreme Being *is* love, no intellectual approach is required. Since the Supreme Being is omnipresent, no approach at all is actually required. The only requirement is to stop believing in what is not, to stop creating false idols to replace the One True God.

What are false idols? It is possible to be devoted to money, cars, people, fame, practically anything. Therefore devotion (sutra 14) is insufficient. Again, one can have faith in people, books, history, fantasy, science, practically anything. Therefore faith (sutra 20) is insufficient. What *is* sufficient is surrender to the Supreme Being. Surrender is superior to devotion, for devotion can equally well be applied to anything of the material world. Surrender is superior to faith, for one can be faithful to illusions, idols and false gods. True surrender implies falling at the feet of the Supreme Being. It is a movement of direct experience, not a fantasy, dream or a hope.[10]

---

[10] -- Of course, the possibility of meeting the Supreme Being face-to-Face is highly unlikely before Perpetual Consciousness is established. But Patañjali does not mention this fact in this sutra, for it is at least theoretically possible

(continued...)

Surrender and zeal are opposites. The one is the ultimate of passivity; the other, the ultimate of activity. One nice thing about the Ascendant is that it is everywhere. It matters not which direction an individual travels, still the goal can be reached. If activity suits you, fine, *be* active. But be maximum in your activity -- be zealous in your growth to enlightenment. If passivity suits you, fine, *be* passive. But be maximum in your passivity -- surrender your every thought and word and deed to the Supreme Being and do nothing of yourself. Either will work just fine, which is why Patañjali says here, "Or."

(...continued)
even in ignorance to surrender to the Supreme Being completely.

Pada I. Sutra 24

क्लेशकर्मविपाकाशयैरपरामृष्टः पुरुषविशेष ईश्वरः ॥२४॥

Kleśa karma vipāka āśayair aparā mṛṣṭaḥ puruṣa viśeṣa īśvaraḥ

The Supreme Being is the most extraordinary and wonderful aspect of the Ascendant.

From the Ascendant, the Supreme Being wipes away the deep impressions that set in motion the fundamental tendencies which lead to the fruition of unenlightened action.

This sutra is the antidote to the incorrect understanding mentioned in the eighth sutra. It shows the result of the surrender of the last sutra and also clarifies what the Supreme Being is.

The Supreme Being is an aspect of the Ascendant. Rather, the Supreme Being is the most wonderful and extraordinary aspect of the Ascendant. This language can easily lead to misinterpretation, for the Ascendant cannot exist apart from the Supreme Being, nor can the Supreme Being exist apart from the Ascendant. Both are omnipresent, Eternal, Infinite -- but when we mention the Ascendant, we imply more of an "it"; when we mention the Supreme Being, we imply an active agent that purposefully pursues our good and the good of everyone else.

These concepts and distinctions are virtually meaningless in the Waking State. But in Perpetual Consciousness, once one has recognized that the innermost Self is in fact not different from the Infinite Ascendant, the quest to discover the Primal Actor becomes relevant. And extremely fascinating. This quest is exactly what impels one to grow beyond Perpetual Consciousness.

"Wipes away," mṛṣṭaḥ, can also be translated "cleanses" or "makes bright" or "puts in proper order." Without ever leaving the Ascendant, the Supreme

Being reestablishes life in harmony.

"Fundamental tendencies," kleśas, will be defined in the third to the ninth sutras of the second pada. They consist of ignorance, ego, desire, aversion and obstinancy. These are the channels that keep life separate, isolated and bound.

"Fruition," vipāka, can also be translated "results" or "consequences." The fruition of unenlightened action will be listed in the thirtieth and thirty-first sutra. Basically, the fruition or results of unenlightened action are those experiences of pain, suffering, disharmony and ill health that result from action that is not fully conscious, i.e., action that is not in tune with the force of Evolution, action that is based on self-destructive beliefs, tendencies and deep stresses -- in short, downward-directed action in the Waking State.

"Deep impressions," āśayair, can also be translated "stresses." Previous unconscious actions have created stresses or impressions in the nervous system; energy rising resonates with these, turning them into afflicting, self-destructive desires; this leads to action to fulfill these desires; such unenlightened action forms further and deeper impressions. The stored impressions lead to distorted desires which lead to distorted actions which strengthen the stored impressions. Impression-desire-action-impression-desire-action-impression. This I-D-A cycle is endless and impossible to break without movement from the side of the Ascendant, for the most damaging consequence of unconscious action is new stress in the nervous system which reinforces the stored impressions and leads to stronger self-destructive tendencies. This I-D-A cycle of action-impression-desire-action-impression-desire is exactly what makes the bondage of the Waking State impossible to break without Ascension.

It is impossible, it is worthwhile to repeat, to break the I-D-A cycle without movement from the side of the Ascendant. Attempting to root out the causes of self-destructive behavior from the Waking State of Consciousness is at best a waste of time, at worst likely to be psychologically damaging. This is why the approaches of modern psychiatry and psychotherapy are often so woefully inadequate for true Healing. Even identifying the cause of any destructive behavior from the surface of the mind is extremely difficult and time-consuming. Imagine trying to fix a leak in the basement plumbing of your neighbor's house from the roof of your own ten-story office building. Who could even begin to succeed? And yet this is exactly what most practitioners of mental health are attempting to do! From the surface of their minds, the 10% level of their thinking, they attempt to direct others to the sources of their afflicting addictive behaviors, which are buried deep in their subconscious! Small wonder they so often fail.

The alternative is to Ascend to the Source of all thoughts. By touching the Source, the energy contained in the Ascendant automatically moves to purify the nervous system. Said another way, the perfect orderliness contained in the Absolute disallows the continuance of any disorder: the deep stresses of stored impressions dissolve; the inherent, self-destructive tendencies automatically fall away; action spontaneously changes to be in harmony with Natural Law. Since no action springing purely from the Ascendant is ever performed that is not in harmony with the upward-directed currents of creation, the results of such action are wholly positive, beneficial and uplifting. This kind of action creates impressions that lead to desires which create more harmony, health and happiness; quickly the whole structure of life moves away from suffering into greater and greater joy.

It is useful to note that the Supreme Being acts in our favor whether we believe in Him or Her or not. If we take our awareness to the Ascendant, the

Almighty Forces of Nature will heal our damaged bodies and minds automatically. It is therefore not difficult to change the trends of our time; it is not difficult to have Ideal Lives. It is in fact quite simple, if we just create the appropriate conditions for change. With perfect ease, life transforms to perfection. We need only give it the chance.

Pada I. Sutra 25

तत्र निरतिशयं सर्वज्ञबीजम् ॥२५॥

Tatra niratiśayaṃ sarvajña bījam

The Ascendant, the Source of all knowledge, cannot be surpassed.

It is not possible to go beyond the Infinite Ascendant. If it were, it would not be the Infinite. The Ascendant is the Source of everything, all knowledge, all thought, all that exists. This is how it is possible to rewrite the internal programs that limit individual consciousness. By experiencing the Absolute, all the previous impressions are purified. Since this is so, it becomes absurdly easy to transform life -- no problem, regardless how tenacious, can lie beyond the flawless subtlety of the Ascendant, and therefore no problem can be beyond the power of the Absolute to solve. Regardless how deeply we dig ourselves into difficulty and trouble, still beyond that is the Supreme, awaiting only our attention to heal us. Thus is the path to freedom from our problems utterly simple, whatever the problems may be -- take the awareness to the Ascendant, and there you are. All done for you, automatically.

Pada I. Sutra 26

स पूर्वेषामपि गुरुः कालेनानवच्छेदात् ॥२६॥

Sa pūrveṣām api guruḥ kālena anavachchhedāt

Not limited by time, the Ascendant was also the Teacher of the Ancients.

All true instruction in the Ascendant has always come from the Ascendant. The Ascendant reveals Itself to Itself by Itself. This sutra also says that the Ancient Teachers of enlightenment also spoke from the Ascendant. Any teaching that does not have as its basis constant contact with the Ascendant will not last long, for it has no connection to the Source of all knowledge. Without a root in the permanent, omniscient, timeless, Infinite Ascendant, any teaching will be of little permanent value to humanity; it will wither and die before very long. But a Teaching that is rooted in the Ascendant has timelessness at its deepest root and therefore endures.

Indeed, there is in fact only one Teaching, appearing over and over at different times and places and languages in the world. Just as there is only one Ascendant, just so there is only one completely direct, automatic and natural path to the Ascendant; there is only one Teaching. Regardless of how very different all True Teachings appear on the surface; they unite in their common Source and Goal -- in the Unbounded Awareness of the Ascendant.

Pūrveṣām, translated in this sutra "Ancients" (past) contrasts with apara, "beyond" (future) of I.24. Go as far as you wish into the past, there will the Ascendant be, shining in its perfect glory. Go as far as you would like into the future, there is the Ascendant, ever Perfect, ever Pure.[11]

---

[11] -- "I am Alpha and Omega, the beginning and the ending, saith the Lord, which is, and which was, and which is to come, the Almighty." REV 1:8.

Pada I. Sutra 27

तस्य वाचकः प्रणवः ॥२७॥

Tasya Vāchakaḥ praṇavaḥ

Its Sound is OM.

OM is the fundamental vibration of creation. Literal translations of pranavaḥ are: "the Great Exaltation," "the nourishing voice of Praise," "the Eternally new voice of God." In Western terminology, OM is called the Word, the Omega and the Amen, it is the Voice for God, the Holy Spirit. OM is the ultimate sound of everything. It contains within its vibratory matrix all vibrations.

All of matter is vibrating energy. For those with sufficiently developed perception, these sounds can be heard (see the commentary on III.17). Even with a slight inward movement of consciousness, it is common to hear the first stages of OM. It can sound like "the voice of many waters" (PSALMS 93:4), like the roar of an ocean wave, like a rainstorm, like a choir of angels singing, like a chorus of tinkling bells, like the wind sighing through a pine forest, like a deeply resonating bass drum.

Those unfamiliar with the possibility of hearing OM are often very disturbed when they hear any of these or other manifestations of its energy; they may race to their friendly allopathic physicians who, equally unknowing and concerned, prescribe medication to cure their patient's tinnitus. In severe cases, surgery or psychiatric care is counselled. All of which goes to prove the old adage, "Little knowledge can be a dangerous thing."

Pada I. Sutra 28

तज्जपस्तदर्थभावनम् ॥२८॥

Tat japas tat artha bhāvanam

From Ascension on OM, its purpose is born.

What is the purpose of OM? To create the Universe and maintain its direction in harmony with evolution. If one uses OM as a vehicle for Ascending, one discovers the purpose and meaning of individual life and Cosmic Life. What is the purpose of individual life? To rise to complete consciousness, enlightenment, full and continual awareness of the Ascendant. What is the purpose of Cosmic Life? To bring joy, fulfillment, healing and enlightenment to all created beings.

"Purpose," **artha**, also means, "cause," "reward," "advantage," "use," etc. OM is the cause of creation. By Ascending on it, one learns the cause. OM is the reward or goal of creation. By Ascending on it, one learns the goal of creation. OM is the advantage of creation. By Ascending on it, one learns the advantage of creation. OM is the use of creation. By Ascending on it, one learns the use of OM and of all creation. Thus this one sound vibration is a master key to unlock all of the fundamental issues of creation. For this and other reasons, OM is an integral part of several of the Twenty-seven primary techniques for Ascension.

"Its purpose is born," **artha bhāvanam**, can also be translated, "Its purpose aligns with Being." The purpose of OM is always aligned with Being, for OM is the primary manifestation of the Ascendant. But in the Waking State, the human is unaware of this purpose. Through Ascension, the human aligns in purpose with Being.

There are four primary aims of human life, according to the most ancient understandings of the enlightened. The first of these is known as **Dharma.** Dharma is the path of life that is aligned with the upward current of creation, the Natural Laws that uphold the structure of the Universe (see III.14, commentary).

Artha, the second goal of life, is to understand one's purpose, one's individual meaning, source and goal. Counting this sutra, Patañjali mentions Artha no less than nineteen times in the Yoga Sutras, demonstrating the vital significance of mastering full knowledge of one's individual purpose in the scheme of Creation.

The third aim of life, **Kama**, is desire. Mastering Kama means that every desire is life-supporting for oneself and everyone else. It is never possible to have a desire that is not in harmony with the Divine Plan for Creation.

The fourth aim, **Mokṣa**, is liberation or enlightenment and is of course the aim of the entirety of the Yoga Sutras, of Yoga in general, of all true meditation, of prayer, of Ascension, of the Science of Union.

All four of these aims are deeply intertwined; it is not possible to realize one fully without also mastering the other three; any step toward one is a step toward all. If any one leg of a table is pulled, the other three obediently follow.

If the four aims of life could be compared to the flowing of a river, Dharma would be the path the river follows, Artha would be the direction the river flows, Kama would be the impelling force of the water, and Mokṣa would be the goal of the river, the Unbounded ocean.

Whether one knows anything of the goal or not, effortless flowing with the river of life will carry one to the goal, for every desire is at its root a manifestation of Cosmic Desire and the ultimate purpose of all creation is indissolubly linked to every aspect of creation through the Universal vibration, OM.

Life, therefore, is supremely simple -- one need do nothing but let go; the fundamental forces of Natural Law take over and bring one to enlightenment.[12]

Pada I. Sutra 29

ततः प्रत्यक्चेतनाधिगमोऽप्यन्तरायाभावश्च ॥२९॥

Tataḥ pratyak chetana adhigamaḥ api antarāya abhāvaś cha

From that, one turns inward, gains Pure Consciousness and obstacles cease to exist.

One begins by seeking answers on the outside, but with sincerity, the aspirant quickly learns that all true Teachings ultimately point back at his/her own heart. There is no other way to discover the Kingdom of Heaven than by looking within. After repeated frustrations on the outside, an individual eventually discovers Ascension, which naturally leads one to reverse one's focus and look inward. From that instant, it does not take long, given an appropriate vehicle, to discover the Ascendant lying within.

The development of Pure Consciousness, consciousness by itself, devoid of thought, is accompanied by the destruction of all obstacles standing in the way of that development. These are two aspects of the same process. As one recognizes the Ascendant more and more clearly, the stresses in the nervous system and the self-destructive tendencies in the mind naturally decrease. Conversely, if the obstacles to the experience of Pure Consciousness decrease,

---

[12] -- "Be still and know that I am God." PSALMS 46:10.

awareness of the Absolute ceases to be blocked by the false, limiting and self-imposed judgments about the nature of the Self. Every step toward the East is a step away from the West; every step away from the West is a step toward the East.

Pada I. Sutra 30

व्याधिस्त्यानसंशयप्रमादालस्याविरतिभ्रान्तिदर्शनालब्ध

भूमिकत्वानवस्थितत्वानि चित्तविक्षेपास्तेन्तरायाः ॥३०॥

Vyādhi styāna saṃśaya pramāda ālasya avirati bhrānti darśana alabdha bhūmikatva anava sthitatvāni chitta vikṣepās te antarāyāḥ

The obstacles which scatter consciousness are: illness, dullness, doubt, negligence, laziness, not desisting from self-destructive habits, mistaken perception, not being grounded, and instability.

When it is one-pointed, consciousness experiences the Ascendant. That which stands in the way of the movement to the Absolute are these nine obstacles. These are what keep the awareness divided and not one-pointed on the Ascendant.

"Scatter," **vikṣepās**, also means "distract," "move to and fro," "wave about." Consciousness scattered is active; it chaotically moves because of these obstacles. Vikṣepās is the strong tendency to be outward-directed and many-pointed instead of inner-directed and one-pointed.

Illness includes all mental and physical disease. Any bodily ailment has its counterpart in the mind -- both are healed together.

Doubt also means “indecision,” “hesitation,” “uncertainty” and “misgivings.”

Negligence also means “inattention,” “heedlessness,” “intoxication” and “carelessness.”

Laziness includes sloth and indolence.

Mistaken perception also means “confused or deluded opinions and understanding.”

Instability can also be translated “faithlessness,” “helplessness,” “tendency to vacillate or waver.”

Pada I. Sutra 31

दुःखदौर्मनस्याङ्गमेजयत्वश्वासप्रश्वासा विक्षेपसहभुवः ॥३१॥

Duḥkha daurmansya aṅgame jayatva śvāsa praśvāsā
vikṣepa saha bhuvaḥ

The natural counterparts of this scattering are:
suffering, unhappiness, lack of mind-body coordination
and deranged breathing.

This sutra explains the counterparts of the outward-directed many-pointed mind, subject to vikśepās.

"Suffering" translates **duḥkha**, which is written दुःख in Sanskrit. The form of this word is quite fascinating: there is a break or gap between the halves of the word. Suffering comes from having a break in the connection of the individual with the Universal. This is an illusory break only -- at all times, the individual *is* established in the Ascendant. If this were not so, he or she could not continue to exist. But when one *believes* in this gap, it has certain unfortunate or even disastrous consequences, not the least of which is the possibility of experiencing suffering and pain. The literal meaning of duḥkha's constituent parts echoes this theme. "Du" means to burn, to be pained, to be consumed with sorrow or remorse; "kha" means cavity, hole or wound. So duḥkha is the wound or emptiness that burns. What is this painful nothingness? The illusion of separation.

If consciousness is not stable in the Ascendant, the body-mind is subject to an endless variety of unfortunate occurrences. These can be roughly and somewhat arbitrarily divided into mental suffering, emotional unhappiness (which includes anxiety, worry and despair) decrease of successful coordination between the mind and body, and imbalance in all bodily functions. The breath is mentioned here as the root cause of all physiological afflictions, for it is exactly derangement in the breath that creates all bodily disease and abnormality.

It is interesting that Mahāṛṣi Patañjali calls these the innate or natural counterparts of a scattered mind rather than the causes of a scattered mind. Those in the Waking State tend to externalize all mental, emotional and physical imbalances and assume that they have an independent existence, quite apart and separate from the way of thinking that creates the Waking State. The reality is quite other, as the next sutra will make clear. Heal consciousness first, all the aspects of the personality will be automatically healed.

Pada I. Sutra 32

तत्प्रतिषेधार्थमेकतत्त्वाभ्यासः ॥३२॥

Tat pratiṣedha artham eka tattva abbhyāsaḥ

One purpose of approach to the essence of the One is to negate these.

Purpose also means "advantage," "reward," "use" and "cause" (see the commentary on the twenty-eighth sutra). Approach is defined in the commentary on the twelfth to the fourteenth sutras.

The essence of the One is Ascendant Consciousness, the Self's True Form (see the Commentary on the third sutra). When consciousness becomes single, all the obstacles and their inherent and destructive effects are negated.[13] **Pratiṣedha**, here translated "negated," also means "prevented." To prevent the obstacles and their effects from occurring, establish One-pointedness of consciousness in the Ascendant.

There is nothing in this sutra to imply that it is difficult to experience one-pointedness of the intellect and Ascendant Consciousness. Trying to heal mental, emotional or physical disease is extraordinarily difficult without experiencing the root of all knowledge. But it *is* easy to approach the Ascendant; when this happens, all undesirable aspects of the Earth-life are negated (if they already exist) or are prevented if they are impending. This is the intelligent way to live human life: gain Ascendant Consciousness in enlightenment and thereby enjoy health, peace, clarity and joy continually and forever.

---

[13]-- "If therefore thine eye be single, thy whole body shall be full of light." -- MATTHEW 6:22. Cf. LUKE 11:34-36.

Pada I. Sutra 33

मैत्रीकरुणामुदितोपेक्षाणां सुखदुःखपुण्यापुण्यविषयाणां

भावनातश्चित्तप्रसादनम् ॥३३॥

Maitrī karuṇā mudita upekṣāṇāṃ sukha duḥkha

puṇyāpuṇya viṣayāṇaṃ bhāvanātaś chitta prasādanam

From friendliness toward happiness, from compassion toward suffering, from joyfulness toward virtue, and from indifference toward vice is born clarity of consciousness.

See the commentary on the twenty-fourth sutra of Pada III for a further discussion of these four. This sutra lists four separate techniques for freeing consciousness from the nine obstacles (I.30) and the four resultant troubles (I.31) while simultaneously stabilizing one-pointedness of consciousness (I.32). If zeal (I.21), surrender (I.23), or OM (I.28) are not sufficient to stabilize Pure Consciousness, this and the following six sutras describe the mechanics of a series of techniques to assist in the process. These, properly taught, can be practiced as a complement to those already mentioned.

It might be useful to reiterate here that attempting to structure enlightenment without the assistance of the enlightened is rather like trying to write a novel in Greek possessing as your only tool the Greek alphabet. Patañjali never intended his Yoga Sutras to stand independently of personal instruction. As an adjunct to personal instruction, they can be marvelously clarifying. But without guidance from an enlightened Teacher, they are bound to be disappointing in result, if not completely confusing.

Friendliness toward happiness does not simply mean to be friendly to happy people, it means primarily to be friendly to those parts inside of each of us that are happy. Thus also for the other three techniques here. It is not our attitude toward those on the outside that is the subject of the Science of Union, it is how to integrate our personalities into harmonious perfection. A compassionate touch for our suffering inside is necessary, as is joy for our virtue and simple indifference toward our vice. Why indifference? Because evil resisted gains in power by our negative energy.[14] That which is forcibly repressed seeks other ways to manifest. Like green branches thrown on a fire, attempting to repress tendencies creates a thick smoke which smothers clarity.

Forcing down any self-destructive habit only results in more and stronger ones manifesting to take its place. With great effort, alcoholism is broken; the former alcoholic now smokes three packs a day. By greater effort, smoking is curbed; now the former smoker weighs in at 350 pounds. Repression leads to undesirable consequences.

Prasādanam, clarity, also means, "purification, soothing, calming, gladdening, brightening, serenity-producing, gratifying," etc. As one's consciousness is more and more saturated with pure Being, all good aspects of consciousness naturally develop and all negative aspects wither away. Prasādanam also means, "the Sacred remnant," for consciousness reestablishing itself as part and parcel of the Ascendant is the ultimate Sacred act. What is left over after one experiences the Sacred movement of Ascension? The personality becomes increasingly harmonious and balanced, every movement of consciousness is possessed of the fullness of all the qualities of the Ascendant and therefore *is* Sacred.

Puṇyā, "virtue," can also be translated, "good, righteous, pure, purifying, holy, lucky, favorable, propitious, auspicious." And "vice," Apuṇyā, therefore means the opposite of all of these.

---

[14] -- This is why Christ said, "Resist not evil." MATTHEW 5:39.

Pada I. Sutra 34

प्रच्छर्दनविधारणाभ्यां वा प्राणस्य ॥३४॥

Prachchhardana vidhāraṇā bhyāṃ vā prāṇasya

Or, by mastering exhalation and retention of the breath.

Consciousness can also be purified and its obstacles removed through mastery of breathing exercises. Such techniques are in general slower and more difficult and therefore most teachers of True Ascension use them sparingly if at all. It is certainly possible to travel from Rome to Beijing in any number of ways. One can walk. One can take third class trains. One could take a boat. One could also fly. If one is interested in speed, comfort and safety, flying is today the preferred method.

It is also true that as the mind settles into the experience of the Ascendant, the body and the breath gradually still. Even during the first days of the practice, it is common to experience a physiological reduction about twice that of sleep. This deep rest naturally allows the body to heal itself; mind-body coordination dramatically improves, happiness grows and pain and suffering of all kinds naturally fall away. This is the result of stilling the breath, which is itself the result of experiencing pure Being. So this and the previous sutra can also be validly read in the opposite direction -- the experience of Pure Consciousness stills the breath and naturally re-organizes the mind to culture positive mental habits of feeling and thought. More of this in the commentary on the thirty-ninth sutra.

Pada I. Sutra 35

विषयवती वा प्रवृत्तिरुत्पन्ना मनसः स्थितिनिबन्धनी ॥३५॥

Viṣayavatī vā pravṛttir utpannā manasaḥ sthiti nibandhanī

Or, the development of Ascension on objects can bind the mind to stability.

What are the mechanics of moving to the stability of Ascendant Consciousness? Repeated practice with a suitable vehicle. Development implies a repetitive and consistent effort to reach the goal (see the commentary on the twentieth sutra). This gradually leads the consciousness to higher and higher perception of Truth.

Pravṛttir, translated here, "Ascension," is literally, "upward-directed movements of the mind."

"Ascension on objects" -- theoretically, any external or internal object can serve as a suitable vehicle for Ascension. But if the object chosen is not charming to the mind, the mind will tend to become distracted easily and/or get bored and fall asleep. Thus, if the vehicle is strictly meaningless, the mind will find it difficult to continue long enough with the practice for much progress to be made.

On the other hand, taking as an object a thought or perception that *seems* charming on the surface of the mind may or may not draw the mind inward. As far as the object is increasingly pleasant, so far will the mind move. And no further. So the secret of successful Ascension is actually no secret at all but very obvious -- for Ascension to lead directly to the Infinite, the object we choose for an Ascending thought must become increasingly charming at every deeper level of thought until we arrive at the Source of Thought, the Ascendant.

Finding such thoughts is not only difficult from the Waking State of Consciousness, it is impossible -- one would simply never know whether or not the vehicle chosen was going to run out of gas before it reached the goal. It might seem utterly charming for months or even years but stop far short of Ascendant Consciousness. It seems that there are many such techniques in the world today. Not coming directly from enlightened minds, they certainly lead many people somewhere, but just as certainly not to enlightenment!

This is why the only sure path to enlightenment is to receive the appropriate vehicle for Ascension from the tradition of the enlightened. Historically, this has been an oral tradition -- techniques of Ascension have only been written down in the most general of ways, for the individual variations of nervous systems make it unlikely any one vehicle will work for all. Some people are just too big for little sports cars, for example.

Even though this is true, there are some common features at the beginning of the practice of Ascension which could perhaps be universally taught -- for example, of the twenty-seven techniques we teach, the first four are universal in application and could be learned by everyone. For this reason, clear descriptions of them have been included in my book, FIRST THUNDER.

Learning Ascension from any book would prove difficult for anyone: even if Ascending correctly, one would never know it without personal feedback. If the unexplained occurred, the understanding might be insufficient to continue with the practice. And then, too, the tendency to add to the techniques from other sources or subtract that which might not seem important would derail many from the simplicity of practice, thereby ending the effectiveness of Ascension for them. This is why the actual First Sphere techniques are not included in FIRST THUNDER; anyone who has attempted to Ascend from reading that book is strongly encouraged to come for personal verification and in-depth training in all the Seven Spheres. Courses are available throughout the United States, taught by qualified Teachers of Ascension.

Pada I. Sutra 36

विशोका वा ज्योतिष्मती ॥३६॥

Viśokā vā jyotiṣmatī

Or, by cutting away sorrow, the brilliant light of the Self dawns.

What is the root of sorrow? A mind that is caught by the past. Once one has released the connection with the beliefs in past pain and suffering, the perfect light of the present dawns. The great curse of the human mind is also its greatest blessing: it can only do one thing at a time. If it is caught by regret or worry, it is not going to be open to the glory of the only time there is, *Now*. Therefore, if one can firmly and completely break the tie with that which afflicts, life is freed for perfect joy.

Sorrow is simply a movement in the mind. Another translation of sorrow, viśokā, is "flame" or "glow." As long as the mind is absorbed and moves with the flame experience of the lower light of ego-based thinking, the brilliant higher light of the True Self cannot be seen. Said another way, as long as the mind experiences movement, Union cannot occur. This sutra does not describe how to detach from grief; it does not give the means for removing the lesser movement of mourning or sorrow; it only says that if it happens, the result will be the experience of the Transcendental Light. Perhaps for some, simply learning that sorrow is not necessary is by itself sufficient to break the bondage of the ego. Or, perhaps Mahārṣi Patañjali simply meant to observe that the movement from misery to the highest joy is as simple as the decision to change.

There can be no progress unless one is willing to change. Unless one is willing to drop the old self-destructive habits and beliefs, the supernal wonder and joy of life Here and Now cannot enter in. The whole wealth of the Universe can be (and is!) waiting just outside our door, knocking to come in, but until we loosen the bolts and turn the handle, it will wait -- forever, if it must. But let us only decide to break the attachment to suffering; joy rushes in and lifts us up on eagle wings into the Indescribable Beauty of the Divine Presence.

Life is a great deal simpler than we commonly believe or allow it to be. It is not difficult to be enlightened; on the contrary, it takes a huge investiture of our mental and physical energy every day to hold back the Infinite. This is the main reason so much sleep is required at night; this is the primary cause of all disease and aging. Let us for even the briefest of instants relax our firm grip on our beliefs and judgments, the Infinite Light will burst into our souls, forever transforming us.

Pada I. Sutra 37

वीतरागविषयं वा चित्तम् ॥३७॥

Vīta rāga viṣayaṃ vā chittam

Or, by taking as object freedom from attachment, consciousness is purified.

The mind that is filled with attachment is a mind that is constantly moving. If one can Ascend on the idea of freedom from attachment, consciousness naturally stills.

This sutra does not advocate desirelessness or say that desires are somehow wrong or bad. It merely says that desires lead outward, into activity (they cause the mind to move), whereas consciousness moving inward (away from the natural direction of desire) causes the mind to become stable and still.

It is a common experience that if we have two or more mutually contradictory desires, the result is not very rewarding. For example, we may sincerely desire an Ideal Relationship, but another part of our personality, built solidly on the foundation of our previous experience, tells us, "You don't deserve that," "You can't have that," "It will end up just like your parents anyway," "It will only fail in the end. Why bother?" or any of a myriad of other self-sabotaging movements of consciousness. These may be operating on such a deep, pre-verbal level that we are unaware of them except by their results -- continual failure to have a happy, successful, long-lasting relationship.

By stabilizing the mind in Ascendant Consciousness, we learn to entertain only one thought or desire at a time. Since we do not undermine the desire with contradictory thoughts and desires, it receives the full support of all the Laws of Nature and therefore quickly rises to fulfillment.

If one can innocently take *any* movement of the mind in the direction of its Source, one will arrive at the Ascendant. Or, if one can reverse any attachment of the mind and follow it back inward, one will arrive at the Ascendant. This is a great deal more difficult to describe than to do. Ascension is perfectly simple and natural and leads quickly to the goal of Ascendant Consciousness, but talking about it or thinking about it leads at best to the inspiration to do it. A thought of stillness is not the same thing as being still any more than the thought of an orange gives the taste of the orange. The Yoga Sutras are a technical description of the smooth development of higher states of consciousness. But they are not a step-by-step do-it-yourself manual for enlightenment. Regardless how many have interpreted them so does not and will never make them so.

Pada I. Sutra 38

स्वप्ननिद्राज्ञानालम्बनं वा ॥३८॥

Svapna nidrā jñāna ālambanaṃ vā

Or, by adhering to the knowledge of dreams and sleep.

There are many paths to the Ascendant. One can take any road to arrive at this goal, for the Ascendant is omnipresent. By focussing on the images veiled by dreams, True Knowledge can be born. Or by focussing on the thought of nothing that is sleep, one can stabilize the mind in the Ascendant. The means are unimportant. The goal is everything.

This sutra can also be translated, "Or, by the knowledge of the foundation of sleeping and dreaming." What is the foundation of sleeping and dreaming? The support of all states of consciousness is the Ascendant. In the gap between the experience of states of consciousness, the Ascendant can be seen if one is awake enough to be looking for it. The result of finding it anywhere is to find it everywhere. So any place will do; what is required is simply to begin to look.

Pada I. Sutra 39

यथाभिमतध्यानाद्वा ॥३९॥

Yatha abhimata dhyānād vā

Or, Resonate to what pleases.

As Joseph Campbell said, "Follow your bliss." That is always and forever the shortest and most direct path to fulfillment.

If the building is burning down, anything that inspires you to pick up the firehose is going to serve you. As an inspiration to evolve, it is extremely useful to be charmed by the experience (see the commentary on the thirty-fifth sutra). Else why would anyone want to do it? The pull of some abstract future reward is hardly sufficient to impel anyone to change in the present. But, if there is immediate gratification (as there is if one has for an object of Ascension something that is increasingly pleasant at ever-deeper levels of the mind), then the desirability of change Now is naturally increased. So the vehicle for the inward ride of the mind must be pleasant even from the perspective of the Waking State.

This sutra could also be translated, "Resonate to the proper desire," or "Resonate to the correct desire." What is the proper or correct desire? That which leads to the Absolute, to mental clarity, to stability of awareness of the Ascendant. This implies that underlying all other desires is the one root desire to know the Self. Underlying all the hidden, obscure and twisted movements of the mind remains the one desire to realize God -- and that desire is crystalline, pure, never-changing, waiting patiently throughout all of Eternity to be recognized. This is the one True or permanent desire in every human heart, regardless how jaded or atheistic the mind believes it has become. The desire to know the Maker of the Soul underlies all lesser desires. Taking this as the object of meditation naturally propels progress forward, as one focusses on the root of the tree of individual life. "Who am I?" "Why am I here?" "What am I?" "Why is all this?" These are the great questions, those that lead most quickly to the goal. If one can devote oneself for a long time without interruption (I.14) with zeal (I.21), surrender (I.23) and be one-pointed (I.32) to this goal, the result of stability in the Ascendant will develop very quickly.

That is why Patañjali puts this last in this series of techniques for purifying consciousness; that is why he uses yatha to begin this sutra (yatha is the word that can also be translated, "proper" or "correct"); that is why he for the first time in this series introduces dhyanā, Resonance, here. The mind prefers to enjoy; sugar is more attractive to a fly than vinegar. The wise recognize this and use the natural tendency of the mind as the motivating force to fuel Ascension.

It is also valid (and perhaps preferable) to read sutras thirty-three to thirty-eight in the opposite direction. Thus, from purification of consciousness is born friendliness toward happiness, compassion toward suffering, joyfulness toward virtue and indifference toward vice (I.33); this also leads to mastering of the exhalation and retention of the breath (I.34); binding the mind to stability develops the ability to Ascend on objects (i.e., see the subtle or celestial value of objects, which is a hallmark of the second stage of enlightenment, Exalted Consciousness -- I.35); when the brilliant light of the

Self dawns, all sorrow and past attachment is cut away (I.36); when consciousness is purified, freedom from desire naturally results, freeing one from fear and worry for the future (I.37); and this leads to knowledge of the foundation of dreaming and sleeping (I.38).

Given this quite viable interpretation, the suggestions for mastering Ascension to stabilize Ascendant Consciousness given by Patañjali are actually quite few: practice continuously for a long time with devotion (I.14), have faith in the goal (I.20), be zealous in the practice (I.21), surrender to higher power (I.22), Ascend with OM (I.28), be one-pointed (I.32) and follow your bliss (I.39). What could be simpler or more productive of reward?

Pada I. Sutra 40

परमाणुपरममहत्त्वान्तोस्य वशीकारः ॥४०॥

Paramāṇu parama mahattva anta asya vaśīkāraḥ

The Ascendant has dominion over every limit;
it is beyond the smallest and beyond the greatest.

The all-pervading nature of the Ascendant is here described. It lies beyond the furthest limit of the Universe; it is larger than the largest; yet it is also smaller than the smallest, more subtle than the subtlest. Remove every scrap of matter and energy and what is left is the Infinite. It is all-pervading and the same everywhere.

One who has stabilized the experience of Ascendant Consciousness knows the underlying Reality of everything. This is dominion; this is mastery. One has recognized the omnipresence of the Absolute -- not as a dry, intellectual understanding but as a direct, living, continual experience. The Ascendant is beyond space; it is also beyond time. There never was a time when it was not, nor will there ever be a time when it ceases to be. The world may end, the sun may burn out, the entire Universe may cease to exist, but still the One Ascendant will continue on, unchanging, forever.

Pada I. Sutra 41

क्षीणवृत्तेरभिजातस्येव मणेर्ग्रहीतृग्रहणग्राह्येषु तत्स्थतदञ्जनता

समापत्तिः ॥४१॥

Kṣīṇa vṛtter abhijātasya iva maṇer grahītṛ

grahaṇa grāhyeṣu tatstha tadañjanatā samāpattiḥ

When the movements subside completely, the mind is like a transparent crystal.

The knower, the process of knowing and the known are adorned with the stability of the Ascendant. This is Attainment.

This is an amplification and explanation of the third sutra. When the movements of consciousness are completely gone, the mind abides in the experience of its essential nature, which is Absolute. The mind is always reflecting whatever is placed before it. When there are no longer movements in consciousness, what is experienced is the crystal of the mind reflecting clearly the undifferentiated or colorless Reality of the Ascendant instead of the variegated nature of thoughts or sensory data. The mind is *always* a crystal, but it is not always a *clear* crystal -- this does not occur until the movements of consciousness have stilled in the experience of the Fourth State of Consciousness, Ascendant Consciousness (see the commentary on sutras two and three).

In this state, the knower, the known and the process of knowing fuse to become one in the Ascendant. Like a turtle drawing in its limbs, all three return to their Source. This will be explained further in II.17 and III.17. Attainment will be further defined in the next ten sutras.

This sutra also has meaning in the Fifth, Sixth and Seventh States. In the Fifth State, Perpetual Consciousness, the knower has realized his/her self to be one with the Infinite. In the Sixth State, Exalted Consciousness, the process of knowing rises to perception of the Infinite. In the Seventh State, all the objects in creation are perceived as being Infinite. So this sutra lays out the whole story of the evolution from the Waking State to the highest value of realization in Unified Consciousness.

Pada I. Sutra 42

तत्र शब्दार्थज्ञानविकल्पैः संकीर्णा सवितर्का समापत्तिः ॥४२॥

Tatra śabda artha jñāna vikalpaiḥ saṃkīrṇā savitarkā samāpattiḥ

Attainment has stages. First, the Surface Stage clarifies the illusory mixture of sound, purpose and meaning.

This and the next three sutras are explanations of the stages of the growth of Ascendant Consciousness first introduced in the seventeenth and eighteenth sutras.

Consider the word, "cow." As we think the word, there is a sound vibration, composed of the sounds composing the word; there is a meaning that is structured by all of our previous experiences and beliefs about cows; there is a purpose behind the existence of the object, quite independent from the meaning we put onto it. These three are mingled in the Waking State, on the surface of the mind; there is little true comprehension of sound, purpose or meaning.

This sutra lists the next three levels of Ascension in reverse order: meaning relates to the Meaning Stage. In its purest state, meaning gives the full experience of exactly what the word means. Purpose relates to the Feeling Stage. In its purest state, feeling gives the full experience of exactly what is the purpose of the object represented by the word. Sound relates to the Knowing

Stage. The purest experience of the sound value of an object gives complete knowledge of the object.

In a perfect language, the word representing an object is a perfect expression of the object. In language as it is found in the world today, there is often little true relation between the words and the objects they represent. Therefore the ability to influence objects by speech and by thought is diminished.

Nothing is seen as it really is in the Waking State. The sensory impression of the external object resonates with the previous impressions of experience -- our minds connect these memories together with the current sensory data, we give the object a name. This is the state of waking dreams. All these three -- name, memory and impression of external object -- are intermingled; nothing is perceived innocently, as it really is. The name we give it rarely correctly reflects the object's inherent sound value; our memories, born of repeated limited experiences of similar objects, blind us to the object's meaning; for the same reason, our sensual impression of the object is distorted so that we never discover its inherent purpose.

Ascension must begin from wherever one is when one comes to the process, and therefore must begin by sorting out the dream-like confusion of these three. The left hemisphere of the brain, the rational/verbal hemisphere, needs a name to focus its energy; the right hemisphere, the spatial/intuitive hemisphere, needs a purpose or direction of emotive energy; and both need true meaning, not illusions. Only when all the three come together to function in harmony instead of confusedly overlapping can True Ascension begin. Thus each of the techniques of Ascension consists of three parts.

It is not by accident that Patañjali uses the word, vikalpaiḥ, "illusions" or "dreams," here. The Waking State *is* a dream, a particularly cunning dream, with three dimensions, five senses, sound, fury, complete and enveloping motion -- but it is nevertheless a dream. Escaping from the gripping nature of the dream is the whole purpose of Yoga and of Ascension. And the first step in doing this it to begin to separate the confusion of disparate elements back into their true and original structure of being distinct.

At its best, the Surface Stage can just begin to discriminate between these, but it takes the complete development of the next three subtler levels to grasp fully what each of these three is.

Pada I. Sutra 43

स्मृतिपरिशुद्धौ स्वरूपशून्येवार्थमात्रनिर्भासा निर्वितर्का ॥४३॥

Smṛti pariśuddhau svarūpa śūnya iva artha mātra
nirbhāsā nirvitarkā

Second, as the mind moves into the Meaning Stage, memory is completely purified, the True Form of the Self is experienced as if it were a void and all meaning shines forth clearly.

As one practices the progressive refinement of consciousness by Ascending, memory, the subtlest and most important movement of consciousness (see the commentary on the sixth and eleventh sutras) is quickly purified. There is no stress that can withstand this wholly natural and beneficial process. When memory is purified, one no longer judges objects by past impressions; everything is seen as it really is.

In this second stage, the mixture of word and meaning have sufficiently separated so that meaning appears as it truly is. Since it is no longer colored by previous impressions, the meaning shines forth in its own brilliance. This is not the highest stage of growth to full realization of Ascendant Consciousness -- when the mind has fully reached its Source, there is no perception whatsoever of other meanings. But it is a distinct stage of progress -- the knower is beginning to separate from identification of the Self with meaning. And this is true no matter what the meaning is -- thoughts, bodies, girlfriends, houses, universes -- in short, all that keeps the awareness divided and bound and therefore gives life to the ego's dominance in the Waking State. So this is a significant stage of progress.

It is still confused, however, for the knower has not yet discovered fully what the Self is. The True Form of the Self is still absent -- Ascendant Consciousness has not yet fully dawned -- but at least the dream-like admixture within is beginning to separate into distinct realities. The knower, known and process of knowing must first separate their illusory union in order to unite in the Ascendant.

In this stage, the Self is experienced as if it were a void. Ascendant Consciousness, awareness with no thought moving, is not empty, it is not a void, it is the state of complete fullness, of Being, the Source of everything. Words cannot adequately describe the experience (see the commentary to the third sutra), but saying it is like a void is a fairly close approximation.

Patañjali's use of "as if it were a void" is quite significant for other reasons as well. The Self can never in reality be away from its True Nature. Regardless how deep the confusion of the illusory mixture of knower, known and process of knowing, still the reality remains, hiding just beneath the surface of the waking dreams. The Self can never be devoid of its True Nature, but it *can* believe that it is -- and this is exactly what gives life to the Waking State with its myriad of bizarre beliefs about the nature of life and death. Fortunately, illusions do not become real simply because of belief. A rope does not become a snake simply because we misperceive it.[15] The Self will always be Absolute, will always be Infinite, even if no one anymore recognizes this fact. Reality is not democratic.

Pada I. Sutra 44

एतयैव सविचारा निर्विचारा च सूक्ष्मविषया व्याख्याता ॥४४॥

Etaya eva savichārā nirvichārā cha sūkṣma viṣayā vyākhyātā

This also explains the next two stages, Feeling and Knowing, in which Ascension focusses on ever-increasing subtlety of objects.

After the previous impressions are eradicated so that objects can be seen as they really are, the awareness begins to appreciate subtler or more delicate levels of the reality of the focus of attention. If memory was completely purified in the previous stage, what impels this further growth? It can only be the incomplete nature of the True Nature of the Self in the second or Meaning stage of the inward march of consciousness.

---

[15] -- Of course, perceiving the rope as a snake can and does have disastrous consequences -- the heart may stop from fear, or we may step off a cliff to avoid it. But it is of course all a mistake of the intellect -- there is not now nor was there ever a snake in the rope.

From the seventeenth sutra, we know that these two inward-directed stages of Ascension are associated with bliss and Self-sense. Bliss increases as subtlety of experience increases, for every new level of perception is more perfect, more beautiful, more glorious than the one before. Therefore the natural tendency of the mind to enjoy impels the seeking mind inward -- as long, of course, as the vehicle continues to become increasingly charming with each inward step of the mind (see the commentary on the thirty-fifth sutra).

This culminates, in time, in the experience of pure bliss. The vehicle for Ascension has refined completely, the process of Feeling meditation has so thoroughly fathomed the depths of feeling that the Self has moved into a state of happiness so intense it can only be described as bliss.

The fourth stage goes even beyond this into Pure Knowingness, the limit of which is pure knowing of the ego. Here words fall short, but the experience is that of the Self expanding closer and closer to its true Nature -- awareness is less and less identified with even the subtlety of objects and more and more with Infinite, Absolute Silence. Yet still persisting is awareness of the I as separate from the Universal Self; this means that there is still room left for the ultimate Ascension, into the Infinite Itself.

The second stage of inward growth finishes separating the three intermingled elements -- knower, known and process of knowing, so that meaning (the known) is clearly perceived. The third stage, Feeling, clarifies the essence of the process of knowing so that bliss is discovered as the essential reality of all perceptions; this reveals the true purpose of all objects, to expand joy. The fourth stage, Knowing, focusses on exactly what the individual knower is. This reveals, among other things, complete knowledge of the sound of all objects.

Each of these is much easier to experience than describe, for the movement into the heart of the Ascendant is in fact one seamless and direct dive. These sutras are easy to misinterpret as four distinct practices to accompany each of the four stages. Nothing could be less well deduced: if the vehicle is adequate, it will refine itself as the questing soul journeys effortlessly inward.

It is interesting that this inward march of the mind from the gross to the subtle mimics exactly the outward march of the growth of consciousness: first the knower rises to full knowledge of the Self, this is Perpetual Consciousness; then the process of knowing refines through the mechanics of blissful experience until everything is perceived clothed in celestial light, this is Exalted Consciousness; and finally, the perfect Unity of the knower, the known and the process of knowing gives rise to the ultimate fulfillment of life in Unified Consciousness, where everything in Creation is simultaneously perceived as an aspect of the Infinite. So the process of rising to full perception of Ascendant Consciousness in the Seventh State is a reverse echo of the outward march of the Infinite from its Ascendant status in the structure of the individual mind.

Pada I. Sutra 45

सूक्ष्मविषयत्वं चालिङ्गपर्यवसानम् ॥४५॥

Sūkṣma viṣayatvaṃ cha aliṅga paryavasānam

The ever-increasing subtlety of objects culminates in the Unmanifest.

If the object of attention continues to become increasingly subtle during Ascension, and if one does not fall asleep, the experience will lead to the Unmanifest, the Absolute. This is so because the Ascendant pervades everything, it underlies everything.

"Unmanifest," aliṅga, can also be translated, "without sign, mark, token or characteristic." There are no qualities in the Infinite; it is beyond every division of space, time or thought. The very last stages of even the subtlest reality of the vehicle must fall away to experience Ascendant Consciousness. The Ascendant lies *beyond.* For this reason, it has been commonly thought that it also lies beyond the capability of the human to experience, but this is not so. The consciousness of the human is sufficiently flexible to stretch to Infinity. This is true because the consciousness of the human is nothing other than the Infinite itself. The Universal Divine Consciousness already shines within everyone, always; it is only necessary to stop blocking it to experience it fully.

Pada I. Sutra 46

ता एव सबीजः समाधिः ॥४६॥

Tā eva sabījaḥ samādhiḥ

That is also the origin of Ascendant Consciousness.

In reality, Ascendant Consciousness has no origin; it is the eternally non-changing, omnipresent Infinite Absolute (see the commentary on the fifty-first sutra). So when Maharṣi Patañjali says that the culmination of the inward march of the mind in the Unmanifest is the origin or source of Ascendant Consciousness, he means that the recognition of the Ascendant dawns when the questing soul has reached this level of inward expansion. It is as if born to the individual; the individual is as if re-born through the recognition of this level of awareness, for the old, self-destructive beliefs and damaging internal programs cease to dominate the mind.

In this state, the individual experiences who he or she really is, free from the limiting and restricting past. Freedom is born in the experience of Now; this is the natural by-product of systematically reducing the activity of the movements of consciousness, returning the nervous system to the perfect innocence of Absolute Silence. This is the birth of joy, of life, of Truth, of permanent stability, of human life as it was designed to be lived.

The experience of the Ascendant in the Fourth State of Consciousness is also the beginning of the development of the higher states -- Perpetual, Exalted, Unified. Without Ascendant Consciousness, these higher states cannot exist, for Perpetual Consciousness means living the Ascendant permanently, and obviously stabilized Perpetual Consciousness is the requirement for the further refinements of enlightenment known as Exalted Consciousness and Unified Consciousness. So this sutra also carries these meanings.

Another implication of this sutra is that this experience of Ascendant Consciousness is not yet quite perfect, for there are still connections with the past. This experience of the Absolute could be described as being hazy, for all stress has not yet dissolved, only enough to allow conscious contact with the Ascendant, not permanent awareness of the Ascendant. The next five sutras will describe how to refine away the final tints of limitation from the pure experience of the Absolute.

Pada I. Sutra 47

निर्विचारवैशारद्येऽध्यात्मप्रसादः ॥४७॥

Nirvichāra vaiśāradye adhyātma prasādaḥ

Full experience of the Knowing Stage of Ascension clarifies the Supreme Soul.

"Clarifies," prasādaḥ, can also be translated, "purifies, soothes, calms, gladdens, brightens, pacifies, gratifies, the Sacred remnant" (see the commentary on the thirty-third sutra). If the individual becomes more and more familiar with the Ascendant through repeated experience of it, the mind, heart and body are naturally purified, soothed, calmed, gladdened, brightened and gratified. The experience of the Absolute brings fulfillment to every area of mental, emotional and physical life; it is the Sacred remnant of the act of Ascending.

The Supreme Soul needs no clarification in and of itself; this sutra is describing the relationship of the aspirant to the Infinite. Clarity is complete in the full experience of the Ascendant, in the Fourth State of Consciousness, but the nervous system is not sufficiently refined to hold onto it permanently. As a result of repeated and persistent practice, the experience of the Ascendant purifies the nervous system, clarifies the mind and soothes the heart sufficiently so that the experience becomes permanent. That is known as Perpetual Consciousness. Having firmly established Ascendant Consciousness permanently inside, the Universe of experience is split between the Infinite, clearly known inside, and the relative external cosmos, which continues very much as it was on the outside.

Such a duality is not acceptable to the heart, which only wishes to unite, however impossible such union may seem to the rational mind. The heart, increasingly soothed and gladdened by the experience of the Infinite within, rises in larger and ever-larger waves of bliss, love, appreciation and gratitude. This naturally begins a process of deepening or refining sensual experience that leads to the perception of the celestial in everything -- this is known as Glorified Perpetual Consciousness or Exalted Consciousness.

In time, this movement of extreme joy and love brightens the objective world so much that the Infinite Light of the Absolute shines forth clearly in every object; the recognition that the Ascendant perceived everywhere outside is the same as the Ascendant experienced inside is known as Unified Consciousness.

In Perpetual Consciousness, the Supreme Soul has been completely clarified within -- the knower's relationship with the Supreme is reestablished (or rather, remembered, for it is always established, even if utterly forgotten). In Exalted Consciousness, the Supreme Soul has been completely clarified in the perceptual machinery -- the process of knowing is no longer cluttered with artificial and therefore false limitations of thought or belief. And in Unified Consciousness, the Supreme Soul has been completely clarified in the objects of perception -- the known is perceived as it truly is, Infinite. The Sacred remnant of the process of Ascending is the Fourth State; the Sacred remnant of the Fourth State is the Fifth; the Sacred remnant of the Fifth State is the Sixth; the Sacred remnant of the Sixth State is the Seventh.

Pada I. Sutra 48

ऋतम्भरा तत्र प्रज्ञा ॥४८॥

Ṛtam bharā tatra prajñā

Therein lies the level of consciousness that upholds Divine Truth: Ṛtam bharā prajñā.

"Upholds," **bharā**, also means "filled with" and "praises."

"Divine Truth," **ṛtam**, also means "Divine Order." So **ṛtam bhāra prajñā** also means, "the level of consciousness that is filled with Divine Truth" and "the level of consciousness that praises Divine Order."

Consciousness while experiencing the Ascendant is not flat. It upholds, praises, and is filled with that which is Eternally True, that which organizes and maintains the entire structure of Creation. For one who can consciously touch this level of Pure Consciousness, there is no request that will not be granted, no question that will not be answered, no desire that will not be fulfilled.[16]

There is no limit to the ability of this level of consciousness; there is no limit of the power for good that can be attained by any human being, fully in

---

[16] -- Knowing full well this level of consciousness, Christ could say, "And all things, whatsoever ye shall ask in prayer, believing, ye shall receive" (MATTHEW 21:22); "Ask, and it shall be given you; seek, and ye shall find; knock, and it shall be opened unto you" (LUKE 11:9); and "If ye have faith, and doubt not... if ye shall say unto this mountain, Be thou removed, and be thou cast into the sea; it shall be done." (MATTHEW 21:21) The fact that He recognized the omnipresence of this level of Reality reflects in His assertion that those who would follow His path would do greater things than these: "The works that I do, shall he do also; and greater works than these shall he do." (JOHN 14:12)

contact with the Divine. It is precisely this level of consciousness that is upholding or bearing the entire structure of Creation from the smallest to the largest. It is precisely this level that maintains the integrity of all Natural Law, everywhere, always. Therefore the mechanics of re-ordering Creation in any desired way are really quite simple -- take your consciousness to its Source, the Infinite, Absolute Self, and there you will see the two faces of Deity -- the one forever facing the Ascendant, the other forever facing the manifest Creation. And these two (which are truly only one) are responsible for all that was, is or will ever be. By making their acquaintance, any request will be answered, any desire fulfilled. INSTANTLY.

Pada I. Sutra 49

श्रुतानुमानप्रज्ञाभ्यामन्यविषया विशेषार्थत्वात् ॥४९॥

Śruta anumāna prajñā bhyām anya viṣayā viśeṣa arthatvāt

Its extraordinary and wonderful purpose is different from that of the highest logical reasoning and even from that of perfected cognition.

Perfected cognition is capable of directly experiencing the Natural Laws which create and maintain the Universe. The highest logical reasoning is that which can intellectually understand, formulate and use the descriptions of the Natural Laws which maintain the Universe. These, then, are the two highest functions of the human mind. If the purpose of the experience of the level of consciousness that upholds Divine Truth, ṛtam bhāra prajñā, is not to cognize, manipulate or understand the laws that govern the Universe, what then is its purpose? What could be more important than full mastery of Creation? The final two sutras of the first pada of the Yoga Sutras answer this question.

Pada I. Sutra 50

तज्जः संस्कारोन्यसंस्कारप्रतिबन्धी ॥५०॥

Tajjaḥ saṃskāra anya saṃskāra pratibandhī

The impressions born from that dissolve past impressions and prevent future impressions.

Past impressions and future impressions are stresses in the nervous system. Only present impressions of Ascendant Consciousness dissolve the stress of the past; only the continual experience of the Now prevents the formation of new stresses. This is the highest function of the experience of the level of consciousness that upholds Divine Truth -- ṛtam bharā prajñā burns the seeds of past events, it soothes away the scars of limited and painful experience.

As these past impressions subside and are erased, the individual is freed to experience life innocently, as it is right NOW (see the commentary on the first sutra). The experience of life Now is the goal of Yoga; Union is the result of burning away all the dross of limited and limiting belief and experience that keeps life bound to the harsh and narrow demands of the Waking State. This is the highest function of the experience of this level of consciousness, not gaining the ability to know or manipulate Natural Law.

It is exactly the impressions in our mind that determine our level of consciousness, our level of peace, our level of joy, our level of health, our level of success in every way on Earth. If the stored impressions in our nervous system are of a life of pain, suffering and limitation, our consciousness will reflect and be colored by this. If, on the other hand, our deepest impression is of the unlimited freedom and perfect joy of the Ascendant, every moment of our waking life will be lived in freedom, bliss and love.

Consciousness and bodies are intimately intertwined here. Stress in one affects the other. To be free, the entire structure of life has to be shaken loose from its hard knots of stress. It is the tightly bound areas inside that lead to dysfunctional life in every way -- mental, emotional, physical. So the impressions born of this level of consciousness not only overshadow and melt away all the past impressions of limitation, pain and suffering, they prevent the formation of new impressions of limitation, pain and suffering.

Because the weight of the bliss of the experience of the present is so great, no other experience can begin to challenge it, and, therefore, no other impressions form, just as in the presence of the sun, no other stars are visible in the sky. Stars only seem bright when the daystar is absent; so too, the stresses of ignorance only seem significant in the absence of the experience of the Self. With the dawn of the sun of perfect understanding, the stresses gracefully vanish into the perfect clarity of the azure sky of Pure Consciousness, no more to influence us with their feeble light.

This, then, is the result of experiencing ṛtam bharā prajñā. Full cognition of the Natural Laws of the Universe is of no interest to one who possesses Infinity; neither is any amount of intellectual understanding about reality worth even the slightest moment of attention. One drop of experience is worth an ocean of analysis. One moment of Eternity is worth a Universe of Time.

Pada I. Sutra 51

तस्यापि निरोधे सर्वनिरोधान्निर्बीजः समाधिः ॥५१॥

Tasya api nirodhe sarva nirodhān nirbījaḥ samādhiḥ

Also, its stillness stills all. That is Originless Ascendant Consciousness.

The highest use of ṛtam bharā prajñā is not to erase previous impressions nor even to prevent the formation of new impressions. The highest use of ṛtam bharā prajñā is to desire the Ultimate. Any desire entertained in that level of consciousness is fulfilled instantly; the whole trick of continuing up the scale of evolution once Ascendant Consciousness is gained is to desire to make the experience of the Ascendant permanent *during the experience of Ascendant Consciousness.* By desiring the Ultimate Stillness, the Stillness that can still all else, during the experience of the Ultimate Stillness, the individual rises to complete fulfillment. This is the state of praying without ceasing, in which the peace which passeth understanding has become a continual reality.

This is called the experience of Originless Ascendant Consciousness, for during the pure experience of Ascendant Consciousness, one no longer remembers anything of a lesser evolved state. It is absolutely freed from even the slightest tinge of duality -- the knower, the known and the process of knowing have all united into Absolute, undifferentiated Oneness.

This is the ultimate refinement and final completion of the Fourth State of Consciousness and is beyond the operation of any technique. After the vehicle for Ascension has carried the individual to the level of ṛtam bharā prajñā, the need for it drops away. After one gains proficiency with the use of ṛtam bharā prajñā and desires the Ultimate Stillness during the experience of the Ascendant, one experiences the perfection of Infinite Awareness, the Ultimate level of Reality in and beyond the Universe.

Again, this experience is called Originless because it has no beginning -- it is ever the same, forever, everywhere, always. It is impossible to describe in words, but negations at least point our understanding in its direction. The Ascendant Consciousness of the forty-sixth sutra has an origin, for there are still residual impressions functioning when one first Ascends. But after the Ultimate Stillness stills all previous impressions, after all false belief and judgments are unmade through direct experience of the Reality of the Inner Divine Self, the Ascendant is experienced as it truly is -- free from limitations of any kind, including the limit of having had a beginning. The Ascendant is called the Unborn for this reason. In other words, it is not that ignorance rises to enlightenment. Enlightenment always is, shining in its perfect glory. There is an illusion of ignorance; one does something and experiences the Ascendant. Through repeated experience of the Ascendant, the memory of the previous dream falls away in favor of the unending experience of the Reality of the Absolute.

This is the pure experience of the Fourth State. The Ascendant Consciousness of the forty-sixth sutra is still as if hazy, for there are still impressions of limitation in the nervous system of one who has only begun to Ascend. The experience of ṛtam bharā prajñā during the experience of the Ascendant creates new impressions that erase the old impressions.

Every time one experiences pure thought in ṛtam bharā prajñā, the old structure of the internal programming is shaken. This can take many different forms; one of the most common is that of a beautiful male or female voice, offering what often seems unrequested advice. This is the Voice for God, and actually is speaking in response to a desire we may or may not have recognized having, a desire that was dropped back into the Stillness of the Absolute Self, sometimes even before we are aware we had it.

Another common form of contact with ṛtam bharā prajñā is the instantaneous fulfillment of a desire. You want to speak to someone and pick up the phone to dial her, only to discover she has just called you. Or you want an apple and someone walks into the room and offers you one. The more clear the awareness, the more perfect and instantaneous the response -- desire can be completely fulfilled instantly. Or it can take longer, it depends entirely on how much consciousness is being lived.

In either case, whether fulfilled at once or over time, the impression of the new style of functioning of the nervous system replaces the old impressions and prevents new impressions from forming. The mind can only do one thing at a time; if it is floating in the pure experience of ṛtam bharā prajñā, it has no time left to be caught responding to the impressions of the old internal programs. This gradually frees life to experience more and more of the new style of functioning; the old habits fall away ever more rapidly.

What accelerates the growth of ṛtam bharā prajñā is, of course, Ascension, for each of the Ascension Attitudes is a pure thought from the level of the Ascendant. As the individual picks up each of these thoughts from wherever he or she happens to be in consciousness, the mind is naturally impelled inward toward the Absolute; the new impressions formed by Ascending gradually become stronger and stronger; the old impressions fade and eventually disappear altogether.

And then the final step, desiring Ascendant Consciousness to become permanent naturally develops. And once this desire is entertained on the level of ṛtam bharā prajñā in the Ascendant, it is instantly fulfilled. Ascendant Consciousness rises in one short step to become a permanent reality -- Perpetual Consciousness is established.

Entertaining this ultimate desire in the Ascendant thus creates enlightenment.

Thus Ends the First Quarter of the Science of Yoga: Ascendant Consciousness.

SECOND QUARTER: FULFILLMENT

Just as the First Quarter of the Yoga Sutras described the growth to Ascendant Consciousness, the Second Quarter describes the growth to Perpetual Consciousness, the first stage of enlightenment. Perpetual Consciousness is called fulfillment as it is the primary goal of human life.

The First Quarter discussed only in the most general of terms the means to realize Awareness of the Absolute; just so, this chapter describes the characteristics of this stage of evolution without describing the means to attain it. The Second Quarter has been widely misinterpreted as being a description of the path to Perpetual Consciousness. The word used (II.29) by Patañjali himself to describe this growth, **aṣṭaṅga**, is considered by most to mean the eight *steps* to Divine Union. But this chapter describes aspects of Perpetual Consciousness, not the conditions necessary to gain it; therefore, Patañjali meant the eight *limbs* of Yoga. Steps are consecutive, but limbs grow simultaneously.

The entire teaching of Yoga has been turned upside down from this one misunderstanding. If there are eight steps to enlightenment, Ascendant Consciousness is listed last and therefore must be the eighth and final step, following exercises, breathing techniques and the various other characteristics described in this chapter. This would make for a *very* long time before Absolute Awareness could be gained! In reality, Union begins with Ascendant Consciousness -- without that, none of the aspects listed in this chapter have any point at all.

With the experience of Ascendant Consciousness, all the other seven limbs naturally and spontaneously develop; the result of this eight-fold development is the permanent stabilization of the experience of Ascendant Consciousness, which is known as Perpetual Consciousness, the first stage of enlightenment.

Pada II. Sutra 1

तपःस्वाध्यायेश्वरप्रणिधानानि क्रियायोगः ॥१॥

Tapaḥ svādhāya īśvara praṇidhānāni kriyā yogaḥ

Austerity, study of the Self and surrender to the Supreme Being are the actions that stabilize Union.

The First Chapter discussed the Fourth State of Consciousness, Ascendant Consciousness. The Second Chapter discusses the mechanics of making the experience of the Ascendant permanent. These are emphatically *not* techniques for Ascending! Rather, they describe how the Ascendant infuses into every sphere of activity -- physical, mental and emotional. In this way, the process of developing Perpetual Consciousness can be understood. In other words, the three actions mentioned in this sutra are by-products of successful Ascension; they are not the path to the Ascendant. These three automatically develop in anyone who is Ascending.

Austerity or **tapas** means renouncing the lower, sense-oriented style of functioning of the mind and body for the sake of the higher. It is the withdrawal of the First Chapter (see I.12, I.15 & I.16, commentaries). This is the transformation of **the physical** that makes the experience of the Ascendant permanent. Austerity means renouncing that which does not serve evolution in favor of that which does. It means choosing the Self over the self, the Holy Spirit rather than the ego. Tapas means being intelligent about time and habits, choosing those which serve and giving up those which do not. There are only so many hours in a day; if they are wasted on pointless, ego-gratifying pursuits, the day is lost. If enough days are lost, the life ends up wasted. So tapas means intelligently and willingly adopting useful boundaries in order to stabilize awareness of the Ascendant.

It may sound contradictory to say, "Adopt useful boundaries to stabilize the Ascendant." But it is natural to do so. Human life *is* choice. If, in the name of freedom, we insist that we should be able to do whatever we choose whenever we choose, that is certainly our right. But every choice has consequences, the most unfortunate being that the nervous system may become so damaged or life so short that there remains inadequate ability or insufficient time to reach the goal.

So tapas means adopting useful boundaries. It does *not* mean self-flagellation, abuse or mortification that has as its purpose punishing the body. That is a gross misinterpretation of austerity by extremely gross and sick Waking State bound minds. Willingly accepted boundaries are *not* painful! On the contrary, they are a joy. And this naturally develops in anyone who Ascends.

This sutra addresses the common question, "Well, I've learned to Ascend. What now can I do to hasten my personal evolution?" From the side of the body (which includes all habits that relate to the world), the answer is tapas -- choose a series of self-imposed boundaries that serve the purpose of evolution. The White Novitiate Path of the Ishayas, for example, lays out an ideal series of self-chosen limits to structure enlightenment in the shortest possible time.

In its simplest sense, tapas means: be willing to close your eyes two or three times a day for twenty minutes or so, back away from the chaos of the world and Ascend. That seems like a simple enough act given the profound and extraordinary results that immediately manifest. But, it is shocking to learn how many are incapable of even this.

Studying the Self, **svādhaya**, is the requirement from the level of the mind to stabilize the experience of Ascendant Consciousness. Studying the Self does not mean studying the philosophical nature of the Ascendant, nor does it mean sitting and thinking about it. Study of the Self is the practice of fixing the conscious awareness on the Self -- with or without the eyes being closed, in or out of dynamic activity.

Surrender, **īśvara praṇidhānā**, is the activity most beneficial to stabilizing the experience of the Ascendant from the perspective of **the heart** (see I.23, commentary). These three together pull the entire personality -- body, mind, heart -- into permanent Ascendant Consciousness. Just as tapas is the withdrawal of the first pada, these two -- study of the Self and surrender -- are the constituents of approach (see I.13 & I.14 commentaries).

Pada II. Sutra 2

समाधिभावनार्थः क्लेशतनूकरणार्थश्च ॥२॥

Samādhi bhāvanārthaḥ kleśa tanūkaraṇārtha cha

These have the purpose of furthering Ascendant Consciousness and weakening the inherent tendencies.

The inherent tendencies, **kleśas**, were first mentioned in the twenty-fourth sutra of the first pada and will be further defined in the next several sutras. Basically, they are the deep-rooted tendencies that keep the experience of the Ascendant from being permanent and keep life isolated and separate, bound to ignorance.

The beginning of this sutra amplifies the meaning of the first sutra. These three practices do not *create* Ascendant Consciousness, they *further* it -- they make it permanent, they extend it. The primary means of stabilizing Perpetual Consciousness is tapas; the primary means of developing Exalted Consciousness is study of the Self; the primary means of stabilizing Unified Consciousness is surrender (see II. 43, II. 44, II. 45, commentaries.) So this sutra states that these three carry the experience of the Ascendant from the Fourth State to the highest degree of enlightenment in Unified Consciousness.

"Furthering Ascendant Consciousness" and "weakening the inherent tendencies" are the approach and withdrawal of the First Chapter applied to stabilizing the experience of the Ascendant. One withdraws from the inherent limiting tendencies of the mind in order to stabilize the experience of the Absolute; conversely, as one becomes more and more established in the permanent awareness of the Ascendant, the less and less the mind is caught by the old limiting beliefs and concepts. It is the same process, seen from opposite angles. It doesn't matter which angle is taken -- Ascend to gain permanent bliss and freedom, or Ascend to escape from pain, illness and slavery. It makes no difference, for the ultimate goal in either case is the same.

Pada II. Sutra 3

अविद्यास्मितारागद्वेषाभिनिवेशाः क्लेशाः ॥३॥

Avidyā asmitā rāga dveṣa abhiniveśaḥ kleśāḥ

These inherent tendencies are:

Ignorance, ego, attachment, aversion and obstinacy.

Ignorance will be further explained in sutras four and five, ego in sutra six, attachment in sutra seven, aversion in sutra eight and obstinacy in sutra nine.

None of these five will stop the mind from experiencing the Ascendant, for the natural tendency of the mind to move inward will accomplish this naturally and automatically once a suitable vehicle is present. But these tendencies *will* keep the dominance of the old impressions intact. These five are the causes of the nine obstacles (I.30) and their accompanying results (I.31). By erasing the subtlest level of these tendencies, the more manifest level of the obstacles will naturally be removed. So the mechanics of *permanently* expanding the mind to the Ascendant is to heal these, as will be explained in the tenth and subsequent sutras.

Pada II. Sutra 4

अविद्याक्षेत्रमुत्तरेषां प्रसुप्ततनुविच्छिन्नोदाराणाम् ॥४॥

Avidyā kṣetram uttareṣāṃ prasupta tanuvichchhinna udārāṇām

Ignorance is the source that rules and animates the others.
The ego slumbers here; attachments are small, weak, inconsequential;
aversions continually interrupt, wound and obstruct;
obstinacy is always active.

This is a lovely verse in the Saṇskrit. The word translated "source," kṣetram, also means "field" -- ignorance is the field where the other four inherent tendencies grow. It also means, "the womb." This is an interesting choice of words, for the modifier of obstinacy -- here translated "always active," udārāṇām -- also means "abdominal swelling." The first fruit of ignorance is obstinacy, stubbornness.

Stubbornness is always active in the Waking State; it underlies all thoughts and feelings, just as Nature permeates everything. One is stubborn about what? One is stubborn about the beliefs in separation that keep alive the existence of the limited ego; one is stubborn about the attachments and aversions that maintain the boundaries of the Waking State. Thus obstinacy keeps the other three tendencies alive.

"The ego slumbers" means that it is not the completely and dynamically awake ego of Perpetual Consciousness. When the self rises to full awareness of the Self, it is fully awake in the realization of Universality, no longer deeply asleep in the fantasies of limitation.

"Small, weak and inconsequential attachments" are not the desires of the enlightened. Every desire that manifests in the human mind has at its inception enough power and significance to be fulfilled instantly. But in the Waking State, by the time the desire reaches the surface of the mind, it is colored by previous impressions of stress and limitation, is therefore weak, often pointless, self-contradictory or even damaging. Such a desire often degenerates into a shallow attachment, small, powerless, of no significance at all. It is a boon that such desires have little energy left in them, else all the vagrant thoughts of the Waking State might be fulfilled and transmute life instantly into chaos.

The "interruption, wounding and obstruction of aversions" affect peace of mind as well as the natural flow of desire. An aversion towards anything means that, at some point in time, a limited judgment was made about the undesirability of a person, place, thing or experience; this arises from its storage place in the nervous system to collide with current experience, coloring and distorting it. The breaking of the stream of desire wounds and obstructs the flow of life, forcing it into painful and limited boundaries. The greatest break is, of course, the awareness of the Absolute into scattered and limited shards of Infinity -- so broken and wounded that the individual pieces no longer remember that they are in reality nothing other than the Infinite Ascendant.

Now begins the definition of each of the five inherent tendencies.

Pada II. Sutra 5

अनित्याशुचिदुःखानात्मसु नित्यशुचिसुखात्मख्यातिरविद्या ॥५॥

Anitya aśuchi duḥkha anātmasu nitya śuchi sukha ātma khyātir avidyā

Ignorance is the perception of the transient as the Eternal, impurity as purity, suffering as happiness and the not-self as the Self.

"Perception," khyātir, can also be translated, "knowing, supposing, celebrating." One not only misperceives, the entire structure of the personality -- mind, heart, self-sense, body -- all align to agree that the belief system, based on limited, painful experience, *must be* the truth.

Mistaking the ephemeral and constantly changing for the never-changing causes every aspect of life to be distorted. The Waking State becomes a race for subsistent survival; growth is stunted, there is little happiness, meager meaning. Mistaking the Eternal for the temporal leads to identification with the ever-changing body rather than the never-changing spirit. This leads to greater impurity in habit, in the mind, in the heart, in the body. This in turn leads to greater and greater confusion about exactly what is and what is not the individual self and therefore inevitably to suffering.

Ignorance means that values are built upon the ephemeral -- the body, possessions, cherished beliefs -- and not on the experience of the unchanging Absolute. Since this is so, suffering becomes certain, for if our treasure is stored where moth eats and rust decays, we will weep for our lost idols in the end, for these eventually pass away. Only the Ascendant endures forever; if the Ascendant is our prime focus, if the Ascendant is our treasure, then life will be lived in purity, in joy, in love, in health.

This is a simple choice, but we don't commonly realize it. We don't feel responsible if we pretend to believe we just didn't know. This is true throughout the belief structure of the ego. "Ignorance is bliss" is a common way of viewing the Universe, if it is recognized as such or not. The deep, internal attraction to maintaining the belief structure exactly as it is will be more thoroughly discussed in the ninth sutra on obstinacy. But this simple stating of the split between what is True and Real and what is not can be a great relief to a thirsty soul. If the root of ignorance is as simple as mistaking black for white, can it be difficult to change our mind and heal it instantly? No, but first stubbornness *must be* transformed.

This sutra relates to the ignorance of the knower; the next sutra applies ignorance to the process of knowing; the seventh and eighth sutras discuss ignorance in the known; the ninth sutra deals with the ultimate value of ignorance -- ignorance in the Unified Field of all the Laws of Nature itself. These four together constitute the full range of ignorance.

Pada II. Sutra 6

दृग्दर्शनशक्त्योरेकात्मतेवास्मिता ॥६॥

Dṛg darśana śaktyor ekātmatā iva asmitā

The ego comes from the apparent identification of the Seer with the power of seeing.

Patañjali says "apparent identification," ekāmatā iva, because there is no true identification of the Seer with the power of seeing; this is an illusory connection only.

The true power of the Seer is the direct cognition of truth in the Ascendant -- this is known as ṛtam bharā prajñā. The Seer identifies with the lesser power of seeing in the Waking State, this gives rise to the belief in separation, in limitation, in suffering and in death.

Seeing here stands for all the senses and the entire internal machinery of the mind and intellect. The sense of sight is chosen because it most strongly reinforces the belief in the body-world here on earth. The entire material creation and our relation to it is built up from the mistaken identity of the knower with the known. This concept will be more thoroughly explained in the seventeenth through twenty-third sutras.

Identification in the Waking State *is* a form of union. But it is a false or apparent form of union only, for the union is with the transient, the impure, suffering, the not-self. By experiencing boundaries, we come to believe in our own limited individuality as separate from our Source. Hence the ego is born and continues.

Pada II. Sutra 7

सुखानुशयी रागः ॥७॥

Sukha anuśayī rāgaḥ

Attachment results from experiencing happiness.

What impels desire? The memory derived from experiencing happiness coupled with the hope of experiencing more happiness. Everyone desires what he/she believes will bestow more pleasure. There is nothing wrong with this deep-rooted tendency of the mind, but when it is misapplied and directs life toward increasing boundaries instead of the Unbounded Absolute, time is lost and life does not progress. This is unfortunate, for it means that suffering continues.

If our experience of happiness is limited to something small, that will typically be the limit of our scope of desire. For example, when we are young, we experience that some pocket change will buy us an ice cream bar that we greatly enjoy. If we hear the ice cream truck playing its song on our street the next day, we desire a similar amount of change to repeat the experience of pleasure. Our vision extends only to the confines of our individual, private Universe. Is this bad? Not in and of itself, but it creates a repetitive cycle that makes it difficult to move beyond self-destructive habits. If we begin to define our happiness by a daily bottle of wine, for example, how long will our body withstand the repeated assaults on our liver? As we desire, we act; as we act, we experience; as we experience, we form new impressions in the subtle recording mechanism of our nervous systems; these impressions impel new desires to form. What can break this cycle? Only the introduction of a higher standard of desiring.

Pada II. Sutra 8

दुःखानुशयी द्वेषः ॥८॥

Duḥkha anuśayī dveśaḥ

Aversion results from experiencing suffering.

No one has to be told to run from pain. It is as natural to life as is running toward pleasure. The problems of human life arise when these tendencies become imbalanced. If our life is filled with fear, if we can't go to certain places or speak with certain people or do certain things because of past stress, our Universe shrinks. The more we exclude, the less there is for us to do. Life becomes extremely narrow as our painful series of self-imposed limits keeps us from acting or enjoying. Breaking our crippling fears can prove an extraordinary challenge; one that is probably all but impossible to master without Ascending.

But with expansion of consciousness, the old, deep-seated fears naturally dissolve as they are exposed to the wholly beneficent influence of evolving awareness. The sweetness of the pure bliss of the Ascendant wipes away every tear in the flawless perfection of God's Imperishable Love. The boundaries of life break, freeing us forever for unlimited joy.

A life of fear is no life but a living hell. But whatever a human being has created can be uncreated. And that is much simpler and more effortless than is commonly believed.

Pada II. Sutra 9

स्वरसवाही विदुषोपि तथारूढोभिनिवेशः ॥९॥

Svarasa vāhī viduṣo api tathā rūḍho abhiniveśaḥ

Obstinacy, flowing by the Self's own taste, flourishes even in the Wise.

What is svarasa, "the Self's own taste?" It is the desires that flow from the Self; chief of which is the desire to realize the nature of Reality. This is why stubbornness persists in the Wise -- it can be quite useful. Obstinacy can be a boon or a curse. When it serves evolution, it keeps one focussed on the goal. When it serves ignorance, it keeps one locked into self-destructive behavior patterns and beliefs. The same energy can be invaluable for growth, can make one arrive quickly at the goal of Infinite Awareness, can quickly lead life out of pain, illness and suffering and into perfect freedom in full consciousness.

Since it is impelled by the Self's inherent nature, this tendency is the strongest of the five. As such, it is at once the most potentially valuable and the most potentially crippling. If one uses this power of the mind to one-pointedly focus on evolution, regardless of whatever obstacles may arise due to past abuses and beliefs, one will quickly arrive at the goal. But if one uses obstinacy to refuse to change, to hold onto the old self-destructive beliefs and habits, life will remain in ignorance indefinitely. Thus is obstinacy the nourishing root of joy and pain.

It is interesting to note that "Obstinacy," abhiniveśaḥ, is almost universally mistranslated as "desire for life" or "will to live." This absolutely bizarre thought attempts to make Patañjali say that the universal intent of all life to stay alive is an inherent tendency, a kleśa, something to be removed with evolution. This is totally absurd. Life *is.* Only the ego can even conceive of death. And only those that understand nothing of enlightenment could possibly so misread Patañjali's intent.

Pada II. Sutra 10

ते प्रतिप्रसवहेयाः सूक्ष्माः ॥१०॥

Te pratiprasava heyāḥ sūkṣmāḥ

These are avoided in the subtle by taking them back inward.

"Avoided," heyāḥ, can also be translated "abandoned" or "rejected." Avoided in the subtle means before they have begun to grip the mind. Taking the impulse of attachment, aversion, obstinacy, ego, or ignorance backward into subtler and subtler states until it dissolves back into the Ascendant obliterates the tendency before it has the chance to manifest fully. Of course, this means that the awareness has already become sufficiently refined to recognize impulses as they arise, which means that the individual has gained proficiency in experience of the Fourth State, Ascendant Consciousness. Attempting to take thoughts back inward without having first developed clarity of Ascending would be rather like trying to put a bomb back together after it has exploded. It is a gigantic waste of time, even were it possible at all.

"Taking them back inward," pratiprasava, can also be translated, "pressing out the Soma inside." Soma is the most refined product of digestion; it naturally occurs in everyone all the time, but not in sufficient quantities to be useful. Or if the quantity is all right, then its function is typically blocked by excessive production of antagonistic molecules. What does Soma do?

Soma is the primary physical source of the glue that sticks the Absolute firmly to the mind. It is the physical carrier or counterpart of the superfluid functioning of the nervous system that maintains Ascendant Consciousness permanently. It is further the source of the transformation in the senses of perception that create Exalted Consciousness and Unified Consciousness. Soma is also the fundamental source of health and longevity.[17] As the Soma is pressed inside, the gripping nature of the innate tendencies starts to relax; those which are useful transmute into vehicles of light and power; those which are not useful fade and are seen no more.

The human mind can only do one thing at a time. If the awareness is continually turning back toward the Ascendant, there is no time left for it to be caught by the old boundaries of belief and habit. This cultures freedom as quickly as is possible.

---

[17] -- The ancient texts would more boldly say, immortality, but we in the modern age tend to scoff at such assertions. To our loss! A world without magic and wonder is a fairly pointless world to inhabit.

Pada II. Sutra 11

ध्यानहेयास्तद्वृत्तयः ॥११॥

Dhyāna heyāḥ tad vṛttayaḥ

These are avoided in their movements through Resonance.

If the mind is not sufficiently subtle to catch the inherent tendencies before they manifest, the path to freedom from them is Resonance, harmonious flowing with the Self (see the commentary on the second sutra of the third pada). Only by learning to turn the mind gracefully inward will the movements of these inherent tendencies gradually fall away.

The effects of these tendencies are the nine obstacles listed in I.30; a primary purpose of the First Chapter was the description of the various methods to remove these manifestations.

Pada II. Sutra 12

क्लेशमूलः कर्माशयो दृष्टादृष्टजन्मवेदनीयः ॥१२॥

Kleśa mūlaḥ karma aśayo dṛṣṭā adṛṣṭa janma vedanīyaḥ

The root of the inherent tendencies is the impressions of actions; they are expressed in seen and unseen manifestations.

What gives life to the inherent tendencies? Just this: previous experiences and the impressions these experiences have left in the subtle recording machinery of the nervous system. When these impressions are impacted by new desire, they breathe forth life into the tendencies of ignorance that reinforce these impressions (see the commentaries on I.24 and I.50).

By "seen and unseen manifestations" Patañjali means that some of the effects of our thoughts, beliefs and actions are known and some are not. For example, one might or might not be aware of the effects of regular inhaling of carcinogenic substances, but the effects will occur nonetheless. Once a rock starts falling down a well, it will fall until it reaches the bottom, if anyone sees it or not.

How then to be free from the five inherent tendencies? Taking them back inward to the subtle dissolves the deep-rooted stresses that are their fundamental root (see II.10, commentary). Or, experience the full power of ṛtam bharā prajñā directed toward Silence and create an impression that is deeper than the impressions of stress (see I.50, commentary). Expansion of consciousness is the universal key to freedom from the past.

Pada II. Sutra 13

सति मूले तद्विपाको जात्यायुर्भोगाः ॥१३॥

Sati mūle tad vipāko jāti āyuḥ bhogāḥ

As long as the root exists, it matures into birth, life and experience.

"Experience," bhogaḥ, also means "enjoyment" -- this is the sticky glue that keeps life bound to the moving wheel. Enjoyment gives rise to impressions that lead to desires that give rise to the birth of new actions. This cycle is endless in its own Universe; only by Ascending beyond it can it be permanently broken.

As long as deep stress continues, it will create manifestations. These manifestations will endure for a certain time (they will have a certain life-expectancy); each will cause certain experiences to manifest. Just as in the case of a tenacious weed that does not die when pulled up but sprouts again from the root, just so the stress in the nervous system will create again its corresponding desires which lead to the actions which will reinforce the stress. This is exactly why it is so frightfully difficult to break any self-destructive behavior pattern without Ascending -- it is not possible (or at least, extremely difficult) to go beyond any deep stress sufficiently to dislodge it and free the nervous system for new freedom and accomplishment without expansion of consciousness.

The new root of the experience of the Ascendant also leads to new birth, life and experience. In this case, however, what is being born is the uninterrupted experience of joy; what lives is Eternal Freedom in Divine Consciousness; what is experienced is fulfillment in every area of human concern. Life in Heaven or life in hell is the consequence of exactly what our deepest root is.

Pada II. Sutra 14

ते ह्लादपरितापफलाः पुण्यापुण्यहेतुत्वात् ॥१४॥

Te hlāda paritāpa phalāḥ puṇya apuṇya hetutvāt

Righteousness causes these to have refreshingly delightful fruits; unrighteousness causes these to have excruciatingly painful fruits.

"Refreshingly delightful," hlāda, can also be translated "cooling" or "rejoicing." "Excruciatingly painful," paritāpa, also means "agonizingly hot, supremely distressing, anguishing, sorrowful."

"Righteousness," puṇya, means life in accord with Natural Law, life that joins the upward spiral of creation into greater and greater joy, love, light and consciousness. "Unrighteousness," apuṇya, means life leading away from evolution into ever-greater bondage.

As life moves upward or downward, Nature acts to restore the balance. Nature is extremely elastic in its functioning; it supports any and every possible lifestyle. The more upwardly-mobile the life becomes, the more Nature responds by inspiring joy, love, life and health. The more downwardly-directed the life becomes, the more Nature responds by inspiring unhappiness, despair, frustration and disease. Choose the tree you wish to grow and enjoy the fruits thereof. But, be careful to recognize that every choice you make is made by you. It is not the fault of any external agent or force. Heaven or hell. Your choice.

Pada II. Sutra 15

परिणामतापसंस्कारदुःखैर्गुणवृत्तिविरोधाच्च दुःखमेव सर्वं विवेकिनः ॥१५॥

Pariṇāma tāpa saṃskāra duḥkhair guṇa vṛtti virodhāt cha duḥkham eva sarvaṃ vivekinaḥ

To the discriminating, not only is the ripening of the impressions of painful fruit suffering, all the conflicting movements of the fundamental forces of Nature, the guṇas, are also all only suffering.

For a discussion of the three guṇas, see the commentary on the sixteenth sutra of the first pada.

The "conflicting movements of the fundamental forces of Nature," guṇa vṛitti virodhāt, are the ultimate root of all suffering. Certainly, it is painful to experience the fruit of self-destructive thoughts and habits; but in this verse, Patañjali observes that *any* conflicting manifestation of even the Natural Laws themselves also only create suffering. This is saying that the range of suffering is from the grossest level of expression to the subtlest disharmonies of the functioning of Natural Law. Thus any thought, desire, action that is not born of the complete harmony of the fundamental forces of Natural Law is necessarily going to lead to suffering, regardless of how plausible it might appear to the surface of the mind.

This sutra explains how some experiences which can seem quite enjoyable are eventually going to produce rather unfortunate results. The wise are not fooled by the surface appearance but quest deeply to understand whether a thought, word, belief or action is truly life-supporting and evolutionary in every way -- or not. For it is only those movements of the guṇas that lead the individual back to the Source that are completely free from any conflict -- only those that are completely dominated by the upward current of creation known as sattva are those which do not lead eventually to suffering (see the commentary on the eighteenth sutra of this pada).

As an example of this, consider the intense focus on the ideal of romantic love in the world today -- virtually every song, movie, book sings the glory of the search for (or the agony of the failure of) romantic love. This focus has become a very effective tool of the ego to keep life from progressing by covering up the true search of a soul with an illusory search that can never be fulfilled.

This is not saying that Ideal Love between two people cannot exist! Ideal Love is most assuredly a real fact. The existence of this is supported by the guṇas working in perfect harmony. What, then, is an Ideal Relationship? It is one in which both partners are rising to full enlightenment together and sharing their dawning perfection with others. Any other motive for togetherness is rooted in conflicting action of the guṇas and will therefore in time inevitably result in suffering.

It is a common experience that if the mind is divided against itself about the desirability of any given action, the support of the mind, body and surroundings is only potential or weak. How much more true is this of the movement of the fundamental forces of Nature. Any conflict, even the slightest, leads to undesirable consequences which take the form of suffering.

How, then, is it possible to be completely free from the effects of conflicting movements of the guṇas? The next nine sutras answer this question.

Pada II. Sutra 16

हेयं दुःखमनागतम् ॥१६॥

Heyaṃ duḥkham anāgatam

Avoid the suffering which has not yet come.

Patañjali in this sutra says nothing about *how* to avoid future suffering, for that is precisely the prime focus of the entirety of the Yoga Sutras. The basic principle is to be established in the Now (see I.1, commentary). Attain perfection in the present instant and the future will take care of itself.

It is vastly easier to cure a disease before it has manifested on the material plane of existence. It is vastly wiser to create a state of being in which suffering of any kind is eliminated in advance of its manifestation.

This comes as a result of establishing invincibility of consciousness. In this state, negativity breaks before it reaches the individual, just as if surrounded by an invisible shield. The hard rocks are vaporized before they can strike; the raining arrows of death and destruction transmute into gentle showers of light and love; all the myriad destructive impulses of returning karma melt into blessings of peace and joy. The desire to attain this state is a perfectly valid reason to attempt to master the Science of Union. Whatever the motivation, to run toward joy or to run away from suffering, it makes no difference in the outcome. The only important thing is to begin to run! There is no winning for those who don't play the game.

Pada II. Sutra 17

द्रष्टृदृश्ययोः संयोगो हेयहेतुः ॥१७॥

Draṣṭṛ dṛśyayoḥ saṃyogaḥ heya hetuḥ

The identification of the Seer with the Seen is the cause of the avoidable.

Compare this sutra with II.6, where the ego is defined as the result of the apparent identification of the Seer with the power of seeing.

"The Seer," Draṣṭṛ, and "the Seen," dṛśyayoḥ, will be further defined in the following five sutras. The cause of "identification," saṃyogaḥ, will be further defined in sutras twenty-three and twenty-four.

How does one avoid the danger that has not yet come? By removing the cause of the impending suffering. What is this cause? Identification of the knower with the known.

The knower in his/her true state *is* the Absolute. But in the Waking State of Consciousness, the knower does not see or remember this; instead, the knower perceives the objects of perception and forgets everything of the Ascendant Self. This is a five dollar gain and a billion dollar loss. Reality hides behind the enticing display of the changing relative, patiently awaiting an enquiring and sincere mind.

"Identification," saṃyogaḥ, translates literally, "connection with the connected." This is an extremely sticky union. The Waking State is a kind of union, only it is an imbalanced union. The subject loses its integrity in the perception of the object. Not remembering its true status, the Self wanders about as the self, believing in its mortality, identifying with its body and the body's suffering; victim to the multitude of infirmities and problems that continually afflict the ego in ignorance.

Fortunately, there is another way to live. And the really good news is that it is not difficult to change the mind and avoid future suffering.

Pada II. Sutra 18

प्रकाशक्रियास्थितिशीलं भूतेन्द्रियात्मकं भोगापवर्गार्थं दृश्यम् ॥१८॥

Prakāśa kriyā sthiti śīlaṃ bhūta indriya ātmakaṃ bhoga apavarga arthaṃ dṛśyam

The purpose of the Seen is enjoyment and liberation. It consists of the senses and the elements and has the properties of stillness, motion and illumination.

"Purpose," artha, also means "cause, meaning, reward, wealth" (see I.28, commentary). "The senses," indriya, include the mind, heart, intellect and ego -- it stands for the inner machinery by which the Self interacts with the Universe.

Why does the Universe exist? To provide for enjoyment and liberation. Neither purpose, correctly applied, opens the individual to suffering. "Enjoyment" also means experience -- see the commentary on II.13 -- ideally, all experience should be enjoyable, a constant and continual upward movement of bliss.

"The Seen," dṛśyam, again here stands for the entire structure of the relative Universe as well as the connecting link to the Universe, the inner machinery of the senses and mind. It represents the entire field of that which can be known by the senses of perception.

The three properties of the three fundamental forces of Nature, the guṇas (see the commentaries on I.16 & II.15) are stillness, motion and illumination.

These three are responsible for everything that is. Illumination is the primary quality of sattva, the guṇa that is in charge of evolution, creativity and purity. Motion is the primary quality of rajas, the guṇa of energy. And stillness or inertia is the primary quality of tamas, the destructive force. Nothing anywhere in creation, from the faintest thought to the largest explosion, the original Big Bang itself, could exist, move or even be without the intertwining energy of these three. So the entire structure of the Seen is thus permeated with these three fundamental Natural Laws. For example, fire is a manifestation of pure rajas, energy. But it is also highly tamasic -- it destroys everything it burns -- as well as very sattvic -- it creates heat and light and new forms from the old. All of matter and energy are composed of the intertwining energies of these three.

Sattva is that property which makes enlightenment possible, for it pervades everything with clarity and light. Rajas is responsible for the energy that permeates all of matter. And tamas makes everything solid or tangible. These three together weave the world and every particle within it.

Pada II. Sutra 19

विशेषाविशेषलिङ्गमात्रालिङ्गानि गुणपर्वाणि ॥१९॥

Viśeṣa aviśeṣa liṅga mātra aliṅgāni guṇa parvāṇi

The limbs of the fundamental forces of nature, the guṇas, extend from the extraordinary to the ordinary, from the whole of the manifest to the unmanifest.[18]

That is to say, the guṇas encompass all of creation. (Cf. I.40). Nothing, from the most wonderful to the most mundane, exists beyond the sphere of their activity; the totality of manifest creation, extending from the unmanifest to the full extent of every created thing, is held by the grip of these three fundamental forces.

---

[18] -- This sutra shows the combination of the three guṇas that creates the four-fold order of creation: extraordinary is the fullest expression of sattva and includes the totality of the celestial and the Natural Laws of the Universe; unmanifest is the fullest expression of tamas and includes the pre-creation state of the togetherness of the knower, the known and the process of knowing called in Sanskrit, *saṃhita*; ordinary is sattva and rajas mixed and includes all living creation; the whole of the manifest is tamas and rajas mixed and includes all physical matter.

Another reading of this sutra identifies extraordinary with the Full Moon, unmanifest with the New Moon, and the other two with the last and first quarters. And it can also be read as descriptive of states of consciousness: extraordinary is dreaming, ordinary is waking, manifest is sleep and unmanifest is Ascendant. Or again, ordinary is Perpetual, extraordinary is Exalted, manifest is Unity and unmanifest is Ascendant. The mind and the senses are contained within extraordinary and ordinary; the elements are described by manifest and unmanifest. Explosions of meaning are everywhere found in Mahāṛṣi Patañjali's Yoga Sutras.

This sutra describes not only the range of the properties of the last sutra, it also defines the extent of the domain of the purpose of creation that is for enjoyment. It is *all* for enjoyment, for experience, for growth, for progress. The culmination of enjoyment *is* liberation. It is not the case that one must cut down enjoyment to be free. Quite the contrary is true, in fact -- it is by *increasing* the level of enjoyment that one rises to higher and higher stages of desiring and eventually rises to the desire for enlightenment. Those that advocate depriving life of enjoyment as the means to gain enlightenment simply don't know what they are talking about, whosoever they may happen to be. Steps of progress follow steps of enjoyment in a thoroughly natural unfolding of life to Life. There is no necessity for suffering on the path of evolution. Rather, all of life can be experienced in increasing waves of bliss and love.

Attempting to cut away enjoyment in order to evolve will always fail, for it is precisely by fulfilling each level of desiring that one naturally rises onto the next stage. Only the fulfilled child rises to healthy adulthood. Whatever the areas of incompleteness as a child, these will continue to exist in the adult personality as dark, shadowy areas that shun the light, as secret wounds that try desperately again and again to be healed. Fulfillment of one stage leads on to the next, spontaneously.

Pada II. Sutra 20

द्रष्टा दृशिमात्रः शुद्धोपि प्रत्ययानुपश्यः ॥२०॥

Draṣṭā dṛśi mātraḥ śuddho api pratyaya anupaśyaḥ

The whole of the Seen is clear to the liberated Seer, even thoughts are witnessed.

Having described in the last sutra the range of enjoyment of the known, Patañjali begins his definition of the purpose of the known to the enlightened. The totality of creation is experienced as clear or pure to those who have completely unmade their self-destructive internal programs. Being completely free from stress inside, they see only Beauty and Truth outside. No longer possessed of darkness and fear, they see only the light of the Divine in every thought, word and experience. This is not blindness! This is seeing life as it truly is, free from all the limiting beliefs and judgments about the nature of the Universe. This is the vision of the enlightened -- *everything* is clear.

Even thoughts are witnessed. Even the subtlest expression of the guṇas in the Universe, thoughts, are separate from the Absolute Silence of the Seer who knows Reality. There is no connection between the Ascendant and the action of the guṇas; this is the experience of Perpetual Consciousness. "Walking, I do not walk; breathing, I do not breathe; speaking, I do not speak; thinking, I do not think." The "I" is established permanently in the Ascendant; the action of the guṇas continues very much as before, creating thoughts, feelings and experiences. Infinite duality is the prime experience of this, the first stage of enlightenment -- the Seer, established in the Absolute Self, watches the entire play and display of creation continue on, very much as before, only now free from the self-created and falsely imposed dark limits of the mistaken understandings of the Waking State. This is liberation -- freedom from the boundaries of false belief and experience, recognition at all times in all places of the Real.

There is a useful analogy to explain the distinction between the Waking State and Perpetual Consciousness: in the Waking State, it is as if water and milk are mixed together. There is no separation between the two, no way to tell where the water ends and the milk begins. The Self and the self are thoroughly mixed together and confused. Perpetual Consciousness is like completely separated milk and water. There is no mistaking the two, for both are perceived in their independent and quite distinct realities.

What desires remain for the enlightened?

Pada II. Sutra 21

तदर्थ एव दृश्यस्यात्मा ॥२१॥

Tad artha eva dṛśyasya ātmā

The liberated Seer's only purpose is in seeing the Absolute Self.

"Purpose," artha, also means, "cause, object, meaning, reward, wealth" (see I.28, commentary).

Once one has discovered the unending bliss of the clear experience of the Ascendant, one quite naturally begins to desire more and more to make it a permanent experience, to establish Perpetual Consciousness. This causes the priorities of life to reverse: instead of being dedicated to the idols of the Waking State, one naturally desires to become ever more firmly and permanently aligned with the Divine.

This does not mean one should cut down other desires in order to evolve! One cannot repress anything if one wishes to be free of self-destructive habits, for anything repressed is only strengthened by the additional energy imposed on it by the act of repression. Freedom from the confines of the ego comes about through enjoyment, as explained in sutras eighteen and nineteen. On the basis of fulfillment, one's standard of desiring naturally rises to higher and higher planes. Only through fulfilling one's desires do they naturally transmute into ever-higher expressions.

This sutra is, then, a description of one who has at least attained the clear experience of Ascendant Consciousness. Only then can a person be said to be a Seer; only then does the ever-rising desire for permanence of enlightenment take hold of the personality ever more forcefully; only then does one's purpose naturally and spontaneously shift from the gross and limiting desires of the Waking State to the subtler and expansive desires of one moving toward Eternal Freedom in the permanent consciousness of the Ascendant.

This sutra also has its extension beyond Perpetual Consciousness, for only when one is continuously witnessing the inherent duality of creation -- Infinite on the inside, finite on the outside -- does the quest to see the Infinite on the outside begin to make any sense. In other words, without the continual recognition of the Divine on the inside, the search for the Divine on the outside is doomed to a rather ignominious failure, for one can project out only what one is carrying within. If one still sees limitation, death, disease and fear inside, it is not very likely that one will well perceive anything very wonderful outside! Cleanse first the mirror of the mind, then turn it in any direction to see the Unlimited Glory of the Cosmos.

Pada II. Sutra 22

कृतार्थं प्रति नष्टमप्यनष्टं तदन्यसाधारणत्वात् ॥२२॥

Kṛta artham prati naṣṭam api anaṣṭam tad anya sādhāraṇatvāt

The connection with Seen vanishes for the liberated Seer who has realized the purpose of all action, but it continues as the common experience of all others.

Perpetual Consciousness is perfect duality -- there is no connection left with the Seen, for the Infinite inside is eternally separate from the finite experienced outside.

One of the most surprising experiences of Perpetual Consciousness is not the Infinite duality between the Seer established in the Absolute Awareness and the Seen, which continues as before (although freed from the imposed beliefs of limitation -- see II.20). This experience, although it may sound very strange indeed from the perspective of the Waking State, is not surprising at all, for it seems utterly natural and logical -- how, after all, could there possibly be a connection between the Seer and the Seen? Rationally, there can be no connection whatever between the Infinite and the finite. No, what is surprising to those established in Perpetual Consciousness is that all people everywhere do not recognize that they share this experience.

This inability to comprehend the identification of the Self with the not-Self[19] is precisely what makes the life of individuals born in Perpetual Consciousness so very frustrating. Such individuals (e.g., Krishnamurti, Mother Meera) who appear to have either been born in that state or moved into it at a very early age, have no memory at all of the illusory identification of the

---

[19] -- Identification was mentioned in II.6 and II.17 and will be further explained in the next sutra.

connection of the Seer with the Seen, and therefore have almost no ability to teach others how to rise above the Waking State into the direct and continual experience of Perpetual Consciousness. For such rare souls, their extremely clear perception of the nature of the Self and of the Universe does not communicate very clearly or well to many. This can lead to a certain degree of frustration on both sides! Without having experienced (or without remembering having experienced) a path to Perpetual Consciousness, their ability to help others realize their inner Infinite Self is typically extremely limited.

Another valid interpretation of this sutra reads, *"The liberated Seer who has realized the purpose of all action is beyond all loss and gain, but these continue as the common experience of all others."* To the enlightened, any change in the relative Universe, the domain of the Seen, does not and cannot overshadow the bliss of continual contact with the Ascendant. This is why the enlightened do not overmuch grieve or rejoice in the changes of the relative Universe.

Pada II. Sutra 23

स्वस्वामिशक्त्योः स्वरूपोपलब्धिहेतुः संयोगः ॥२३॥

Sva svāmi śaktyoḥ svarūpa upalabdhi hetuḥ saṃyogaḥ

The cause of identification is the perception of the Absolute Self as the knower, the known and the process of knowing.

Identification (from II.17) is the connection that vanished in the last sutra. The Absolute Self is experienced as completely separate from the objective Universe in Perpetual Consciousness; but in the Waking State, the Absolute Self is scattered between three very distinct realities: the knower, the known and the process of knowing. The Self becomes the self, the ego; the small "s" self is overshadowed and identifies with the objects of perception. This confusion and loss of Self-awareness is the root of identification and therefore is the source of all the suffering which has not yet come and can still be avoided (see the commentary on the sixteenth sutra).

Pada II. Sutra 24

तस्य हेतुरविद्या ॥२४॥

Tasya hetur avidyā

The cause of that is ignorance.

The ultimate root of all avoidable suffering (II.16) is simply ignorance. Ignorance (as stated in the fifth sutra) is the confusion of that which is not real for the Real; it has innumerable consequences, not the least of which is all suffering. Disease, old age and death itself are the baleful counterparts of ignorance. It could be accurately said that the entire purpose of the Science of Union is simply to remove ignorance. This, from the negative side, is the whole purpose of human life. What is the positive side? Expansion of happiness, joy, love and life.

Pada II. Sutra 25

तदभावात्संयोगाभावो हानं तद्दृशेः कैवल्यम् ॥२५॥

Tad abhāvāt saṃyoga abhāvo hānaṃ tad dṛśeḥ kaivalyam

When ignorance ceases to exist, when identification ceases to exist, when all that is for seeing is abandoned, that is Unified Consciousness.

II.20 defined the first stage of enlightenment, Perpetual Consciousness, in which the knower is established in full awareness of the Infinite Self. This sutra defines the Absolute Oneness of Unified Consciousness, in which the knower's Infinite status is perceived throughout the full range of the Seen. This sutra defines Unified Consciousness as the removal of ignorance from the knower, removal of identification from the process of knowing, and complete cessation or abandonment of all that is known.

"Abandonment of the known" does not mean that a person established in Unified Consciousness gives up his family, his job and his home and lives in a cave somewhere. What it does mean is that one is no longer bound to anything of the Universe. The whole range of creation is perceived as being Infinite by the person established in Unified Consciousness. The boundaries do not cease to exist, but they are no longer the dominant feature of Awareness. Since one is no longer attached to the objects of perception, one is established in freedom.

"Ignorance ceases to exist" means it is utterly gone. What happens to a dream when one awakens? It simply returns to the nothingness from which it sprang. Patañjali also uses this phrasing for identification ("Identification ceases to exist"), for identification is nothing other than the clogging of the process of knowing with false belief and understanding. But he uses a very different phrasing for the objects of perception ("All that is for seeing is abandoned"), for the external world obviously does continue to exist even if the enlightened individual has wholly abandoned the overshadowing connection with it.

Freedom means being able to move through the characteristics of the world without losing the stability and integrity of Consciousness. Slavery means being overshadowed by every experience, forgetting joy, forgetting peace, forgetting love, forgetting everything that is of the Real, the True or the Good and being left with nothing but a handful of broken dreams, a castle of sand, a phantasmal mirage of life.

The next sutra describes the mechanics of developing this process of abandoning which leads to Unified Consciousness.

Pada II. Sutra 26

विवेकख्यातिरविप्लवा हानोपायः ॥२६॥

Viveka khyātir aviplavā hānopāyaḥ

The means of abandoning is stabilizing the awareness of discrimination.

How are Perpetual Cosciousness and Unified Consciousness structured? By making the awareness of discrimination permanent. What is the awareness of discrimination? Discrimination is the act of discerning what is and what is not Real. Obviously, this is impossible without the experience of the Ascendant. When one has risen to stability of Absolute Awareness in Ascendant Consciousness, moving ahead quickly to enlightenment is intimately connected with the ability to tell the difference between that which is Eternal and that which is not.

Culturing the awareness of discrimination is impossible without the experience of Ascendant Consciousness. With it, on the other hand, one gradually learns to discriminate more and more effectively between the thoughts and experiences which lead to greater and greater happiness and eventually to liberation and those which lead to greater and greater bondage and ignorance. From the surface of the mind, this discrimination is extraordinarily difficult (or even impossible) to achieve, for much that can seem enjoyable is in fact going to have painful consequences, and some of that which may appear not enjoyable may in fact be exactly what is required to move ahead.

As an obvious example, wise parents do not give everything to their children on silver platters. Even if they are quite wealthy, they, if they are wise, wish for their children to appreciate what they will one day inherit; this inspires them to introduce their children gradually to their status. The children might not, from their level of experience, appreciate the gift their parents are giving them by making it a slightly more indirect path to fulfillment -- but they will appreciate it and understand it when they are mature.

This is not saying that suffering is desirable! No wise parents wish their children to suffer. But there is a wide range in the potential of human experience. Some paths lead to useless lives; others, perhaps viewed from the surface of the mind as being harder, will lead to much greater levels of progress and accomplishment.

How to stabilize this ability to discriminate is the subject of the rest of this chapter, beginning with the twenty-eighth sutra. Again let me emphasize that *stabilization* of Ascendant Consciousness is not the same thing at all as *gaining* Ascendant Consciousness. Gaining Ascendant Consciousness was the topic of the First Chapter. Beginning here, Patañjali is now focussing on how to make the experience permanent, how to stabilize the higher states of consciousness collectively known as enlightenment. To underscore this simple point, Maharishi Patañjali adds the following sutra.

Pada II. Sutra 27

तस्य सप्तधा प्रान्तभूमिः प्रज्ञा ॥२७॥

Tasya saptadhā prānta bhūmiḥ prajñā

Unified Consciousness is the limit of the sevenfold stages of consciousness.

The "sevenfold stages of consciousness" are the Seven States of Consciousness: sleeping, dreaming, waking, Ascendant, Perpetual, Exalted and Unified. "Unified Consciousness is the limit" means that these seven constitute the full range of human development of consciousness. When one has risen to the state of constant awareness of the Ascendant, both within and without, there is no further development available in terms of expansion of consciousness. Of course there is more to be learned, of course further development continues, but this development is not of the container of knowledge, only of its contents.

Rising to full human consciousness is rather like building a beautiful home with seven rooms. The purpose of the Science of Union is to build the house, it is not to fill the rooms with furniture or decorate the walls. That is the domain of philosophy, science, religion and human life experience of the full range of the Universe that is devoted to experience and enjoyment. One could therefore say that Unified Consciousness is more accurately described as the birth of normal human life. Human life was never intended to be restricted to three rooms, one completely dark, one fantastic but intrinsically meaningless, one fraught with danger, hardship and suffering.

There is an ancient echo, coming down to us from virtually every part of the world, written or whispered in almost every tradition, that the human is born to be the Master of Creation, with dominion over everything that is, every plant, every animal, even over the angels in Heaven.

And yet, what is the average human? A disease-ridden, virtually powerless, miserably unhappy worm of seventy winters. This the Master of Creation? It is scarcely the master of its own body, which falls ill, rots and decays almost from its inception. Obviously if the human is born to be the Master of Creation, the Waking State with its constant change is most assuredly not the seat of this mastery. What then is? The unchanging, Infinite stability of Absolute Awareness is the only suitable ground for this dominion.

Pada II. Sutra 28

योगाङ्गानुष्ठानादशुद्धिक्षये ज्ञानदीप्तिराविवेकख्यातेः ॥२८॥

Yoga aṅga anuṣṭhānād aśuddhi kṣaye jñāna dīptir

ā viveka khyāteḥ

As one accomplishes the limbs of Union, impurities are destroyed and the light of wisdom rises to full awareness of discrimination.

"The limbs of Union" will be listed in the next sutra and explained subsequently. "Limbs" imply simultaneous development. When a child is growing in the womb, all the structure more or less grows simultaneously. It is a complete misunderstanding of this flawless Science to think that it develops in steps, which is the common translation of aṅga, limbs. Thinking that Union is the result of eight physical and mental practices at once cheapens and complicates the practice of Union to make it all but impossible to attain by an average person. Rather, it is impossible to attain by *anyone*, for the requirements of the eight steps are simply impossible to accomplish without the experience of the Ascendant.

Probably the ultimate root of this misunderstanding is the fact that a pseudo or surface value of each of the eight limbs *can* be practiced; some limited success with these leads to a certain modest degree of progress. But full accomplishment of any of the limbs implies and necessitates full accomplishment of all of them. These are the handmaidens of enlightenment, not the stairway to enlightenment.

Destruction of impurities and the rising of the light of wisdom are the same reality, viewed from two opposing viewpoints. The nervous system is freed from stress as consciousness expands; consciousness expands as the nervous system is freed from stress. Both happen simultaneously. Indeed, one is impossible without the other.

Pada II. Sutra 29

यमनियमासनप्राणायामप्रत्याहारधारणाध्यानसमाधयोष्टावङ्गानि ॥२९॥

Yama niyama āsana prāṇāyāma pratyāhāra dhāraṇā dhyāna samādhi aṣṭa aṅgāni

The eight limbs are: the five observances, the five actions, postures, breathing, withdrawal, Focus, Resonance and Ascendant Consciousness.

These will be explained in the next thirty sutras. "Withdrawal" means withdrawal of the senses from their objects. "Focus" means the ability to maintain a single thought or experience to the exclusion of others. "Resonance" means Ascension.

These eight list the effect of experiencing the Ascendant on the various components of the personality from the subtlest -- the Self in Ascendant Consciousness -- to the grossest -- how to manage the body in the world, the five observances. Patañjali here defines eight spheres of life and observes the effect of expansion of consciousness in each.

Those who consider these to be the steps to Union observe that Ascendant Consciousness is at the end of the list and therefore conclude that the previous steps must be mastered first in order to reach the last. But to master any of these could easily require a lifetime of effort. To perfect postures, for example, means that one can hold any position or yogic āsana for at least three hours. All day could be spent in practicing physical Yoga with very little achievement by the end. And when the program of evolution is believed to begin with the five observances, each of which must be flawlessly mastered before one graduates to the five actions, the whole life will be lost before one even begins the approach to the Ascendant.

On the other hand, if these eight are in fact developing simultaneously, then the more one experiences the Ascendant, the less stress is there in the body; therefore, the more effortlessly the postures are mastered. And similarly for each of the limbs. These are the qualities that mature simultaneously with Ascendant Consciousness. Or, if there must be a starting point, then the starting point must be Ascendant Consciousness.

This is why Patañjali puts this list here, half-way through the Second Chapter on Perpetual Consciousness, not at the beginning of the First Chapter on Ascendant Consciousness. Ascendant Consciousness develops first! As one has risen to the clarity of this experience, all the other qualities of the enlightened mind naturally and inevitably develop. This is not a complicated path of strain and effort! This is an ever-increasing movement of pure joy.

Pada II. Sutra 30

तत्राहिंसासत्यास्तेयब्रह्मचर्यापरिग्रहायमाः ॥३०॥

Tatra ahiṃsā satya asteya brahmacharya aparigrahā yamāḥ

Among these, the five observances are: non-violence, truthfulness, non-stealing, self-restraint, and non-grasping.

Those who say that the path to Union consists of eight steps insist that these five observances must be mastered as the very first step. But these five observances (which, literally translated, mean "deaths") are simply impossible to attain without first mastering Ascendant Consciousness.

How could one even recognize if a given thought or action is life-supporting or damaging, if awareness is colored by self-defeating beliefs and judgments? How can any moment be established in "non-violence," ahiṃsā, considering the simple fact that our bodies are continually destroying millions or even billions of invading bacteria at every instant? And how can one survive without eating, an act which pulls life from the environment to nourish ours?

Perfect non-violence is impossible if one desires to stay in a human body. But as one rises to full human consciousness, one stops damaging the mind, body and environment by projecting and acting out destructive impulses. Being fully established in non-violence means that we never contribute to contradictory motions of the guṇas -- from our side, we move in harmony with the perfect operation of the fundamental forces of Nature, the guṇas, which means that all of life flows forward, united with the Divine Plan.

Similarly, "truthfulness," satya, can only be a relative thing unless one has established the level of consciousness that perceives Absolute Truth. Attempting to master non-violence, truthfulness or any of the limbs of Yoga is not in any sense bad, but will never succeed perfectly until Ascendant

Consciousness is attained and stabilized. No one is truthful until established in the Truth.

These two, ahiṃsā and satya, are the two most basic laws in the Universe. Ahiṃsā, non-violence, is an expression of pure love, the Ānanda quality of the Ascendant. Satya is an expression of Truth, the Sat value of the Ascendant. By dedicating the life to these two, the consciousness (Chit) is filled with Truth and Love, bringing all the three elements to completion. Sat-Chit-Ānanda is one of the most ancient definitions of the Ascendant; this sutra recognizes the absolutely basic nature of Non-violence and Truthfulness and thereby demonstrates how consciousness is structured in complete accord with Natural Law.

Similarly, everyone as if steals the authority of the action of the fundamental forces of nature, the guṇas, as long as one is in the Waking State of Consciousness. Everyone thinks, "I do, I think, I feel," but the reality is that the Forces of Nature act on the Forces of Nature. It is not until the Seer or knower is established in the Absolute that all thoughts, words and actions are purely witnessed. This is Perpetual Consciousness -- then and only then is "non-stealing," asteya, fully established.

"Self-restraint," brahmacharya, is typically translated "celibacy" and includes turning away from every kind of sensual enjoyment. But straining to control the physical body is not the path to Union. When one has stabilized Perpetual Consciousness, it is natural for all of life to be directed upward. The literal meaning of "Self-restraint" is "student of the totality of the Absolute." How does one become such a student? Only by experiencing the Ascendant. Thus this observance applies to a state of mind rather than to an artificial practice of control. If one is experiencing Infinite bliss from upward-directed thoughts, what potential will there be for downward-directed thoughts and activity? Not a whole lot.

"Non-grasping," aparigrahā, is the tendency *not* to amass possessions. Possessions include everything physical and mental that one attempts to hold onto. Sometimes fear drives people on such a deep level that they see no hope for fulfillment without amassing much more than they can ever use, of things as well as knowledge. The tendency to hold on at all costs is one of the major stumbling blocks to the growth of consciousness, for if possessions are valued more than the Ascendant, possessions will be owned as long as the body endures, but the Absolute will remain hidden. It is not that there is anything wrong with possessions! It is the *attachment* to possessions, the desire to hold them close from fear, that keeps life bound to the Waking State.

Healing attachment without the experience of the Ascendant is all but impossible and largely pointless. Giving up one's possessions and family accomplishes absolutely nothing except that one would no longer have possessions or contact with a family. The path to enlightenment is not through renunciation. But when Perpetual Consciousness is stabilized, one's experience is that the inner Self is Infinite, the outer world completely separate from it. In this state, non-grasping is naturally perfected (just as are the other four observances), for *nothing* is held by or even can be held by the Self. Even though the Self underlies and pervades everything, it is eternally separate from all of space and time -- *knowing* that, one does not tenaciously grasp that which is meaningless.

This is the only understanding of the five observances that makes sense; indeed, this is the only understanding of the five observances that makes them possible to achieve. These are not the steps to Union, these are the natural counterparts of Union. Any other thinking on this subject serves to divide the mind, weaken it and slow down the growth to enlightenment. These are not the steps to Union! *These are not the steps to Union!*

Pada II. Sutra 31

जातिदेशकालसमयानवच्छिन्नाः सार्वभौमा महाव्रतम् ॥३१॥

Jāti deśa kāla samaya anavachchhinnāḥ sārva bhaumā mahā vratam

The observances are perfected when they apply to all that proceeds from the Earth with no distinction for species, place, time or circumstances.

Another valid translation of this sutra is, "The observances become great vows when they apply to all that proceeds from the Earth with no distinction for species, place, time or circumstances."

As long as one continues to make exceptions for the observances, for so long has one not attained full and continual Perpetual Consciousness. Misreading this sutra is easy. People could, for example, say that George's non-violence is not perfected because they know that George eats chickens. George could be violent toward no human or any other animal, but since he eats chickens, his non-violence is obviously not perfected. Or perhaps George only eats French chickens (Chicken Cordon Bleu), or in Russia (Chicken Kiev), or only in March (Spring Chickens) or perhaps only if it was a bad chicken, such as a rooster that was terrifying George's wife and children. Since George violates species, place, time or circumstances, his observance can't be perfected. Right?

Wrong! These are all outward actions and reveal nothing at all about George's inner state of mind when he wrings the neck of the chicken, plucks it, cooks it and eats it. Perfecting the observances is impossible without realizing Perpetual Consciousness, for until one recognizes the separation of the Self from all that is, one will be violent, will be dishonest, will steal, will not be restrained and will grasp -- these are the inevitable counterparts of ignorance.

One might wonder just how established one's own awareness truly is. Test it! Does the body's unending violence touch you? Does anything of the world overshadow your serenity? Starvation in Africa? Violent crime in our cities? Corruption? Drug abuse? Intense movies? Anything anywhere at any time by anyone? Do you hate or resent anyone or any class of beings? Do you feel contempt for anyone anywhere at any time? How do you feel about traitors? Murderers? Rapists?

If anything at all still upsets you, non-violence is not yet perfected in you.

This sutra does not suggest that the path to enlightenment is to make a mood of non-violence or any of the other four observances. It does not suggest pretending to be peaceful if you are enraged inside. Such attempts only end in greater stress to the nervous system and dramatically slow down the growth of consciousness. Nor does this sutra mean that the enlightened necessarily exhibit what the Waking State defines as non-violence or any other of the observances. The fact is, it is perfectly possible to kill and yet to have perfected non-violence. Ahiṃsa is entirely based on the level of consciousness inside, not at all on the external behavior.

This is perhaps the most confusing truth of the Science of Union to those in the Waking State. These have so very many opinions about the nature of the enlightened -- how they walk, how they talk, how they dress, how they eat -- and misinterpretations of sutras such as this one only serve to complicate these misunderstandings even more. There are no external signs of enlightenment. That bears repeating! *There are no external signs of enlightenment.*

Enlightenment is an internal reality. What one does with it on the outside is up to the Absolute Self, lived forever on the inside.[20]

Pada II. Sutra 32

शौचसंतोषतपःस्वाध्यायेश्वरप्रणिधानानि नियमाः ॥३२॥

Śaucha saṃtoṣa tapaḥ svādhyāya īśvara praṇidhānāni niyamāḥ

The five actions are: purity, contentment, austerity, study of the Self and surrender to the Supreme Being.

The last three of these were the subject of the first sutra of this chapter. There it says that these three stabilize Union. In the second sutra, it adds that these three not only further Perpetual Consciousness, they weaken self-destructive tendencies. Because of their significance, there is a slight degree more emphasis on practicing these five than there was on practicing the five observances of the thirtieth sutra, which is why the literal translation of niyamāḥ, actions, is "leading to the observances." The five observances are the natural counterparts of enlightenment; these five actions are also the natural counterparts of enlightenment, but they also have the effect of furthering enlightenment, particularly the last three.

---

[20] -- Christ said, "For John came neither eating nor drinking, and they say, He hath a devil.

"The Son of man came eating and drinking, and they say, Behold a man gluttonous, and a winebiber, a friend of publicans and sinners. But wisdom is justified of her children." MATTHEW XI:18&19. Those that seek verification of another's consciousness through their senses or minds will forever fail.

The interpretation of this sutra closely follows that of II.30. There is no purity, śaucha, without Ascendant Consciousness -- the best of thought, feeling or action in the Waking State is colored by previous impressions of limitation, lack and fear. One can strain to be pure but never truly know if one is acting purely or not. On the other hand, it is impossible for the Ascendant ever to be impure. For one who knows that, life *is* purity.

Similarly for contentment, saṃtoṣa. As long as the Infinite Self is unknown, there is no true contentment -- diverse desires continue to rise in all times and places. For those who do know the Self, however, the goal of all desiring is attained; contentment is the natural by-product of establishing permanent awareness of the Ascendant.

And austerity, Self-study and surrender to God are impossible without Ascendant Consciousness (see the commentaries on I.23, II.1 & II.2). These last three, however, are descriptive of the growth to enlightenment. Even so, one must first have the clear experience of the Ascendant -- this is the Absolute requirement for these three to function.

Pada II. Sutra 33

वितर्कबाधने प्रतिपक्षभावनम् ॥३३॥

Vitarka bādhane pratipakṣa bhāvanam

When the Surface Stage is distressed,
ride opposing thoughts back onto the Self.

The Surface Stage is the first level of Ascension defined in I.17 & I.42. When the mind begins its inward march, there may be times when large quantities of stress are dissolving from the nervous system and the body; this makes the experiences rather less than rewarding. ("Distressed," bādhane, can also be translated, "harassed, tormented, afflicted, molested.") What is the poor beginner to do? Not start to concentrate, for that would only raise the physiological rate and tire the mind. Patañjali suggests culturing the opposite thought to the one that is causing the distress, then continue to Ascend on that.

This will work, of course, only if one has already become familiar with the act of Ascending. Only if one has risen to the level of clear experience of the Absolute, at least occasionally, is it possible to do this. Once the mind has become familiar with Ascending, any thought at all can become a vehicle for further Ascending. Thus one begins to create one's own program for evolution, based entirely on the need of the moment. If one feels hate, one Ascends on love. If one feels unhappy, one Ascends on happiness. This process will be further explained in the next ten sutras.

Patañjali specifically mentions the Surface Stage here because it is only the first of the levels of Ascension that can be so afflicted. The Meaning, Feeling and Knowing stages are too deep for distressful experience of any kind to occur.

Pada II. Sutra 34

वितर्का हिंसादयः कृतकारितानुमोदिता लोभक्रोधमोहपूर्वका मृदुमध्याधिमात्रा दुःखाज्ञनानन्तफला इति प्रतिपक्षभावनम् ॥३४॥

Vitarkā hiṃsādayaḥ kṛta kārita anumoditā lobha krodha moha pūrvakā mṛdu madhya adhimātrā duḥkha ajñana ananta phalā iti pratipakṣa bhāvanam

For example, if your Surface Stage is distressed by thoughts of violence as a result of what was done to you, done by you or approved of by you because of greed, anger or delusion (for subtle and intense inward thoughts produce endless fruits of suffering and ignorance), ride opposing thoughts back onto the Self.

Mahārṣi Patañjali takes an extreme case as his first example. When stress starts dissolving due to the deep rest that results from experiencing the Ascendant, this dissolving of stress activates memory. As the mind moves outward on thought, it can at times be slightly rough, particularly if there is much guilt about past actions performed or permitted, or if there is still some feeling of being victimized by others. As these stresses dissolve, they can trigger past memories or current feelings of anger, greed or delusion.

This cycle, if unbroken, will continue to create further and greater fruits of ignorance and suffering. This is even more true if the intensity of these thoughts is permitted to become increasingly subtle during the inward movement of the mind. Power increases as one approaches the Ascendant -- the power for happiness or suffering is greater, not less, as one dives more and more deeply inward.

"Subtle and intense inward thoughts," echoes I.22 -- but in that sutra, the result of Ascending is extraordinary and wonderful[21]; here it results in endless suffering and ignorance.[22] What makes the difference? Subtlety, inward focus and intensity are the same; therefore the difference must lie in the vehicle used for Ascending. If the thought chosen for Ascension does not become increasingly life-supporting at every deeper level of thinking (that is, if it is not wholly positive at every level of Reality), it will not produce positive results. It is theoretically possible to Ascend on any thought, even destructive ones such as the memory of violence mentioned in this sutra. But what will be the fruit of such an inward march to increasing subtlety and power? Endless suffering and ignorance. So the particular thought one wishes to ride back onto the Self is *vitally* important.

This sutra has almost universally been misinterpreted to say that the unending ignorance and suffering that inevitably result from violence is the opposing thought for the distress of violence in the Surface Stage. This is saying that fear of future horror is the antidote to violence. Nothing could be more ridiculous. The fear of future harm (fear of any sort, for that matter) is itself a distressing thought that disturbs the Surface Stage. This kind of thinking is common in those kinds of religions and among those teachers that feel there is something to be gained by terrorizing their adherents by fear of eternal damnation or by suffering of some other sort. What could be gained by making your followers terrified? Only their fearful obedience to your laws.

---

[21] -- The fullest development of that inward movement is the Supreme Being -- see I.24.

[22] -- Is this not an excellent definition of hell?

Who would desire such a thing? Only those who are not interested in the spiritual development of their members, but who are very interested in maintaining their power over them would desire to increase fear.

Fear is not an opposite thought anyone thinking clearly would ever dream of riding back into the Ascendant. Fortunately, any such effort will poorly succeed, for the mind is not charmed by fearful thoughts. It is easy to see how faulty interpretations of such sutras would lead to self-mortification or to concentration -- "Since the mind does not naturally respond to thoughts of fear or threats of damnation, it must be necessary to whip it and beat the body to enforce obedience." Such ignorance, and all in the name of evolution! Eternal peace to such foolish attempts to gain enlightenment.

If fear is not the opposite thought of violence, what is? Non-violence is, of course, as the next sutra will make perfectly clear. This also conclusively demonstrates that the proper sphere for the practice of the five observances is internal, during Ascension, not by attempting to modify external behavior -- that is a pointless and all but impossible task.

Pada II. Sutra 35

अहिंसाप्रतिष्ठायां तत्संनिधौ वैरत्यागः ॥३५॥

Ahiṃsā pratiṣṭhāyāṃ tat saṃnidhau vaira tyāgaḥ

From reversing to stability of non-violence,
all hostility is renounced in your presence.

Mahāṛṣi Patañjali begins to list the opposing thoughts which still the various kinds of distress that can afflict Ascension. These eleven sutras (35 - 45) are also going to describe the result of riding back onto the Self these ten opposing thoughts -- the five observances of sutra 30 and the five actions of sutra 32.

"Reversing," prati, means to pull these thoughts back into the Ascendant. "Stability," ṣṭhāyām, means that the thought, having reached the Ascendant, is maintained in Absolute Awareness. This is the result of mastering the fourth or Knowing stage of Ascension, which causes the full development of ṛtam bharā prajñā. In this state, the full ṛtam effect of the thought is spontaneous and natural. Perhaps it is obvious by now that this is impossible without intimate familiarity with the process of Ascending.

From reversing back onto the Self and holding onto the thought of non-violence in the Ascendant, all violence is abandoned in your presence. This includes your own violence -- there is no room in any human mind for more than one thing at a time. It also includes everyone else's violence -- if there is no functioning violence in you, it is impossible for any person or creature to feel violent toward you.

This may sound surprising to those who deeply believe it is possible to be hurt, damaged or victimized by another in any way. And yet, it is so. It is possible to walk up to an enraged tiger and calm him with your glance, once your non-violence is stably entertained in the Ascendant. Ahiṃsā is Universal Love. Since it is love that unites all the seemingly sundered sparks of individuality into their one Source, the consciousness of the master of ahiṃsā resonates at the core of every heart and mind, bringing joy and peace.

It must be reemphasized that practicing non-violence in the field of action is most assuredly not what Patañjali is talking about here. It may or may not be useful to be non-violent in your actions, but it is largely irrelevant. What does matter is that the mind learns to Ascend; having learned this, holding onto certain thoughts *while experiencing the Ascendant* will have certain predictable, extraordinary and wonderful results.

Why list these? Surely not simply to gain the ability to charm snakes or deranged criminals in dark streets. No -- the prime reason for this is to smooth the ride into the Ascendant and to make the experience of the Ascendant permanent.

Pada II. Sutra 36

सत्यप्रतिष्ठायां क्रियाफलाश्रयत्वम् ॥३६॥

Satya pratiṣṭhāyāṃ kriyā phala aśrayatvam

From reversing to stability of truthfulness,
all actions quickly result in their fruits.

This sutra means that we no longer undermine our thoughts, speech, desires and actions by self-contradictory and self-destructive thoughts, speech, desires and actions. Therefore, whatever we do, we receive full support from all the Laws of Nature; all desires are quickly fulfilled.

It is interesting that truthfulness is intimately connected with the connection of result to thought, word and action. This may not be intuitively obvious, unlike the result of maintaining non-violence in the Ascendant discussed in the last sutra. The nature of the Ascendant *is* Truth. As one aligns more and more perfectly with that, one naturally finds that all the Laws of Nature rise to support, for all the Laws of Nature exist only to serve the Ascendant.

It is said that the masters of the observance of Truthfulness can speak anything and it will be instantly fulfilled. For a person who resonates in perfect clarity with the fundamental power of the Ascendant that is Truth, one moves the Universe according to one's desire. One has risen to the level of Cosmic Universality, of the Self of all that is. All desires of the Self are Holy and reach instantaneous fulfillment.

Pada II. Sutra 37

अस्तेयप्रतिष्ठायां सर्वरत्नोपस्थानम् ॥३७॥

Asteya pratiṣṭhāyāṃ sarva ratna upasthānam

From reversing to stability of non-stealing, all precious treasure presents itself.

Once one stops usurping the authority of the three guṇas by establishing Perpetual Consciousness, all of Nature comes forth to be of use. "Presents itself," upasthānam, can also be translated, "approaches to serve," or "assembles to venerate," or "comes to live nearby." The whole of Nature is available for the use of the enlightened; this is the natural by-product of the full development of consciousness.

One could spend an entire lifetime not stealing anything and yet not have any precious treasure appear. The reason for this, of course, is that the outermost sphere of activity only reflects the inner. Even if one steals nothing in thought, still the power of this particular Ascendant realization will not be very likely to manifest all precious treasure. This sutra describes a state of consciousness in which all attachment to the Universe is broken. When one masters the ability to remain forever in the Ascendant, all of Nature comes forth to support.

It is the common experience in the world that the employees do their master's will, even in advance of her need, automatically, if they are talented or love their master.

It is safe to assume that the Laws of Nature are talented -- look at all the variegated wonders of this Universe with its thousand billion galaxies of two hundred billion stars each -- and it is not much of a stretch to conclude that they exist in a relationship of love to the Ascendant. When one aligns with the Master of Creation, all employees and servants run to assist. This is the art of fulfilling desires in advance.

This is a step of progress beyond the last sutra, which is itself a step further than the previous. These three thus define a gradual progression of the stabilization of Perpetual Consciousness. In sutra 35, violence of others falls off; in sutra 36, action reaches fruition completely, thoroughly and quickly; in this sutra, Nature starts spontaneously rising to fulfill desires even in advance of our recognizing their existence. Life becomes simpler and more complete as one rises in consciousness.

Pada II. Sutra 38

ब्रह्मचर्यप्रतिष्ठायां वीर्यलाभः ॥३८॥

Brahmacharya pratiṣṭhāyāṃ vīrya lābhaḥ

From reversing to stability of Self-restraint,

heroism is acquired.

Self-restraint means that all energy is directed upward (see the commentary on II.30). When this is maintained in the Ascendant, a self-referral loop in the Absolute is created that manifests unlimited power. What is this power? The power to be a hero. What is a hero? A hero is he or she who rises to protect and serve others. What is the ultimate act of heroism? To be able to save others from their suffering.

This is not done through self-sacrifice -- at least not in an Ideal State. This is done by giving of one's own vital energy, one's own life-force -- the ultimate act of healing others is a spontaneous flowing of energy from the Infinite into the finite boundaries of their minds and hearts.[23] This flow of energy naturally

---

[23] -- Compare this with the spontaneous flowing of Christ's healing energy (continued...)

breaks their boundaries. It breaks the boundaries of disease in their bodies; but more importantly, it breaks the boundaries of belief, habit and judgment in their minds.

So the ultimate use of heroic energy is to move the Ascendant to break the bondage of ignorance in the minds and hearts of others. This is the most important function of a true Teacher, and the only one that is capable of saving the student from suffering permanently.

Pada II. Sutra 39

अपरिग्रहस्थैर्ये जन्मकथंतासंबोधः ॥३९॥

Aparigraha sthairye janma kathaṃtā saṃbodhaḥ

Stability of non-grasping calms the intellect so it knows the how, whence and why of existence.

When a pond is still, it is possible to see the reflections on its surface clearly. When the mind stops trying to hold onto the limiting boundaries of its belief and experience, all knowledge naturally dawns in its awareness.

It is precisely the tendency of the mind to hold onto *everything* that obscures the vision of its past, future or present. Like a television tuned to a specific channel, a mind holding onto anything is not free to experience anything else. When one channel is playing, the television cannot pick up another. This is immediately obvious, but the tendency of the mind to hold on is very, very deep. It can never be broken or even much lessened without the experience of Ascendant Consciousness.

(...continued)
when an ulcerous woman simply touched the hem of his robe. (MATTHEW IX:20-22; MARK V:25-34; LUKE IX:43-49)

It is interesting that Patañjali here for the first time drops "from reversing to stability" (II. 35 - 38) in favor of the simpler, "stability." The reason for this is that non-grasping is something that is entirely internal. The previous four have some external application: non-violence, truthfulness, non-stealing and celibacy all relate directly to our relationship with the world. But non-grasping is purely a mental thing, which is why a purely mental result ensues. There is no need to reverse back the natural function of the mind; indeed, to try to do so would not only be impossible but also potentially mentally imbalancing. One cannot reverse back a state but only a thought. The Self is eternally non-grasping in all that was, is, or ever will be by Its very nature.

This sutra also implies that in the natural state of the mind, all knowledge is available for use. It is only a perverted or deranged style of functioning of the nervous system that clouds awareness of the reality of all that is.

Pada II. Sutra 40

शौचात्स्वाङ्गजुगुप्सा परैरसंसर्गः ॥४०॥

Śauchāt svāṅga jugupsā parair asaṃsargaḥ

From purity, one's body is protected and preserved from contamination by others.

Those who are devoted to renunciation translate this sutra to say that purity results in aversion to one's own body and also to the bodies of others. While technically a valid translation, that kind of feeling about bodies is not the result of enlightenment but only the result of straining to be enlightened by those who know very little about how to be enlightened.

"Protected," jugupsā, means protected from accidents, injuries and failure of bodily systems and organs. "Preserved from contamination by others" means being immune to their diseases as well as from their violence of thoughts, words and actions. The natural by-product of purity, then, is physical security and invincibility.

Purity can be practiced, for there are some actions and habits and foods that lead life forward quickly on the path of evolution, and there are some actions and habits and foods that slow the growth of consciousness. But of course flawless purity is impossible without stabilizing Ascendant Consciousness, for a mind not established in the Self is inevitably caught in thralldom to the past, to limiting and painful beliefs and judgments, to the entire play and display of the three guṇas in created time. The only Absolute purity is contained within the Absolute itself -- it is only when one is fully established in that Ascendant Reality that one can be said to be pure. This purity is not the result of diet or vow; it is the natural by-product of full human consciousness. And full human consciousness will *never* result from straining to be pure.

Pada II. Sutra 41

सत्त्वशुद्धिसौमनस्यैकाग्र्येन्द्रियजयात्मदर्शनयोग्यत्वानि च ॥४१॥

Sattva śuddhi saumanasya ekāgraya indriya jaya

ātma darśana yogyatvāni cha

Perfection of purity leads to gladness, one-pointedness,

clarity of the senses, and the capability of seeing the Self.

It is also valid to read this sutra in sequence; i.e., the perfection of purity leads to gladness and one-pointedness which clarifies the senses and bequeaths the capability of seeing the Self. Happiness or gladness of the heart and one-pointedness of the intellect are thus the two motivating forces that lead to the refinement of the senses that culminates in Unified Consciousness, when the enlightened sees the Self in all things and in all beings.

"Perfection of purity" means that purity becomes completely dominated by sattva -- the guṇa that is responsible for all evolution and illumination. Joy and clarity are the primary adjuncts of one whose life is dominated by sattva. When life is dominated by the other guṇas, rajas or tamas, life is open to suffering, for the only ordering of the guṇas that does not lead to conflict is when sattva predominates. So a life fully established in sattva is fully established in harmony with all the Laws of Nature; as a result of that, any stress in the senses of perception quickly runs away and the Infinite is revealed in all its glory, shining on or through everything, everywhere, always.

"Capability of," yogyatvāni, literally means, "qualified for Union with" (see II.53, commentary).

Pada II. Sutra 42

संतोषादनुत्तमः सुखलाभः ॥४२॥

Saṃtoṣād anuttamaḥ sukha lābhaḥ

From contentment, supreme happiness is gained.

It is not difficult to attain supreme happiness -- one must only be established in perfect contentment. The problem, of course, is that this is simply impossible without enlightenment. As life moves on, energy rises due to the action of rajas; this rising energy collides with previous impressions stored in the nervous system to produce desire.

There is nothing wrong with this; indeed, it is by fulfilling desire that one naturally rises to higher levels of desiring. Those that advocate cutting off of desire and enforcing a false contentment from the surface of the mind are therefore impeding the natural flow of evolution; continued for a long enough time, this will lead to greater and greater stress and artificiality of functioning of the mind and body.

Nothing superficial of this sort is meant by this sutra. When one is established in the permanent experience of Perpetual Consciousness, one is naturally content; this is the by-product of evolution. Contentment comes *from* fulfillment; it does not and cannot lead *to* fulfillment.

This sutra does *not* say that the enlightened have no desires, nor does it say that the enlightened are content with suffering in others or in the world. It *does* say that one's joy is Absolute -- Supreme Happiness is pure bliss. When one has recognized identity with the Source, one lives Eternal bliss at all times. From this platform of Unchanging Stability, one dynamically acts for the good of the entire world. No longer acting from limited beliefs, habits or judgments, one's vision is perfectly clear -- it is easy to see how best to assist the upward current of creation, sattva. One's desires are the desires of God. And with that, one *is* content.

Pada II. Sutra 43

कायेन्द्रियसिद्धिरशुद्धिक्षयात्तपसः ॥४३॥

Kāya indriya siddhi aśuddhi kṣayāt tapasaḥ

Austerity destroys impurities and perfects the body and senses.

"Destroys impurities," aśuddhi kṣayāt, repeats II.28, showing the deep importance Patañjali attaches to austerity as the means to fulfill Union. Again it is important to emphasize that austerity, tapas, does not mean self-abuse (see II.1, commentary). Standing in freezing water only stresses the body, it does not purify it. And thus also with any other technique of bodily mortification. Austerity means the willing assumption of a set of self-chosen boundaries to realize a goal.

This is true, whatever your goal happens to be. If you are studying for a mid-term in chemistry (and it is a test on which you need to do well and for which you need to study hard) and some of your friends come by your room to invite you to a party to which you would very much like to go, it is austerity for you to continue studying instead of going partying. But it is your choice, caused by your desire to do well in school. If you did not desire to go to the party and simply used studying as an excuse, it would not qualify as tapas.

Correctly applied, tapas leads directly to bliss, for it continually redefines what is and what is not enjoyable, what does and what does not serve as our ultimate goal, and therefore, what will make our path to enlightenment shorter or longer. As one chooses more and more intelligently for the upward current of evolution, impurities of thought, belief and habit naturally fall away, along with their corresponding stresses in the body and nervous system. As the body and nervous system become less and less stressed, the entire structure of the physical machinery rises to a state of perfection.

Tapas destroys the ego and aligns the soul with the Holy Spirit, thereby opening the door to Perpetual Consciousness.

Perfection of the body will be further defined in III.46 as the by-product of another technique.

Pada II. Sutra 44

स्वाध्यायादिष्टदेवतासंप्रयोगः ॥४४॥

Svādhyāyād iṣṭadevatā saṃprayogaḥ

Study of the Self leads to complete Union with the most agreeable form of the Supreme Being.

Study of the Self does not mean via books, or attending seminars, or philosophical enquiry (see II.1, commentary). Study of the Self means that the awareness of the Self unfolds its Self to its Self by its Self -- what we can do to help is to focus on this process. Our active attention brings the process to fruition more quickly.

Study of the Self is the functional opposite of austerity, just as approach is the functional opposite of withdrawal. These are the same process, seen from opposite angles. Every step away from something is also a step towards something else. But it is easier and smoother to move toward instead of away. The mind and heart find this a much more compelling reason for consistency in the practice.

What is the end of this ever-increasing subtle inward development? Enlightenment, of course, and this sutra lists as the ultimate result of approach the Sixth State of consciousness, Union with an aspect of the Supreme Being. This is an inward Union, the result of the inward march of approach, just as physical perfection is an outward gain, the result of the outward withdrawal of tapas.[24] The aspect of the Supreme Being with which you become united depends entirely on what your conception of the Supreme Being is. If you think of the Supreme Being as being the Ultimate of Harmony, for example, upon mastering the study of the Self, you will be united with Harmony. This

---

[24] -- In the Waking State, it is not common to view the body as external, but this is the experience in enlightenment -- everything is external to the Self.

is why the choice of the name to describe the Supreme Being, the choice of each person's left hemisphere, must be individually made, for everyone's mind has been structured by a different lifetime of experience and belief. What will work for one will not necessarily work for all -- or even for anyone else (see I.39, commentary).

In Ascension, the left hemisphere focus, the conception of the Supreme Being, will change as the experience of life changes. It need not remain the same -- indeed, it must not remain the same if our conception of Reality changes, else we will remain united with a lesser level of reality, not the ultimate glory of the Ascendant. So one by-product of study of the Self is a constantly evolving conception of exactly what the Supreme Being is.

Does this go on forever? No -- once the human mind has directly realized its Absolute status, the focus on the Supreme Being becomes very clear and one-pointed. Before then, however, any attempt to focus on or surrender to the Supreme Being is mostly going to occur on the level of mood-making, for the Waking State perceives nothing clearly or consistently.

Is it bad, then, to focus on divinity before Perpetual Consciousness is gained? No, but the full depth of permanent experience -- complete Union with the Supreme Being -- can only occur after Perpetual Consciousness, for only then does the perfected individual aspect of the Infinite have anything significant to Unite. Absorption may be possible before Perpetual Consciousness, but not Union.

Pada II. Sutra 45

समाधिसिद्धिरीश्वरप्रणिधानात् ॥४५॥

Samādhi siddhiḥ īśvara praṇidhānāt

Surrender to the Supreme Being perfects Ascendant Consciousness.

See I.23 and II.1 & II.2.

After Perpetual Consciousness is stabilized, the desire naturally develops to know the maker of the soul. Entertaining this desire in the Ascendant leads directly to the perception of the most agreeable form of the Supreme Being. Having discovered the Supreme Being, it becomes possible to surrender to the Supreme Being.

Surrender to the Supreme Being can occur at any time in a soul's evolution. What this means is that at any time, one can permanently renounce all the false, ego-created beliefs and judgments about the limited and limiting nature of individual life and return permanently to perfect harmony with Natural Law. When this happens, one is said to have surrendered to the Ascendant, for there is no longer an individual basis for thought or action; everything is structured from Universality.

One could do this at any time in a soul's evolution, but for all practical purposes, the intensity of the internal programs are simply too great in the Waking State for this to happen with any depth or consistency. And dreaming is too illusory and sleep too dull to allow this to occur. There is no question of surrender in the Fourth State of Ascendant Consciousness either, for in that, the individual Self simply Is, experiencing the Infinite, with no motion of thought or belief rippling its perfect Silence.

So the first time that surrender becomes truly significant or consistent is in the state of permanently established Ascendant Consciousness -- in the first stage of enlightenment, Perpetual Consciousness. Then the quest to find the Maker of this Infinite Self as a continual, direct experience becomes significant. And as one seeks more and more deeply into the fundamental structure of the Universe, one does indeed in time find the Supreme Being, dancing on the surface of everything -- and then only does surrender become practical.

Before this time, to what is one surrendering? A belief? A dream? An occasional, fleeting experience of light? A vision? Surrender becomes significant when it is a continual, every moment repeated experience. And this can only be possible when one sees the Supreme Being in everything -- every particle of light, every drop of water, every grain of sand, every human face, every thought.

When one's consciousness never wavers from the continual perception of the Supreme Being, surrender becomes a practical reality. And when this happens, Ascendant Consciousness is perfected. What is the ultimate perfection of Ascendant Consciousness? Unified Consciousness. One could say that Perpetual Consciousness is a state of perfection of Ascendant Consciousness, and this is certainly true; Exalted Consciousness is also a state of perfection of Ascendant Consciousness. But the ultimate perfection of Ascendant Consciousness is Unified Consciousness, and that is what this sutra addresses.

So tapas or austerity (adopting relative boundaries for the sake of Eternal Freedom) is the path to Perpetual Consciousness, study of the Self is the path to Exalted Consciousness and surrender to the Supreme Being is the path to Unified Consciousness. These are the stages of the growth of enlightenment.

The most agreeable form of the Supreme Being is not a complete expression of the Supreme Being. This is why mastery of the Study of the Self, Svādhyā, results in Exalted Consciousness and mastery of surrender, Īśvara Praṇidhānā, results in Unified Consciousness.

Pada II. Sutra 46

स्थिरसुखमासनम् ॥४६॥

Sthira sukham āsanam

Postures lead to stability and happiness.

Mahāṛṣi Patañjali continues here with his analysis of the eight limbs of Yoga listed in II.29. "Postures," āsanam, mean moving the body into various positions for the purpose of increasing flexibility and removing stress. This is what most people in the West are thinking of when they think of Yoga. The various yogic postures *can* be practiced to increase flexibility and remove stress, but to think that they are a necessary step to be mastered before Ascension can begin is simply an error. The result of reduction of stress in the body naturally makes the body more flexible. This means that the mastery of the postures is the by-product of a perfectly healthy mind and body, rather than the path to it.[25]

---

[25] -- It is at least theoretically possible to remove all the stress from the central nervous system by bending and twisting the body, but in order to make much progress toward removing all the stress, it is usually necessary to practice the various postures as a full-time occupation, for a minimum of twelve and preferably eighteen hours every day.

(continued...)

When one's body is freed from stress, the mastery of the postures leads to an upswelling of joy inside and to the ability to hold any given position indefinitely. "Stability," sthira, also pertains to stability of consciousness. It is a common experience that if the body is uncomfortable, the mind tends to be distracted by the feeling of discomfort. This is why it is important to sit comfortably when one Ascends. Minimizing distractions, both internal and external, is always wise. But forcing the body into uncomfortable postures is most assuredly *not* a prerequisite for Ascension. This point will be clarified in the next sutra.

"Happiness," sukha, can also be translated, "comfort, pleasure, mildness, ease, enjoyment." None of these translations implies anything even vaguely like strain or effort.

(...continued)

In other words, it *is* possible to gain enlightenment with a strictly physical approach, but this angle is not viable for the average person in the world who simply does not have sufficient time to devote to such a practice. This does not imply that some short time daily spent practicing the postures is not valuable. On the contrary, yogic exercises are an ideal way to relieve tension and can very much smooth the process of the release of stress. As an adjunct to Ascension, then, postures can be quite useful.

Pada II. Sutra 47

प्रयत्नशैथिल्यानन्तसमापत्तिभ्याम् ॥४७॥

Prayatna śaithilya ananta samāpattibhyām

By attaining the Endless comes suppleness and diminution of trouble.[26]

Patañjali here clarifies the source of success in mastering the physical postures.

When one is established in Perpetual Consciousness, one's body naturally becomes increasingly flexible and supple. What is the basis of aging? The organs and cells become less and less flexible, more and more rigid. For example, a baby's veins and arteries look like flexible plastic tubing; the average octogenarian's veins and arteries look like cast iron water pipes that have become completely filled with foreign deposits, calcium and plaque; they are brittle, fragile and rigid.

The convolutions of the human brain gradually flatten out and become more and more hard and stiff with aging in the those caught by the Waking State; only through evolution, by stretching the mind to the Infinite, does the body become increasingly flexible. Aging reverses as one becomes permanently established in the Absolute; this naturally protects the body from unwanted disease and premature failure of its various constituent organs and systems.

---

[26] -- Given the utter simplicity of this sutra, it is a little shocking that anyone could conclude that mastering postures is required to gain Absolute Awareness. Without knowing Reality as a direct, living and permanent experience, any conceivable theory can arise to explain how to raise consciousness. Most of these theories will of course fail to lead anyone to enlightenment, but they might well occupy a lot of people's time in trying!

"Trouble," prayatna, can also be translated, "pain, labor, effort." Reduction of pain, labor and effort is the natural by-product of experiencing the Infinite. The postures become easier and easier as flexibility increases in the nervous system. This naturally leads to freedom from trouble of all kinds, including sickness, pain and suffering.

"The Endless," Ananta, also means the cosmic serpent, Śeṣa, the full embodiment of tamas guṇa -- perfect stability or inertia. Ananta thus symbolizes the fluid state of Silence that accompanies physical mastery -- it is the opposite of rigidity, which coarsens the body and mind. Śiva, the master of Yoga, wears Ananta around his neck, symbolizing at once his mastery of tamas, the powers of death, Eternity, and his own body.

The Earth is said to rest on Ananta. What does this mean? The universal property of matter is gravity, which is endless and omnipresent. Gravity holds the Earth together and binds the Earth to the Sun. The path our planet follows around the daystar is an endless spiral, as eternal as are the Sun and the solar system. Nature works with perfect economy and unending superfluidity of grace -- all characteristics developed by awareness of the Endless, Ananta.

Pada II. Sutra 48

ततो द्वन्द्वानभिघातः ॥४८॥

Tato dvandva anabhighātaḥ

Thereupon, the pairs of opposites stop having a noxious effect.

"The pairs of opposites," dvandva, mean the entire structure of change in the created Universe. This is the development of complete freedom from trouble -- no aspect of the inherent duality of life strikes individual life painfully. This sutra says that life becomes free from all conflict, including all doubt and fear.

The full mastery of the postures also means that one is not much affected by any of the pairs of opposites such as heat and cold; comfort of the body is maximal in any environment. When one's focus is exclusively on the Infinite and the body is established in perfect flexibility, one is naturally freed from bondage to the environment.

One remains bound to the relative Universe as long as one is not established in Perpetual Consciousness. Patañjali mentions this result of enlightenment here as the body is the connecting link between the Absolute Self and the external Universe, and is therefore the part of us that is affected by any physical transformations.

The ultimate range of the pairs of opposites encompasses the two absolutely opposed forces of tamas and sattva guṇas, Infinite destructiveness and Infinite creativity, the two fundamental forces of Nature that hold permanent sway over the entire structure of relative existence. Only by stabilizing the Ascendant can one be permanently freed from these ultimate opposites -- and there, in enlightenment, their ultimately noxious effect, suffering, ceases to afflict.

Birth and death are two more opposites that cease to trouble the enlightened. When one is permanently established in the Eternal Now, there remains no question of loss or gain of any kind whatsoever.

Pada II. Sutra 49

तस्मिन्सति श्वासप्रश्वासयोर्गतिविच्छेदः प्राणायामः॥४९॥

Tasmin sati śvāsa praśvāsaya gati vichchhedaḥ prāṇāyāmaḥ

In that experience of the Now, the motions of exhalation and inhalation are interrupted. That begins the death of the breath.

When the mind experiences Ascendant Consciousness, the body encounters its deepest possible state of rest. That is the beginning of the death or cessation of the breathing process.

Practicing of breathing techniques is not going to lead very quickly or effectively to this state. Decrease of the rate of breathing is the natural by-product of the awareness being established in the Absolute, it is not the path to that goal.

As the mind settles down during the practice of Ascension, the breath naturally stills. Even in the first few days of practice, it is common to experience very deep rest -- typically about twice as deep as the deepest sleep at night. And this occurs within just the fifteen or twenty minutes that are normally spent Ascending. Because of this very deep rest, stress starts dissolving from the nervous system; as the body becomes less and less stressed, the over-all physiological rate drops even after the process of Ascension. Stress and tension quickly vanish in daily life; this leads to greater health, happiness and success in every area of human concern.

Refinement of the breath, then, can be considered the cause of the increasing health and happiness that are the common results of Ascending. But stilling the breath is not the source of Ascending -- it works quite the other way around. The body needs a certain amount of oxygen to maintain its metabolic rate. Forceful reduction of breathing without reduction of the metabolic demand will only stress the body further. The breath drops during the practice of Ascension because less effort is required to think at subtler levels in the mind. So reduction of the metabolic rate with its concomitant reduction in the breath is the by-product of correctly practiced Ascension, not the path to it.

Pada II. Sutra 50

बाह्याभ्यन्तरस्तम्भवृत्तिर्देशकालसंख्याभिः परिदृष्टो दीर्घसूक्ष्मः ॥५०॥

Bāhya abhyantara stambha vṛttir deśa kāla saṃkhyābhiḥ paridṛṣṭo dīrgha sūkṣmaḥ

As the modifications of outer and inner breathing still, the volume becomes inobservable, the duration becomes long and the frequency becomes rare.

As one dives more and more deeply into silence, the entire physiology settles farther and farther down into very deep rest. Breathing becomes subtler, slower and less frequent, with longer and longer pauses between breaths. Less and less oxygen is consumed, meaning the metabolic rate is dropping. This deep rest allows the deep stress in the nervous system to dissolve. This is a natural by-product of the inward march of the mind. Patañjali is describing the natural counterparts of Ascension, not giving instructions on how to still the breath, as most commentators try to make him say. Less oxygen is consumed because less is required; this naturally causes the breath to slow and the volume to decrease.

Pada II. Sutra 51

बाह्याभ्यन्तरविषयाक्षेपी चतुर्थः ॥५१॥

Bāhya abhyantara viṣaya ākṣepī chaturthaḥ

In the Fourth State of Consciousness, the entire range of inner and outer breathing is abandoned.

The progression inward of these three sutras (49 - 51) demonstrates the increasing refinement or subtlety of the breath as one settles into the Ascendant. In sutra 49, the word translated "outer breathing," śvāsa, literally means, "panting, snorting, hissing, wheezing." This is breath at its coarsest; this also reflects in the word used to describe its activity, gati, "motion." In sutra 50, violent breath moving is transformed into breath modifying -- this is a subtler state. And by this sutra, the entire range of breathing moves to silence.

As one slips more and more fully into the Absolute, the necessity for breathing decreases; eventually the breath stills completely, as long as one remains in the pure experience of the Fourth State of Consciousness.

Ākṣepī, translated here, "abandoned," also means "ravishing" or "charming." The experience of the Ascendant is so wonderful that the breath stops -- it is quite literally breathtaking. In this state, the body functions with absolute perfection. Since there are no mutually contradictory thoughts moving, the body flows with maximum efficiency, which has perfect health as a natural by-product.

"The entire range," viṣaya, can also be translated "object." Thus the object or purpose of breathing has been reached in the experience of the Ascendant. When one has accomplished the purpose of all living, the need for the vehicle is over. The breath's purpose is to keep life continuing until this moment. In the presence of the master, the servants stand still out of respect. The master of the breath is the Ascendant: the Master of Creation remains forever the Lord of all its creatures.[27]

Breathlessness as a technique is meaningless. Breathlessness does not lead to Ascendant Consciousness. Breathlessness leads to death -- and that very quickly. Breathlessness is a by-product of the goal, not the path to the goal. In the Ascendant, the entire physiology enters a state of superfluid functioning in which any motion of breath is so long and shallow that it is beyond observation.

The refinement of the breath or praṇa is thus the physical counterpart of expansion of consciousness. The breath is the connecting link of life between the inner machinery -- the mind, intellect, ego and senses -- and the outer machinery -- the physical body and its world. It is precisely the breath locked into narrow boundaries of stress, belief and judgment that maintains ignorance. Conversely, when the subtlest breath, the ūdana praṇa (see III.40) enters the suṣumna (see Appendix 2: The Chakras), enlightenment is absolutely guaranteed, as the next two sutras clarify.

---

[27] -- See *AUTOBIOGRAPHY OF A YOGI* by Paramahansa Yogananda for a marvellous description of some of the experiences that can accompany the breathless state.

Pada II. Sutra 52

ततः क्षीयते प्रकाशावरणम् ॥५२॥

Tataḥ kṣīyate prakāśa āvaraṇam

Thereupon, the obstruction of illumination is destroyed.

When one clearly experiences the Fourth State of Consciousness, all obstructions to the experience of illumination naturally fall away. The questions might naturally come, "What is this obstruction? Whence does it come? And why?"

That which obscures the perfect light of Self-realization is the belief in separation, in limitation. Ignorance, in other words. And ignorance means, after all, to ignore. One ignores Reality and substitutes instead false idols of beliefs which cannot and do not save one from suffering and destruction.

From where does this obstruction come? It is as old as the human. We are endowed with free will, which permits us to choose anything, even the most bizarre if we wish it. We can choose to remain in ignorance for as long as we please. Conversely, we can choose at any moment to move away from our self-destructive beliefs in suffering and death; as we move closer and closer to the omnipresent divinity within, we naturally find that everything of our life improves -- happiness, success, intelligence, health. These are the hallmarks of an evolving life.

Where does the obstruction go when we abandon it? It goes nowhere; it simply ceases to be. This is the fate of all dreams when we awaken, to vanish back into nothingness. This is the fate of ignorance when we cease supporting it. It simply disappears, and we realize it never was real.

Maintaining a legion of false and faulty beliefs is exhausting to the body and mind; as these begin to fall away, it is completely natural that the body has to work less hard, which requires less and less breath. At first this happens only during the experience of Ascending, but as the stress systematically decreases in the nervous system as a result of that deep rest, soon the breath starts being more and more refined, even in the midst of activity. Breath sounds less and less labored; it is deeper, fuller, more rich and full as the body rises to greater health and efficiency of functioning.

This process culminates in the perfect experience of Ascendant Consciousness, in which the breath stills completely and ignorance is thrown off like an old, worn-out cloak that is no longer needed or desired. Perhaps for an instant, we might think fondly of the old garment, for it served us for many years; but we will surely not dwell on such thoughts for long -- one needs no cloak in the warm spring sun; even the memory of the cold dark days of winter past are too burdensome to continue to carry long. Gratefully we drop them and run joyfully ahead into the magnificence of our destiny.

Pada II. Sutra 53

धारणासु च योग्यता मनसः ॥५३॥

Dhāraṇāsu cha yogyatā manasaḥ

And the mind becomes capable of Focus.

When the obstruction to illumination is destroyed, the mind is no longer pulled out from the Ascendant -- it becomes capable of focussing on the Absolute permanently. This quality of the mind, to stay continually in the Ascendant, is an inherent feature of what the mind is. The natural style of functioning of the mind, once the stress is dissolved from the nervous system, is to remain in Ascendant Consciousness always.

Said another way, once we have gone beyond the belief in individual limitation, we remember fully and continually that we are an indivisible part of the One. So it is not so much that the mind is gaining fitness for holding onto the Ascendant, for that capability already exists within it. Rather, the mind ceases to turn away from the Reality of its Oneness with the Absolute. When this happens, it is united permanently with the Ascendant; this is called Perpetual Consciousness.

"Capable of," yogyatā, literally means, "qualified for Union with." This is the epitome of Yoga. No longer confined to an occasional experience of the Ascendant (in the Fourth State), the mind has attained a degree of clarity that permanently unites it with the Absolute. The experience of the Self is never again lost. This is the beginning of human life and the beginning of true freedom, for one is no longer bound by the limiting beliefs and judgments about the nature of Reality carried over from past experience.

Pada II. Sutra 54

स्वविषयासंप्रयोगे चित्तस्वरूपानुकार इवेन्द्रियाणां प्रत्याहारः ॥५४॥

Sva viṣaya asaṃprayoge chitta svarūpa anukāra iva indriyāṇām pratyāhāraḥ

From withdrawal, the senses cease to be united with the objective world and resemble, as it were, the True Form of Self Awareness.

"Cease to be united" translates asaṃprayoge, the opposite of the "complete Union," saṃprayogaḥ, of II.44. From growth of consciousness, one merges completely into the Absolute and separates completely from illusions. The senses are never truly united with the outer world, but from habitual use, one believes that they are. One sees a house and forgets the Absolute Self; one sees a dog and forgets the Absolute Self; one sees *anything* and forgets the Absolute Self. But from the natural development of withdrawal, the fifth limb of the Science of Union, one naturally learns to separate from the overshadowing nature of the boundaries in preference to the experience of the Unbounded Absolute.

This sutra is descriptive of Perpetual Consciousness beginning to grow into Exalted Consciousness and Unified Consciousness. It cannot be considered to apply to the Waking State, for when one withdraws one's senses in the Waking State, one falls asleep, one does not experience the Absolute with the senses. Closing the eyes may well be the prerequisite for not only sleep but for the experience of deep Ascending, but the senses of the sleeper are still connected with the outer world and will reactivate immediately upon awakening.

When one has fully stabilized Perpetual Consciousness as described in the last sutra, the senses naturally begin to refine their activity, begin to move more and more in the direction of experiencing the Infinite even in the field of diversity. The senses can only be used in one direction at a time -- if they are turned toward objects, they cannot be turned toward the Self and vice verse.

The reason Patañjali says "resembles as it were," is that of course the senses cannot experience the Infinite. They can only experience boundaries. But they can experience the reflection of the Infinite, they can approximate the True Form of the Self. This is descriptive of the growth of Exalted Consciousness. And therefore this chapter on Perpetual Consciousness is drawing to a close, providing a bridge to the Third Chapter, which has for its subject the Sixth State of Consciousness -- the second degree of enlightenment, Exalted Consciousness.

Pada II. Sutra 55

ततः परमा वश्यतेन्द्रियाणाम् ॥५५॥

Tataḥ paramā vaśyatā indriyāṇām

From that, the senses become obedient to the Supreme.

No longer do the unruly senses drive away the mind. Complete control is the natural by-product of the mind being fully established in Perpetual Consciousness. The senses are the servants or tools of the mind, but when the mind is not established in its True Nature, the senses are not submissive to the mind's will. This is so primarily because the directives from the mind in the Waking State are self-contradictory. The senses exist to bring enjoyment and experience of the outer world to the mind; when the mind is not sure what it wants or is inconsistent in its desires, the senses become confused in their attempt to respond to conflicting commands.

It is therefore simply not the case that the senses are somehow bad or corrupt or need to be punished for their natural tendency. Their desire is simply to serve, but if their master is weak or corrupt, their service will necessarily not be very glorious. The fault is not theirs; the fault lies with the thinker.

Conversely, when the mind has turned inward sufficiently to be established in the Supreme, the senses naturally respond to this manifest strength and stability. If there has been a build-up of stress in the sensory mechanisms due to long abuse by the mind, it may take some time for the senses to return to perfect functioning. But they will stop accumulating more stress when the mind is established in stability; in time, the natural tendency of the body to heal itself will restore them to ideal functioning. And that ideal functioning will not only bring clear vision, hearing, touch, taste and smell of the surface of matter -- that ideal functioning will bring complete experience of the celestial and full perception of the Infinite in everything, everywhere, always.

Thus ends the Second Quarter
of the Science of Yoga:
FULFILLMENT.

THIRD QUARTER: SPLENDOR

The Third Quarter of the Yoga Sutras describes the second stage of enlightenment, Exalted Consciousness. As with the first two padas, there are no techniques here to accomplish this. The Third Quarter is a treatise on the mechanics of this growth; it is not a how-to manual.

This pada begins with a discussion of the final three limbs of Union: Focus, Resonance and Ascendant Consciousness. These three together carry consciousness to the final two levels of enlightenment: Exalted Consciousness and Unified Consciousness. These three are the most intimate or internal of the eight limbs; together, they constitute a process which is called, saṃyamaḥ, "the Bestower of Union," which will be further defined in the fourth and fifth sutras of this pada.

A very large part of this chapter lists the results of saṃyamaḥ applied to various objects, for the purpose of stabilizing Exalted Consciousness and Unified Consciousness. It should probably be observed now and again later that saṃyamaḥ is absolutely a waste of time without Perpetual Consciousness being established first. More correctly stated: saṃyamaḥ is *impossible* without Perpetual Consciousness, for without the stabilized experience of the Ascendant, the most important part of the triad is missing.

Pada III. Sutra 1

देशबन्धश्चित्तस्य धारणा ॥१॥

Deśa bandhaś chittasya dhāraṇā

Focus is consciousness fastened on a point.

This means that the mind is sufficiently stable to focus on one object without wavering. This is a by-product of the awareness being stabilized in the Ascendant -- which is known as Perpetual Consciousness -- it is not the path to that goal.

This and the next two sutras define the three constituents of the practice that leads Perpetual Consciousness to Exalted Consciousness and Unified Consciousness. By mastering these three, consciousness naturally rises from the Infinite duality of the first degree of enlightenment to the perfect Unity of the final degree. Focus deals with the object of attention -- the field of the known; Resonance (III.2) deals with the process of knowing; and Ascendant Consciousness (III.3) deals with the knower.

The mind could theoretically fasten onto any point to grow to Exalted Consciousness; but practically speaking, there are a specific and finite number of objects that will serve the growth of consciousness best. Patañjali will devote a large part of this chapter to discussing some of these.

Pada III. Sutra 2

तत्र प्रत्ययैकतानता ध्यानम् ॥२॥

Tatra pratyaya eka tānatā dhyānam

In Focus, when thoughts vibrate to the One, that is Resonance.

This sutra defines the seventh limb of Union, Resonance.

As the mind focusses on a single appropriate object, the fluctuations of thought naturally settle into the One, the Ascendant. As the mind thus stills, the ability to cognize the full range of the meaning of the object naturally blossoms in the mind. Every object has a gross level of reality and a subtle level of reality. The subtle is typically not known because of absorption in the gross. But as the mind becomes familiar with the three aspects of one-pointedness, it learns to cognize an ever-deeper level of experience. This is the mechanics of the growth of consciousness from Perpetual Consciousness to Unified Consciousness.

"Vibrates to the One" means that all thought begins to be in perfect harmony with the Ascendant. In the Waking State of Consciousness, thought is often out of harmony with the fundamental forces of Natural Law, the guṇas, and with their Lord, the Ascendant. This leads to disharmonious thought, feeling, desire and action, which in turn leads to pain, suffering, illness, unhappiness, lack of success in every area of human concern, and eventually to death.

When, through Ascension, the mind learns to function in perfect harmony with the Universal Source of All That Is, all of Nature serves to bring greater happiness, health, success and fulfillment to every area of human concern. As one naturally rises in this perfect harmony, all of life starts developing and progressing toward fulfillment. How is this done? By removing stress from the nervous system (from the perspective of the body) or from expansion of consciousness to the Infinite (from the perspective of the mind). Either leads to perfect harmony with the One Ascendant; and from perfect harmony comes success and power.

Consider the example of the laser -- all the photons march together in step -- this leads to great power. A 75 watt beam of laser light can be bounced off of the moon. Seventy-five watts of random, diffused light will scarcely travel a few miles. This is an analogy of the difference between the incoherent functioning of the Waking State and the coherence of Ascendant Consciousness. This difference is measurable by the EEG -- the Waking State is characterized by a chaotic admixture of brain waves, almost randomly flowing through the cortex. During the experience of the Fourth and higher states, however, the brain exhibits perfect orderliness -- the brain waves vibrate in perfect harmony with the One. This is a measurement of the subjective experience of the perfect silence and peace of Ascendant Consciousness.

Pada III. Sutra 3

तदेवार्थमात्रनिर्भासं स्वरूपशून्यमिव समाधिः ॥३॥

Tadeva artha mātra nirbhāsaṃ svarūpa śūnyam iva samādhiḥ

In Focus also, when all meaning shines forth clearly and the True Form of the Self is experienced as if it were a void, that is Ascendant Consciousness.

The eighth limb of Union, Ascendant Consciousness, is here defined in a virtually word-for-word repetition of I.43. This is not the highest or fullest experience of Ascendant Consciousness, this is the stage that corresponds to the second stage of Ascension, Meaning (from I.43). The Self is experienced "as if it were a void," for the complete experience of Ascendant Consciousness is not Emptiness; rather, it is the Fullness beyond all qualities (see the commentary on I.43). This sutra does not describe the highest experience of Ascendant Consciousness, but it describes a level which is good enough for saṃyamaḥ to function.

"All meaning shines forth clearly" means that in this state of Ascendant Consciousness, any object that is held in the attention reaches the level of ṛtam bharā prajñā. When this happens, its entire meaning and purpose is instantly and fully known. In other words, by curling back onto the Self with any object of attention, the full ṛtam value of its existence is understood. This becomes the primary tool for the development of consciousness beyond Perpetual Consciousness, for it is precisely by understanding the full range of meaning of the senses and the process of knowing that one experiences Exalted Consciousness, and it is by understanding the full range of meaning of the known that one rises to complete consciousness in Unified Consciousness. Thus this development is the by-product of being able to hold any object of attention one-pointedly in the mind while simultaneously experiencing the Ascendant.

This is not only difficult in the Waking State, it is simply impossible. Firstly, there is no clear experience of the Self, so there is no clear experience of the Ascendant; therefore, the eighth limb of Union is dysfunctional. Secondly, the mind does not vibrate strictly with the One, as it is continually swayed by previous impressions. As these distort its calm mirror, it moves continually from object to object, from thought to thought, in the vain effort simply to be happy. Therefore, the seventh limb, Resonance, is dysfunctional. And thirdly, there is no possibility of Focus either, because consciousness is too scattered to be stable on a single point. Without the maintenance of one-pointed attention in Ascendant Consciousness, there is no possibility for ṛtam to function efficiently or consistently, and therefore the purpose and meaning of anything cannot be known with certainty.

In Perpetual Consciousness, on the other hand, the Self is established in the Ascendant; the mind vibrates in harmony with the One; and the intellect is one-pointed. Thus the last three limbs of Union function in perfect harmony; this leads to the capability of cognizing the full value and purpose of anything and everything.

Pada III. Sutra 4

त्रयमेकत्र संयमः ॥४॥

Trayam ekatra saṃyamaḥ

When these three function together as one, that is saṃyamaḥ, the bestower of Union.

Saṃyamaḥ bestows Union because it is precisely the ability to move the Absolute into the process of knowing that structures Exalted Consciousness and the ability to move the Absolute into the known that structures Unified Consciousness. As Ascendant Consciousness begins to become more and more firmly established in the mind, thought resonates more perfectly with the One and the senses of perception lose their dross and learn to cognize the subtle. This naturally gives rise to the use of the full range of the senses, which is called Exalted Consciousness.

As this process continues, one-pointedness of the mind becomes ever more firmly established, which has the curious effect of moving the Absolute out from its status of being separate from all of space and time, isolated inside a single knower, until it is perceived in everyone and everything. This is Unified Consciousness.

So it is through the practice of saṃyamaḥ after Perpetual Consciousness is established that one naturally rises to Exalted Consciousness and Unified Consciousness. These are not separate techniques, for Exalted Consciousness naturally develops into Unified Consciousness, given sufficient time of practice. As the full ṛtam value of more and more objects of perception are perceived, the boundaries of the external world gradually fall into the Infinite until there is no thing anywhere at any time that is not directly cognized as Infinite. This is the highest state of fulfillment in Unified Consciousness and is almost impossible even to conceive in the Waking State. But it is the natural result of the evolution of consciousness.

Pada III. Sutra 5

तज्जयात्प्रज्ञालोकः ॥५॥

Taj jayāt prajñā lokaḥ

By mastering saṃyamaḥ comes the level of consciousness of Heaven.

That is to say, Exalted Consciousness, the subject of this chapter. Why is Exalted Consciousness called "the level of consciousness of Heaven?" Because in this, the second stage of enlightenment, everything appears in celestial light. The individual has unmade all -- or at least the most part -- of belief in separation, in limitation, in suffering, in death; this naturally unchains the senses of perception so that they perceive the full range of creation, not simply the most surface value.

It is in the celestial light that the Laws of Nature function; this means that one open to this level of consciousness perceives the functioning of the Laws of Nature. When we are so developed in perception that we perceive the functioning of the Laws of Nature, the Laws of Nature become as it were eager to work for us. This removes our suffering in advance -- even before we are aware of the need, the Laws of Nature are working for us. And any desire, not being undermined by self-destructive thoughts and actions, leads to quicker and quicker fulfillment. When this level of consciousness functions perfectly, all desires are instantly fulfilled. For all these reasons, Exalted Consciousness is called heavenly.

It is also called Heaven because this is the level of perception of the angels, devas, gods and of God. There are no limits to perception in Exalted Consciousness, save only that of seeing the Infinite in everything (this final development occurs in Unified Consciousness). All of perception is supremely enjoyable; the celestial light shining on and through everything is wonderful beyond the means of any words to describe. This state is so replete with knowledge, love and bliss that it can only be called Exalted. It is wondrous in the extreme. Every perception is filled with supernal beauty and radiance; all of life dances in joy and love.

Exalted Consciousness is so fulfilling, a continual delight to the senses, that it is quite possible to remain caught by it and not rise to the ultimate level of Unified Consciousness. But there is nothing to fear: for those who have begun the process of saṃyamaḥ, perfect Union will be bestowed. It is primarily just a matter of time; the celestial light will melt into the Infinite and the purpose of human existence will be fulfilled.

Exalted Consciousness is wonderful, beyond any words to describe or adequately praise, and it is the natural by-product of saṃyamaḥ.

Pada III. Sutra 6

तस्य भूमिषु विनियोगः ॥६॥

Tasya bhūmiṣu viniyogaḥ

Saṃyamaḥ is applied in stages.

The purpose of the different stages of the practice of saṃyamaḥ is to introduce the experience of Ascendant Consciousness throughout the range of experience. In this way, Unified Consciousness is stabilized. The different degrees of development of saṃyamaḥ lead to ever higher plateaus of experience. Saṃyamaḥ is the means of rapid progress after Perpetual Consciousness is gained, for it is through the progressive refinement of experience on the various focal points of attention that Unified Consciousness is found everywhere, always.

"Applied" is a curious word in Sanskrit -- viniyogaḥ -- contained within it is Yoga or Union, ni, that which leads down or into Union and vi, which means literally "separation, sundering, apart, away." So the root meaning of applied is "that which leads to Union and away from Union." This is the effect of a washing machine -- it turns one way and then the other; this reversing effect makes for deep cleansing. This in one word repeats approach and detachment from I.12 and the opposing thoughts of II.33 and the withdrawal from II.54. It is by alternating the inward stroke of Ascension with the outward stroke of thought that Perpetual Consciousness is stabilized; it is by flowing in and out with the subtle fluctuations of saṃyamaḥ that Exalted Consciousness is stabilized.

There is a tale from ancient India that illustrates this: After one of the periodic destructions of the Earth, everything that had existed before did not spontaneously re-manifest from the Ascendant. To cause all that had been great before to return, the gods and the demons picked up Mount Mandara and, turning it over, used it as a churning stick to vibrate the Ocean of Milk. Viṣṇu, the Maintaining Aspect of God, turned himself into a Tortoise and dove beneath the surface of the water to hold up the weight of the mountain. The megacosmic serpent Śeṣa allowed himself to be used as the rope the gods pulled one way and the demons the other to cause Mandara to turn. As they pulled it back and forth, out of the Ocean of Milk flowed various wonderful items, not the least of which was the Amṛta (the Nectar of Immortality), the elephant Airavata and Sarasvatī, the Goddess of Wisdom.

This, in beautiful, mythical imagery, illustrates the growth of consciousness past the fifth state. The gods represent the senses of perception and the organs of action when they function in harmony with the upward current of creation; the demons represent the senses of perception and the organs of action when they are directed outward and downward, under the control of the ego and the old self-destructive tendencies from the past.

Pure positivity pulls the pivot (the nervous system) one way, pure negativity pulls it the other. The serpent Śeṣa represents the power of Life, which can be pulled upward or downward, toward evolution or destruction. The Ocean of Milk is the most refined level of Consciousness, the Ascendant; the Tortoise is the one-pointed focal point (Focus); Mount Mandara is the mind flowing in Resonance. Thus these last three represent the process of saṃyamaḥ. The performance of saṃyamaḥ is structured by approach (the devas) and withdrawal (the demons) alternately pulling on the Power of Life, Śeṣa.

As a result of this churning of consciousness through saṃyamaḥ, many great and wonderful results occur, not the least of which is perfect physical functioning (the amṛta), omnipotent mastery over the entire range of existence (the elephant Airavata) and supernal wisdom (Sarasvatī).

This tale is very deep and rich. It further illustrates that caution is also required -- as the gods and demons churned the Milk Ocean, the very first product released was poison. Śiva (the Destructive Power of God) swallowed it to save everyone and everything in creation from destruction.[28] As consciousness is churned by saṃyamaḥ, the body and mind throw off their toxins and stresses; these can overshadow life and lead to undesirable consequences -- unless one has the support of all the Laws of Nature. In other words, there can be no areas of life still condemned or judged as unworthy, or Śiva, the destructive aspect of God, will not be your ally. And without Śiva, there is no safety from destruction.

---

[28] -- This is why Śiva is traditionally pictured with a blue neck -- the poison he swallowed lodged there.

Pada III. Sutra 7

त्रयमन्तरङ्गं पूर्वेभ्यः ॥७॥

Trayam antaraṇgaṃ pūrve bhyaḥ

These three limbs are more intimate than the five preceding.

"Intimate," antara, can also be translated, "inner, within, special, entrance." These three are strictly an inner manipulation of consciousness; they function within; they are special in that they produce Exalted Consciousness and Unified Consciousness; and they are the entrance to the higher degrees of enlightenment.

Patañjali is generous; he wishes to ensure that no one misunderstand that the final stages of Union can only be accomplished with the focus of the mind on the subtle modifications and manifestations of Ascendant Consciousness. This does not imply that they follow upon mastery of the preceding limbs. It merely means that these three are focussing on the subtlest level of transformation of consciousness, the universal fluctuations *within* -- the fluctuations of the Absolute that bring the experience of Ascendant Consciousness from being isolated inside (Perpetual Consciousness) to being perceived throughout the full range of the operation of the senses of perception and organs of action. The knower is fulfilled in Perpetual Consciousness; the lively but intimate mechanics of saṃyamaḥ is the master key to unlock Exalted Consciousness and Unified Consciousness.

Pada III. Sutra 8

तदपि बहिरङ्ग निर्बीजस्य ॥८॥

Tad api bahir aṅgaṃ nirbījasya

But even these three are outer limbs to the Originless.

"The Originless" is the highest stage of Ascendant Consciousness (see I.51, commentary). In this state, the Absolute is experienced in its totality, not "like a void" (see I.43 & III.3). This state of complete experience of the Absolute is beyond all attributes. The best description for it is found in the Upanishads, the ancient texts about Unified Consciousness, with the descriptive phrase, Neti, neti -- "not this, not this." The fullest experience of the Absolute is beyond all thought, all boundaries, all limits of space and time. This is why even the subtle triad of saṃyamaḥ is considered external to the full experience of the Ascendant. For the experience of the Originless is a very real and distinct experience -- which is why the Upanishads also define the experience of the Ascendant simply as "That." It is more real than any experience of waking or dreaming, but impossible to define in words except in ways similar to those in this text.

Patañjali wishes to make it absolutely clear that no path at all is required to move to complete awareness of the Ascendant. It is present everywhere in all its glory always. Confusing the path for the goal comes from believing that some technique is required to reach the Ascendant. This misunderstanding is the common fate of all great Teachings, regardless how cleverly and carefully constructed. But it never hurts to sprinkle reminders here and there throughout the text, "You don't really need this!" Sometimes just the reminder that, "You are That!" is enough to enlighten a soul fully.

Pada III. Sutra 9

व्युत्थाननिरोधसंस्कारयोरभिभवप्रादुर्भावौ निरोधक्षणचित्तान्वयो

निरोधपरिणामः ॥९॥

Vyutthāna nirodha saṃskārayor abhibhava prādurbhāvau
nirodha kṣaṇa chitta anvayaḥ nirodhaḥ pariṇāmaḥ

When consciousness is attracted toward the joyful moment of stillness, the impressions that lead to outward manifestation disappear and the impressions that lead to stillness appear.
This is called the Transformation to Stillness.

This and the next several sutras explain how saṃyamaḥ leads to the Originless Ascendant Consciousness.

Stillness is here stated to be the natural by-product of the experience of the present instant of time. Whenever opened to the reality of Now, thought stills and Union is found to be the natural experience.

Even so, Patañjali says that there is a transformation that leads to Stillness; therefore he explains the two modifications of consciousness that structure awareness of this Stillness: disappearance of those impressions that lead to outward-directed thoughts and desires and the appearance of those impressions that lead to inward-directed thoughts, to greater and greater Silence.

These opposed impressions already exist in everyone; but in the Waking State, from habit those impressions that lead to outward thought are alone typically active. From birth, we learn to direct our senses and thought outward -- this is required, of course, to survive -- we must learn to relate to the world in order to function here. There is little obvious external necessity to impel us to take an inward path with the mind. So even though there are residual impressions of the inward-directed tendencies of the mind, they are rarely active in the Waking State, and therefore full Union with the Now does not readily or often occur.

Hence, touching the Ascendant is not the common or continual experience of the average person; even though the latent impressions of Silence exist, they are not actualized without the attention of the individual's intention. This is not a difficult or a complicated process, but it does require a shift in awareness from outward direction to inward direction. As consciousness shifts to inward flow, the impressions of Silence naturally begin to manifest with greater and greater strength; the impressions of diversity naturally begin to fade; the intensity of their grip on the mind decreases. This process culminates in time with full appreciation of Originless Ascendant Consciousness.

This and the following seven sutras describe fundamental fluctuations of awareness that create the full value of Ascendant Consciousness and then transform it into Perpetual, Exalted and Unified Consciousness. They deal with the intimate transformation of the four aims of life: Dharma, Artha, Kama and Mokṣa. The transformation of Dharma or Natural Law is explained in sutra ten; the transformation of Artha or purpose is explained in eleven; the transformation of Kama or desire is explained in twelve; and the development of Mokṣa or liberation is explained in fourteen. Nine through twelve describe the growth of Perpetual Consciousness; thirteen explains the growth of Exalted and Unified Consciousness. Fifteen observes that internal transformations in consciousness are the causes of changes in the outer world. Full knowledge of these transformations grants complete knowledge of the past and future; this is explained in the sixteenth sutra.

Pada III. Sutra 10

तस्य प्रशान्तवाहिता संस्कारात् ॥१०॥

Tasya praśānta vāhitā saṃskārāt

Consciousness flows to stillness because of impressions of tranquillity.

What attracts consciousness to the joyful moment of stillness? Previous impressions of the joy and peace of Silence inspire the mind to return again to Silence. This causes the appearance of the impressions that lead to stillness. This sutra clarifies the fact that the impressions that lead to stillness do not come into the mind from the outside. Rather, they already exist within; active choice or attention activates them but does not create them. Another way of saying this is that the natural tendency of the mind to experience Silence is deeply ingrained in the nervous system; this natural tendency pulls us inward to Peace. If it is the natural tendency of the mind, if the impressions that lead to Silence are already present in our consciousness, then it is only necessary to engage them so this process can occur. Ascension is completely natural because it is based on the inherent tendency of the mind to flow to greater Silence. Nothing need be done to actualize these latent impressions other than the simple turning of the attention inward.

This sutra verifies the grace, simplicity and sweetness of the growth to enlightenment. It is not a difficult or even a complicated process; it is only necessary to trigger the mind's latent impressions of calmness. Is this difficult? No, calmness is a natural style of functioning of the nervous system. Everyone experiences this throughout life at different times -- everyone some days feels more relaxed and peaceful than other days; evolution of consciousness simply takes these experiences of Silence and makes them regular, systematic and repeatable. When this happens for a long enough time, the mind is permanently established in peace. Stillness is thus subtly redefined as a wholly positive experience of soft composure, tranquillity and peace.

It is also valid to read this sutra, "*Consciousness flowing to tranquillity strengthens the impressions of stillness.*" What we put our attention on grows. If we focus on violence, the impressions of violence strengthen in us. If we focus on peace, the impressions of peace strengthen in us. We are in charge of whatever we choose to fill our minds with; this sutra reminds us that whatever we choose is going to change our lives for better or worse, because our choice forms impressions that will influence our future behavior.

Pada III. Sutra 11

सर्वार्थतैकाग्रतयोः क्षयोदयौ चित्तस्य समाधिपरिणामः ॥११॥

Sarva artha ekāgratayoḥ kṣaya udayau chittasya samādhi pariṇāmaḥ

The dawning of one-pointedness and the setting of many-purposes in Consciousness is called the Transformation to Ascendant Consciousness.

The Transformation to Ascendant Consciousness occurs within the joyful moment of stillness. This is the movement out of the field of diversity and into the field of one-pointed purpose.

"One-pointedness," ekāgratayoḥ, can also be translated, "bound, joined, strung or woven to the One." When perfected, this is a description of the intellect in Perpetual Consciousness. All of life is focussed on the One. In the growth to Perpetual Consciousness, one-pointedness begins to rise, multiple forms of purpose and desire begin to set. This is the dawn of inward focus on purpose and the setting of outward focus. It is also the beginning of the final disappearance of the impressions of outward manifestation from III.9.

A weak mind is a scattered mind, wandering from experience to experience, never able to hold onto any thought stream long enough to accomplish its purpose. Diversity of focus is an excellent way to accomplish nothing; one-pointedness of attention is a powerful tool for success in all areas. Artha, translated, "purpose," also means "wealth, object, meaning, cause," etc. (See I.28, commentary.) The attention on multiplicity is thus defined as the cause of all weakness and failure. Without transformation to one purpose, one meaning, one object, one cause, one use, life continues to be burdened by mutually contradictory thoughts, desires and actions -- therefore thoughts, desires, and actions are weak.

What is the resolution of this conflicted state of awareness? Simply to focus on the Ascendant. When this happens, the impressions that lead to tranquillity start to dominate and the impressions that lead to diversity naturally decrease. This is the key to success in every area of human concern, for it is precisely by one-pointedness of attention that life proceeds gracefully to the fulfillment of desire. This is in reality the only way to fulfill desire effectively. Otherwise, life is frittered away in multiplicity, with mutually contradictory and often destructive desires leading further and further away from Reality and fulfillment.

This is the tragedy of the Waking State -- with all the good intentions and sincerity of belief and action, life continues to tend toward superficiality, toward unhappiness (for unfulfilled desires lead inevitably to pain and suffering), to disease (for self-contradictory belief and action lead to physical distress), to aging (the body wears out rapidly when it is constantly torn between opposed desires) and even to death itself (for this is the ultimate resolution of contradiction to the Waking State mind -- to rest at all costs, even at the expense of life). One-pointedness, then, is the path to all success, happiness, health and life.

Pada III. Sutra 12

ततः पुनः शान्तोदितौ तुल्यप्रत्ययौ चित्तस्यैकाग्रतापरिणामः ॥१२॥

Tataḥ punaḥ śānta uditau tulya pratyayau chittasya
ekāgratā pariṇamaḥ

Then again, the equalization of subsiding and arising thoughts in Consciousness is called the Transformation to One-pointedness.

This sutra is descriptive of the beginning of the full realization of Ascendant Consciousness. All of thought becomes a faint vibration in the stable field of perfected Silence. This describes the increasing subtlety of experience as the mind settles down into stillness. As one moves more and more clearly into the Absolute, the fluctuations of thought turn back to their Source sooner and sooner. Said another way, one learns to intercept unwanted thoughts closer and closer to their inception and turn them back to the Self before they can produce undesirable effects. Similarly, one learns to introduce or favor desirable thoughts closer and closer to the Absolute. Power is greater and greater as one approaches the Ascendant; the ability to experience thought exactly there opens the doorway to instantaneous and complete fulfillment of desire. The most important thought to be entertained is the desire for one-pointedness, which is the same thing as the desire for full enlightenment.

This sutra says that one-pointedness is the natural result of the mind settling down into Silence. When one looks neither out *nor* in, one simply *sees*. When one is not caught by the past or the future, one simply *is*. This is the experience of Originless Ascendant Consciousness; in this state, consciousness is naturally directed at the One and is therefore perfected in its one-pointedness.

Pada III. Sutra 13

एतेन भूतन्द्रियेषु धर्मलक्षणावस्थापरिणामा व्याख्याताः ॥१३॥

Etena bhūta indriyeṣu dharma lakṣaṇā avasthā

pariṇāmā vyākhyātāḥ

By this is also explained the transformations of Natural Law, purpose, and root desire of the process of knowing and the known.

The previous four sutras relate to the three transformations of the knower: III.9 and 10 describe the transformation of Natural Law (Dharma); III.11 describes the transformation of purpose (Artha); III.12 describes the transformation of root desire (Kama).

In III.10, it is explained that the natural tendency of the knower is to experience Silence. The human comes equipped with other natural tendencies, but these without exception lead outward, into activity. With expansion of consciousness, the knower settles more and more deeply and thoroughly into Ascendant Consciousness; this reorders the functioning of internal Natural Law. The Laws of Nature that function in life are different in different states of consciousness. The Laws which rule the life in the Waking State are not those which guide the life in Perpetual Consciousness.

As this transformation occurs, the purpose of life also naturally changes (III.11). Many purposes naturally change into one, transforming the second aim of life, Artha. When this happens, all fluctuations of consciousness naturally become stable in pure Ascendant Consciousness (III.12), changing all desires into one. This transforms the quality of the third aim of life, Kama, for it is precisely here, in the domain of subtle fluctuation of thought that all desire is instantaneously fulfilled and one learns what is and what is not worth desiring.

So sutras nine to twelve describe the three transformations of the knower that structure Perpetual Consciousness. The growth to Perpetual Consciousness results from the natural tendency of the mind taking over, impelling the transformation of outward or multiple forms of purpose into an inward or one-pointed focus; this naturally results in grounding desire into faint fluctuations of Ascendant Consciousness.

This sutra says that identical processes inspire the growth of Exalted Consciousness and Unified Consciousness as the process of knowing and the experience of the Similarly does the known also settle down into the Absolute. The natural tendency of the senses change as consciousness changes; so does the use or purpose of the senses; so does their desire relationship with the Ascendant. The natural tendency of the senses transforms from dominance by tamas or rajas to dominance by sattva -- this introduces tranquillity into their functioning. The purpose of the senses changes from diversity to one-pointedness; this eventually transforms their function into faint vibrations of one-pointed desire. This develops Exalted Consciousness. Similarly does the experience of the field of the known also change to develop Unified Consciousness.

Pada III. Sutra 14

शान्तोदिताव्यपदेश्यधर्मानुपाती धर्मी ॥१४॥

Śānta udita avyapadeśya dharma anupātī dharmī

Subsiding and arising unite in the Unmanifest;

Natural Law closely follows the Source.

The Source of all fundamental tendencies is the Ascendant. This sutra affirms that all flowing of Natural Law is rooted in the Absolute. Even those functions of Natural Law which seem to be opposed to the nature of the Source, the outward-flowing tendencies, are still tightly connected with the Source. Indeed, no Natural Law ever is or even can be detached from its Source in the Ascendant. The more consciousness evolves, the more all tendencies flow in perfect harmony with the Source; the more all tendencies flow in harmony with the Source, the more quickly consciousness evolves.

As are the natural tendencies of Dharma, so are the changing purposes of Artha and the transformations of desire (Kama). This sutra stands for all of the three. Just as the whole table comes to you if you pull just one leg, so the transformations of natural tendency inevitably effect Artha and Kama.

Sutras nine, eleven, twelve and fourteen point to a gradual stilling of the thought process: in nine, outgoing thought begins to disappear and stillness begins to appear; in eleven, one-pointedness dawns (udaya) and multiple purpose sets; in twelve, arising (uditau) thoughts are equalized with subsiding thoughts; here, the arising (uditau) thoughts settle into the Unmanifest along with the subsiding thoughts. This is a description of the full development of Ascendant Consciousness, Originless Ascendant Consciousness.

Therefore this sutra explains the development of the fourth aim of life, Mokṣa. The processes described in nine, eleven and twelve are called transformations, but the ultimate refinement of this stilling process in this sutra is not called a transformation, for here it is a fluctuation that is completely beyond the operation of movement. "Transformation in the Unmanifest" would make no sense; before the apple tree sprouts, there is no meaning in talking about differences between twigs, leaves, branches and fruits within the seed. Transformations in the fields of Dharma, Artha and Kama are perfectly logical; but there is no transformation in Mokṣa. In the Unified Field of all the Laws of Nature, Natural Law is intimately connected with its source; there are no external manifestations to be transformed.

Pada III. Sutra 15

क्रमान्यत्वं परिणामान्यत्वे हेतुः ॥१५॥

Krama anyatvaṃ pariṇāma anyatve hetuḥ

Differences in transformation cause differences in manifestation.

Dharma changes as a result of changing consciousness. Frequently in the Waking State of Consciousness, people engage in an occupation and a lifestyle that is based on what they feel they should do or have to do, rather than on what they truly want to do, deep inside. If the stress in their nervous systems starts dissolving as a result of Ascension, their activity will naturally change to be in harmony with their deepest desire.

For example, consider someone who, deep in her heart, wants to be an artist, but is making a living as a nurse. When she comes to learn Ascension, she will be presented with a simple choice: whether to learn or not. If the stress in her nervous system is too great for her to appreciate the opportunity being presented to her, the nurse will leave without learning to Ascend and will continue with her life as before. But if she for *any* reason does decide to begin the practice, different Natural Laws will start functioning for her more and more quickly as her stress falls away; this will naturally produce a different purpose in life as the underlying, deeper desire of her heart is revealed to her.

This is the graceful and automatic path to the evolution of life. There is no requirement to force life to change. As one evolves to higher and higher stages of evolution, the Natural Laws functioning with and for the individual automatically change. As Dharma changes, so does Artha -- one's purpose and meaning naturally change in response to one's broader, all-comprehensive vision. And as one's purpose changes, one's desire and ability to desire also naturally transform.

This, then, is the royal road to the transformation of every aspect of life -- change the level of consciousness and every manifestation of consciousness in life will automatically change. All of life vibrates in harmony with the relationship to the Ascendant. The more perfectly in tune with the Ascendant, the more perfectly life dances in flowing rhythms of progress and sings in accomplishment.

As our consciousness transforms to Perpetual Consciousness, to Exalted Consciousness, to Unified Consciousness, the functioning of Natural Law gradually and gracefully transforms for us so that the Natural Laws which uphold our lives become completely different. That which serves us in the Waking State of Consciousness may or may not serve us in Perpetual Consciousness, Exalted Consciousness or Unified Consciousness.[29]

This sutra therefore clarifies the cause of the changes in life -- life changes because consciousness evolves; it is not that consciousness evolves because life changes. The source of success in life is thus the transformation of

---

[29] -- "When I was a child, I spake as a child, I thought as a child; but when I became a man, I put away childish things." I CORINTHIANS 13:11.

consciousness. Many have misunderstood the path for the goal. Life changes as consciousness changes, but to try to change life to change consciousness is not only a waste of time, it is potentially quite destructive, for introduction of strain in order to evolve puts more stress into the nervous system and can therefore significantly slow growth. One will never evolve by copying the behavior of the enlightened. Activity of thought and behavior change with different states of consciousness. Attempting to live the natural activity of a different state of consciousness is potentially deranging. This is not the path to success for anyone.

Pada III. Sutra 16

परिणामत्रयसंयमादतीतानागतज्ञानम् ॥१६॥

Pariṇāma traya saṃyamād atīta anāgata jñānam

By saṃyamaḥ on the three transformations comes knowledge of the past and future.

The three transformations are: the Transformation to Stillness that changes Dharma (III.9), the Transformation to Ascendant Consciousness that changes Artha (III.11), and the Transformation to One-pointedness that changes Kama (III.12). By focussing on each of these three long enough for the mind to resonate in harmony with the One while awareness remains absorbed in the Absolute, the full meaning of each of these three transformations is directly cognized.

What is their full meaning? Knowledge of the past and future. What normally shrouds perfect memory and intuition? Stress in the nervous system. How does this triple saṃyamaḥ eliminate stress? In order for each of the three transformations of consciousness to occur, the corresponding stress in the nervous system that is keeping awareness bound must dissolve. As these stresses dissolve, the mechanics of awareness and perception are loosened, giving rise to enlightened consciousness.

Memory is the subtlest motion of consciousness (see I.6 & I.11, commentaries). When the mind is purified, memory naturally functions perfectly. Typically, memory is blocked because of stress associated with the belief that the experience was in some way painful or damaging, or simply because the nervous system is so polluted with stress that nothing can be seen clearly. As the water of consciousness becomes clearer and clearer, the ability to see clearly in every direction naturally develops. Without the clarity of the water, however, nothing can be seen.

Saṃyamaḥ on any of the three transformations will produce this clarity. But if one is sufficiently conscious to practice these three in sequence, one's rate of growth of consciousness is greatly accelerated; the whole of the past and the future unrolls before one like a royal red carpet laid down for a monarch. One could start the sequential unfolding of saṃyamaḥ (III.6) anywhere, but starting with the fundamental transformation of consciousness to the Originless Ascendant Consciousness is a wonderful place to begin.

Pada III. Sutra 17

शब्दार्थप्रत्ययानामितरेतराध्यासात्
संकरस्तत्प्रविभागसंयमात्सर्वभूतरुतज्ञानम् ॥१७॥

Śabda artha pratyayānām itaretara adhyāsāt saṃkaraḥ tat pravibhāga saṃyamāt sarva bhūta ruta jñānam

Word, object and idea are confused and intermingled. By saṃyamaḥ on their separation comes knowledge of the sound of everything.[30]

When we perceive anything, the previous impressions we have learned to associate with similar objects resonate with our current experience to provide a name for the object. Therefore our perception is never innocent. The word "cow" is not the same thing as a living, three-dimensional energy matrix we see chewing grass by the side of the road, nor does it equal the mental concept of cow. There is a certain practical usefulness that results from this confusion of three separate realities, but it also keeps us from perceiving *anything* as it really is.

---

[30] -- A secondary translation of the last part of this sutra is, *By saṃyamaḥ on their separation comes knowledge of the language of all creatures.* When one has separated the illusory mixture of these three, there are no words of any creatures that are not known.

"And they were all filled with the Holy Ghost, and began to speak with other tongues, as the Spirit gave them utterance. And there were dwelling at Jerusalem Jews, devout men, out of every nation under heaven... Every man heard them speak in his own language. And they were all amazed and marvelled, saying one to another, Behold, are not all these which speak Galilaeans? And how hear we every man in our own tongue, wherein we were born?" THE ACTS 2:5-8.

All of matter is vibrating energy. To those who are sufficiently conscious, these vibrations can be heard. One way for consciousness to develop after Perpetual Consciousness is to practice saṃyamaḥ on the separate realities of word, object and idea. "Object" here translates artha -- meaning, purpose, etc. Contained within all objects are their inherent meanings and purposes. These are rarely or never appreciated in the Waking State, for words are too quickly assigned and artificial meanings derived from previous limiting experience. Seeing nothing as it really is, those in the Waking State do not truly know the purpose or meaning of anything. Without knowing the meaning of anything, it is not possible to perceive anything with sufficient subtlety to understand the true idea that underlies it, nor cognize its essential vibratory nature. Thus previous impressions, ideas and beliefs keep the true meaning or purpose of anything unknown.

As awareness in Perpetual Consciousness develops one-pointedness, all artha settles back into the Unmanifest. This particular development of consciousness bequeaths the ability to hear all the sounds of creation as they really are.

This is known as cognition of the Veda. The Vedas are called the blueprints of creation -- they are the sound vibrations that underlie all phenomena, all objects, all Natural Law. This ability to cognize all the sounds of creation is a by-product of expanding consciousness, a natural result of separating that which is illusorily mixed in the Waking State.

Pada III. Sutra 18

संस्कारसाक्षात्करणात्पूर्वजातिज्ञानम् ॥१८॥

Saṃskāra sākṣāt karaṇāt pūrva jāti jñānam

By bringing impressions to clarity comes knowledge of previous existences.

Every experience makes an impression in the subtle recording mechanics of the nervous system. Whether recognized or not, these remain, influencing every thought, word and deed in the present. Mostly these are invisible, but after Ascendant Consciousness is stabilized in Perpetual Consciousness, it becomes possible to bring these deep recordings to conscious awareness. When this happens, that which created the impression is clearly remembered. This can happen even before Perpetual Consciousness is gained, as a result of Ascension's dissolving of deep-rooted stresses. It is a common experience during the practice of Ascension for ancient memories to drift through with perfect vividness. This is a spontaneous result of stress dissolving.

After Perpetual Consciousness is stabilized, one can do this consciously. But before that day dawns, attempting to fish around for the ancient stresses is a waste of time, for it is *never* possible from the Waking State to see clearly exactly what is and what is not hindering awareness from experiencing its True Nature. This is why any such attempt, even if it is in the effort to heal present aberrant behavior, is going to be very time-consumptive and may or may not have any beneficial effect whatsoever. Life is too short to waste on such dubious endeavors!

Pada III. Sutra 19

प्रत्ययस्य परचित्तज्ञानम् ॥१९॥

Pratyayasya para chitta jñānam

By saṃyamaḥ on thought comes knowledge of the highest consciousness.

After Perpetual Consciousness is established, every thought is purely witnessed. Since this is so, it becomes possible to use the thought process itself as the vehicle of saṃyamaḥ. When this is done, the ultimate level of consciousness becomes known.[31]

Thought is the result of the energy of life colliding or resonating with previous impressions. This movement is itself nothing other than consciousness vibrating. If the vibration is completely understood, consciousness will be understood. This becomes increasingly true as the thought manifesting from the Ascendant is less and less distorted by previous impressions. These pure thoughts are the ṛtam thoughts discussed at the end of the first chapter. By saṃyamaḥ on such thoughts, one rises very quickly to knowledge of Unified Consciousness, for the distance to be traversed is not large. Focussing on a pure ṛtam thought, or rather, resonating with the One while focussing on a pure ṛtam thought and simultaneously experiencing Ascendant Consciousness takes one without delay to the knowledge of the full range of thought.

---

[31] -- Contained within this ultimate value of consciousness are the individual, localized impulses of consciousness of everyone and everything else. Therefore, since one knows his or her own Self, one knows the Self of everyone else. This leads to a secondary translation of this sutra: *By saṃyamaḥ on thought comes knowledge of the consciousness of others.*

Pada III. Sutra 20

न च तत्सालम्बनं तस्याविषयीभूतत्वात् ॥२०॥

Na cha tat sālambanaṃ tasya aviṣayī bhūtatvāt

But this does not result in Union with the Highest, for that is not within the range of the nature of the elements.

Knowledge of Unified Consciousness is not the experience of Unified Consciousness. This sutra explains that Unified Consciousness is not typically gained by focussing on thoughts. Thoughts are, after all, merely movements of physical phenomena. The range of that created by the elements, including thoughts, does not extend to the Ascendant. Patañjali adds this sutra to clarify that knowledge of enlightenment is not the same thing as the experience of enlightenment.

If Union with the highest value of consciousness is not within the range of the nature of the elements, what is? The Ascendant lies forever beyond the elements, indeed, It lies beyond any created thing. But the subtlest level of anything created is not beyond the range of the elements. So saṃyamaḥ on thoughts *will* give full experience of the subtlest level of the process of knowing, or Exalted Consciousness. The next fourteen sutras give various examples of this process of saṃyamaḥ on thoughts, and therefore describe different abilities that can develop as Perpetual Consciousness grows into Exalted Consciousness.

Pada III. Sutra 21

कायरूपसंयमात्तद्ग्राह्यशक्तिस्तम्भे चक्षुः
प्रकाशासंप्रयोगेन्तर्धानम् ॥२१॥

Kāya rūpa saṃyamāt tad grāhya śakti stambhe
chakṣuḥ prakāśa asaṃprayoge antardhānam

By saṃyamaḥ on the form of body comes suspension of the power of comprehension, disconnection of illumination with the eye and disappearance.

By resonating on the body's form in Ascendant Consciousness, mastery of the appearance of the body is attained. The "power of comprehension" resides within the knower, the "connection of illumination with the eye" represents the process of knowing, and "disappearance" relates to the known. What are the practical mechanics of becoming invisible? It is the result of breaking the connection with each of these three -- knower, known, and process of knowing.

This sutra may seem very surprising to those of us in the West who have deeply invested our belief systems in the external reality of all objects. Yet we have already learned there is a great deal we cannot perceive. Humans see a very narrow band of the electromagnetic spectrum, for example. A slightly higher or lower vibratory rate and we cannot see it. The infrared and ultraviolet are more visible to others species of animals; there are vast reaches of vibration perceived by no carbon-based beings.

Similarly for sound. Dogs can hear much higher pitches, for example, than humans. We live in an extremely narrow experiential band; that which lies beyond is not known without sufficiently refined equipment; and there are vibratory rates that no machine has yet been able to measure. So there exists a great deal that we cannot perceive; this sutra affirms that one's increasing level of consciousness opens one to understanding of the knower, the known and the process of knowing in terms of the body. Once one has fully understood their relationships, one can alter the typical flow of individual life into form.

This is actually already happening all the time to everyone -- one's thoughts determine the physical shape of one's body. One's thoughts make one fat or thin, well-muscled or flaccid; they also smooth the lines from the face from peace or deeply etch it from agony. What reflects on the outside also manifests on the inside -- the state of functioning of the body and the bodily organs is a by-product of our continual thought processes.

This truth in the Waking State remains true in enlightenment, but now choice becomes increasingly dominant. With this increasing choice, one's ability to restructure the form of the body naturally follows. There is actually no limit to this process. The body can be restructured into any desired form; it can be translated into any desired frequency. The echoes from the world's scriptures about bodily Ascension were based in truth.[32] The mechanics of this is full mastery of the knower, the known, and the process of knowing.

---

[32] -- "And it came to pass, as they still went on, and talked, that, behold, there appeared a chariot of fire, and horses of fire, and parted them both asunder; and Elijah went up by a whirlwind into Heaven.

"And Elisha saw it, and he cried, My father, my father, the chariot of Israel and the horsemen thereof." II KINGS 2:11

Pada III. Sutra 22

एतेन शब्दाद्यन्तर्धानमुक्तम् ॥२२॥

Etena śabdādi antardhānam uktam

By this is also explained the disappearance of sound.

By saṃyamaḥ on the sounds of the body, full knowledge of the knower, the known and the process of knowing related to sound gives the ability to change these in any desired manner.

It is a common experience that if the mind is distracted, the eyes do not see, the ears do not hear. This is well known by all magicians and pseudo spiritual leaders -- by misdirecting the attention of the audience, the illusion is accomplished. In plain sight, the elephant walks away and no one sees it, for everyone is looking elsewhere. From nowhere, the cheap crucifix or Citizens watch appears to astound the credulous. By not looking where you are expected to look, you do not see the deluder disappear. Those who wish to see such "miracles" will always find those who are eager to appear miraculous. In that case, it is all a part of being bound to the Waking State -- forever looking outside for God.

The inner transformation is a different reality. All the senses can be effortlessly redirected, based on full knowledge of the manifest form of their application. There are no limits to the human condition other than those we artificially impose.

Pada III. Sutra 23

सोपक्रमं निरुपक्रमं च कर्म तत्संयमादपरान्तज्ञानमरिष्टेभ्यो वा ॥२३॥

Sopakramaṃ nirupa kramaṃ cha karma tat saṃyamād

aparānta jñānam ariṣṭebhyo vā

The results of action manifest quickly and slowly.

By saṃyamaḥ on these comes knowledge of death and

other unfortunate events.

Some of our actions return very quickly to us, whereas others return very slowly. By focussing in Ascendant Consciousness on these two kinds of returning action, we can discover the lifespan as well as all events that are coming to us. The purpose of doing this is of course to avert the undesirable. Foreknowledge would be fairly pointless without the ability to change it. From full knowledge of the functioning of returning action, we can redirect it to extend life or avoid any and all extreme losses.

As the mind expands to Infinity, the returning missiles of death and destruction are vaporized, or turn into gentle showers of life. There are no absolutes in the created Universe other than the One Ascendant Reality. By knowing That, all programs can be rewritten, all unfortunate realities erased, before they oppress. There is no mistake, no sin, no crime that cannot be resolved, redeemed, erased. This is skill in action; this is the aversion of future suffering; this is the intelligent way to experience human life. Being a victim is senseless. Anyone can change individual destiny -- it is only necessary to expand to Infinity and there will be no action, no karma left to rebound.

Another way of saying this is that the genetic code is imprinted from its inception with a specific lifespan. As one Ascends, one naturally learns what is written there, and rewrites that which does not serve. There is no life-situation that cannot be healed through the expansion of consciousness. There is no disease, no structural deformity, no hereditary failure that cannot be transformed through the effortless mechanics of Ascension.

Pada III. Sutra 24

मैत्र्यादिषु बलानि ॥२४॥

Maitrya ādiṣu balāni

Saṃyamaḥ on friendliness and the other good emotions leads to strength.

The "other good emotions" refer to the compassion, joyfulness and indifference of Sutra I.33. Strength in these results in purification and clarity of consciousness. This strength effects the unfortunate results of returning karma by averting them before they come. Strength might seem an unlikely result of such positive emotions, but the reality is that it is only the positive emotions that are strong, for only they function in complete harmony with the upward current of creation. A life completely in harmony with Natural Law is a strong life, for every desire is fulfilled in advance. There is no request too small to be granted to the eternally joyful. Friendliness to everyone everywhere at all times brings about personal invincibility, for there can be no enemy born to those who always love.

There is a story from ancient India about Śukra, the God of Love. Śukra alone has never been defeated in battle, for whenever an enemy rushes at him to harm him, he simply loves his attacker so much that his enemy puts down his weapons. Nothing can withstand the power of love. This is why Patañjali mentions friendliness, for friendliness is love, and therefore is the most important of the good emotions.

Compassion does not mean "suffering with," as has often been felt in the world. True compassion raises the consciousness of those who are less evolved. Thus compassion is that emotion which connects humanity vertically together, for there will always be those who are less conscious and those who are more conscious than oneself. Therefore compassion to the lesser evolved and compassion from the more evolved ties the entire human race together in one endless tapestry of forgiveness, atonement and progress.

Friendliness radiates horizontally outward to equals; compassion radiates downward and outward to those less evolved; joyfulness radiates upward. The natural movement of joy upward connects the individual to the higher powers of nature and the more evolved humans throughout creation. This naturally leads to their blessings upon us.

These are the natural directions of these three emotions, but indifference has no natural direction, nor is it ever practiced through saṃyamaḥ, as it relates only to the world of illusions, to that which is not real. As the individual becomes more firmly and clearly established in the Self, it becomes increasingly evident that compassion is the only appropriate emotion for those who are caught by the boundaries of ignorance.

When these three are mastered, there is no longer room for weakness of any kind. Nor is there any longer room for any untoward results of returning action, for all of creation is united with one in love, compassion and joy. What, then, could harm one? There is nothing left, anywhere, at any time. These three are thus the doorway to freedom, immortality, and all success in life.

Pada III. Sutra 25

बलेषु हस्तिबलादीनि ॥२५॥

Baleṣu hasti bala adīni

Saṃyamaḥ on positive strengths leads to the strength of the elephant and others.

It is also possible to develop limitless strength simply by focussing on strength in the Absolute. One small manifestation of this ability occurs when someone without thinking raises a car to save a child. "Without thinking" is the operative phrase in that sentence. If one can, even for an instant, be free from the limitations of belief, judgment and previous experience, the Universe instantly becomes completely different. It is not that one breaks physical laws; rather, one flows in harmony with different physical laws, those that are not commonly known or used. When one is adept with this ability, the full range of the natural Universe is open for exploration and development.

It is not that some precious few are open to higher experience and ability: all are. It is not that only a fortunate few can break the restricting confines of their limited pasts and be born into a new world of manifest splendor. All can.

What is required is nothing more than to stop supporting the old, destructive beliefs by our continual, unconscious choice. How can a choice be unconscious? If we turn often enough from the light, we may forget that we possess the power to turn back toward the light at any instant of time. This act of forgetting makes us as if unconscious of our continual, every-moment repeated choice to believe we are limited, finite beings, not the Sons and Daughters of God. As we believe, so we act.

Stretch your mind with me -- even for an instant will be enough. Imagine for the briefest of moments that the ancient echo coming down to us from all lands and cultures is in fact literally true. Dream with me for just an instant that you -- I mean *you!* You who are reading this right now! You who are looking down at this page with your lovely eyes! You, conscious being, just a foot or so above these words! Dream that you really are born to be *the* Master of Creation, you really were created in God's own image, that all your beliefs about limitation and suffering are nothing other than a particularly cunning lie, created by your own illusory ego.

Where does that leave you now? Flying with the eagles, running with the lions, swimming with the dolphins, uprooting trees with the elephants? Yes, of course, and infinitely more besides, for these are among the least of the strengths in my Garden.

Join with me in this magical dream and I promise you, you will dream no longer -- all of space and time will bow down before you, for you will again remember your oneness with your Maker. Once you have remembered you are one with the Father-Mother-God, if you order the world to move, it will move for you. If you request a new sun to light the sky, it will be born for you. If you wish to create a new Universe, even this is within your power. For when you were created, you were created in the image of your Creator. All God's strength is yours -- not as some ideal fancy but in Reality, both now and forever.

And what need you do to realize this glorious Truth, far beyond the power of any words to adequately describe? Only stop being someone other than who you are. Only stop supporting the dreams of illness and death and suffering. Only stop turning every moment from the light of perfect Silence, burning for you forever in your heart, if you acknowledge it or even remember it or not. You need do so very little and you will gain so very much.

Come, dance with me in the dawn of Love and Peace and together we will reform the world, remake it in the perfection of the Divine Plan.

Pada III. Sutra 26

प्रवृत्त्यालोकन्यासात्सूक्ष्मव्यवहित विप्रकृष्टज्ञानम् ॥२६॥

Pravṛtti āloka nyāsāt sūkṣma vyavahita viprakṛṣṭa jñānam

By applying the light of higher thought comes knowledge of the subtle, the hidden and the distant.

The word translated here as "light," āloka, can also be translated, "seeing" or "praise." The light of Pure Consciousness can see through objects; it is not limited by space or time and can see the entire range of creation -- i.e., it is not limited to the gross level of sensory experience of the Waking State. This level of the light of consciousness sees Heaven (III.5), which is the primary indicator of Exalted Consciousness -- seeing the celestial light and the beings who inhabit the celestial light everywhere, always.

Praise is that level of activity of thought that continually rejoices in the light of Heaven. In the subtle, praise *is* pure light; it is the most active of the Ascension emotions, that which is most closely aligned to the pure quality of bliss. Praise is the primary function of the human in relation to the higher powers of Nature; it is therefore the primary active portion of the upward-directed emotion, joy. Pure praise is not different from pure bliss, nor is it different from pure light.

As this level of consciousness develops, one learns to extend consciousness beyond the illusory boundaries of the Waking State. Consciousness is omnipresent; therefore the ability to automatically extend it everywhere is inherent within it. This is why Patañjali says "applying," nyāsāt, instead of saṃyamaḥ in this sutra. The light of Pure Consciousness develops by other practices; having developed it, it is effortless to move it anywhere to know anything at all that there is to be known.

Pada III. Sutra 27

भुवनज्ञानं सूर्ये संयमात् ॥२७॥

Bhuvana jñānaṃ sūrye saṃyamāt

By saṃyamaḥ on the Sun, knowledge of the worlds.

"The worlds" are not the suns and planets of our three-dimensional Universe (knowledge of those is the result of the next sutra). The worlds are the celestial regions of light that surround and permeate our three-dimensional Universe. There are generally considered to be seven major regions of light (these are the Heavens referred to in III.5). These seven are: bhu, bhuva, svar, mahar, janar, tapas and satya.

"The Sun" translates surya, a word which comes from Sva, the third world of the seven, which literally means, "The Self," "sing the praise of" and "light." As in the previous sutra, consciousness, light, praise and higher perception are intimately linked. This sutra further explains the knowledge of the subtle mentioned in the last sutra; the next two sutras further explain the knowledge of the distant; beginning in sutra thirty, knowledge of the hidden will be explored.

The external Sun can be taken as the object of saṃyamaḥ, but easier than this is saṃyamaḥ on those parts of the body that are intimately connected with the Sun. For example, there is a subtle channel that runs along the right side of the spine known as the piṅgala. This contains the upward-directed, hot, bright, positive, yang, masculine, solar energy. By saṃyamaḥ on that comes this knowledge. Or by saṃyamaḥ on the right side of the body, or on the right breast, or on the right eye. But best is saṃyamaḥ on the upper part of the suṣumna, that part of the central subtle channel up the spine that leads from the heart to the crown of the head. That is called the Solar Path, that is the route the soul in Unified Consciousness takes when leaving the body at death, that is the path that leads directly to the highest level of Heaven, that is the Path of the Sages. For one who has fully mastered that, there is no rebirth nor is there return to this world or any other.

Pada III. Sutra 28

चन्द्रे ताराव्यूहज्ञानम् ॥२८॥

Chandre tārā vyūha jñānam

By saṃyamaḥ on the moon, knowledge of the arrangement of the stars.

"The stars" refers to the entire external Universe. The word translated "the moon," chandra, also means "shining, bright, lovely." As with the Sun, the external moon can be taken as the object of saṃyamaḥ, but easier is the iḍa, the subtle channel that moves along the left side of the spine. The iḍa contains the downward-directed, cool, dark, negative, yin, feminine, lunar energy. Or by saṃyamaḥ on the left side of the body, or on the left breast or the left eye. But the best is the part of the suṣumna that branches at the base of the skull and heads to the forehead. That is called the Lunar Path, that is the route the soul in Perpetual Consciousness takes at death, that is the path that leads directly to the intermediate levels of Heaven, that is the path of the Gods.

For one who has mastered this path, there is no rebirth in this world, but the soul continues to evolve to higher and higher planes of existence until the highest is reached. This is a much slower path to complete realization than that outlined in the last sutra. Fastest is to gain perfected Unified Consciousness in human life -- the Path of the Gods involves slower evolution through the celestial regions. All paths eventually end in the same place -- complete Union with the Ascendant -- but on Earth, it is possible to evolve the quickest. This is why it is said that the angels, the devas and the gods are envious of the humans -- here it is possible to accomplish in one short lifetime what elsewhere can take uncountable ages.

Pada III. Sutra 29

ध्रुवे तद्गतिज्ञानम् ॥२९॥

Dhruve tad gati jñānam

By saṃyamaḥ on the polestar, knowledge of their motion.

The complement to the complete knowledge of space in the last sutra is the complete knowledge of motion. With these two together, full knowledge of the relative Universe is available. Knowledge of motion implies knowledge of time. The past and the future are open to one who has mastered this sutra.

The predictive power of the stars is also herein implied. Astrology has a bad name in the West among many, partly because of the inability to understand how the Universe intimately connects everywhere, partly because of the gross carelessness of many Western astrologers in ignoring the precession of the equinox. The Earth wobbles slowly about its celestial pole, taking some 23,000 years to complete one revolution. This causes the signs of the Zodiac to shift by approximately 50 seconds of arc every year. What this means is that by 1996, each of the astrological signs have shifted some 23°48' from their correct or astronomical position. Since this is so, the predictive power of Western astrology has severely decayed, for there is no longer a measurable relationship of the returning energy of action (karma) with the firmament.

In its pure state, when the zodiac positions correspond exactly with their true astronomical positions, astrology is capable of revealing the entire knowledge of the results of returning action. This sutra, therefore, opens the door to full mastery of the knowledge of returning karma (fulfilling the promise of III.23) and, as a by-product, full knowledge of valid astrology.[33]

Pada III. Sutra 30

नाभिचक्रे कायव्यूहज्ञानम् ॥३०॥

Nābhi chakre kāya vyūha jñānam

By saṃyamaḥ on the navel chakra, knowledge of the arrangement of the body.

This sutra is the complement of III.28 -- there the result is complete knowledge of the structure of the external, physical Universe; here, the result is complete knowledge of the structure of the internal physical Universe.

The seven chakras are subtle energy centers scattered along the cerebral-spinal axis that control various bodily functions and are associated with certain abilities. (See Appendix 2: The Chakras.) From focussing on the navel chakra while resonating with Ascendant Consciousness comes complete knowledge of the body, for all the subtle energy currents (known as naḍis) that control the physical functioning of the body pass through this chakra. Mastery of that gives the ability to see all the internal organs and all the bodily systems; from this direct perception comes the ability to heal any area of the body that is damaged, diseased or aged.

---

[33] -- Valid astrology is called Jyotiṣ in Sanskrit.

The navel chakra is also the connecting point with the external world; full mastery of this therefore also gives full mastery of the physical. This will be further discussed in the commentary on sutras 44 and 45 of this pada. Full mastery of the external world is an inherent property of the third chakra; for anyone who cognizes its full range, there is no inability left in the relationship with the outer world. That is, there remains no possibility for any external failure. This is not the only way to develop this Mastery, but it is among the easiest.

Pada III. Sutra 31

कण्ठकूपे क्षुत्पिपासानिवृत्तिः ॥३१॥

Kaṇṭha kūpe kṣut pipāsā nivṛttiḥ

By saṃyamaḥ on the hollow of the throat, cessation of the attachment to eating and drinking.

The fifth chakra, corresponding to the hollow of the throat, controls all desire. The immediate practical application of this sutra is to normalize excess body size, but this is only the most superficial meaning. The "attachment to eating and drinking" is the attachment to experience in the world, the attempt to control or devour experience, as it were. This naturally ceases when one masters the Ascendant, for one has attained the goal of all desiring.

What are the steps to this mastery? Fulfillment of desire. One does not (indeed, one cannot) attain fulfillment by attempting to cut down desires. Desires are the omnipresent reality of creation, leading forever to evolution and expansion. (This is why the third aim of life, Kama, or mastery of desire, is last before Mokṣa, enlightenment. And this is also why sutra twelve of this chapter, the desire sutra, deals with subtle fluctuations of thought in One-pointedness.)

Desire is effortlessly fulfilled when the individual acts in perfect harmony with Natural Law. As Perpetual Consciousness rises to Unified Consciousness, ṛtam bharā prajñā functions more and more effectively (see I.48-51 commentary); this is the practical mechanics of fulfilling all desire, individually and severally.

A repressed desire lives on, gathering energy inside; if not permitted to manifest, it will in time force its reemergence; this can lead to self-destructive acts. An expressed desire, however, is gone. Its fulfillment may leave impressions that will in time lead to future desire, but at least the manifestation of the desire's energy has been spent. And if in the expression of the desire, it can be subtly directed into wholly life-supporting channels, then the impressions formed by its fulfillment need not lead to undesirable consequences.

How to subtly direct desire? By mastering the desire before it is fully manifest. When it has developed fully, it is impossible to change. The time to move concrete is before it has set; there is nothing simple or effortless about moving it afterward. By full mastery of the throat chakra, one learns to pick up thought before it has permanently congealed. At this level, thought can still be changed, can still be redirected. This is the royal road to freedom from unwanted desire. And it is also the royal road to fulfilling all desire, even those considered miraculous by the Waking State.

Pada III. Sutra 32

कूर्मनाडयं स्थैर्यम् ॥३२॥

Kūrma nāḍyaṃ sthairyam

By saṃyamaḥ on the Tortoise Tube, steadiness.

The Tortoise Tube is the subtle energy channel that flows through all of creation connecting all beings and all humans with the Creator. This is also known as the Sutra Atman (lit.,"the Thread of Souls") and is an experience that comes in Perpetual Consciousness. We are all connected, not just theoretically or ideally but quite literally. Every soul is like a bead on this Infinite thread, winding without ceasing through all of space and time.

Some of the experiences of enlightenment are incomprehensible from the perspective of the Waking State of Consciousness. How can all souls from the innumerable blades of grass to the omnipotent Creator of All be interconnected? It makes no sense to a mind conditioned by the three-dimensional Universe perceived by the senses, a mind deeply invested with the beliefs in separation, division and duality.

The Tortoise is the aspect of God that carries the Universe on its back. If one is established in Perpetual Consciousness and quests with consciousness downward, one will experience the Source of all individual energy, rising through the Infinite Tube. The Source of the tube appears rather like a tortoise from way up here -- although, of course, only rather like!

The Tortoise also represents the lower levels of creation, the pre-conscious, animalistic energies from which we have evolved, and which continue to rule our subconscious minds. This sutra connects us with those instinctive, primal energies lurking in the unconscious. As an additional by-product of this practice comes steadiness. One can only be overshadowed by experience if one is not grounded to the Source. The whole Universe could cease to exist, but the master of this sutra would not be shaken. This is the purest essence of invincibility.

Pada III. Sutra 33

मूर्धज्योतिषि सिद्धदर्शनम् ॥३३॥

Mūrdha jyotiṣi siddha darśanam

By saṃyamaḥ on the brilliant light at the top of the head, the vision of the perfected ones.

The crown chakra, through which the Solar Path passes, is connected with the highest world. Because of this, "the top of he head," mūrdha, also means, "the height of Heaven." When one with stabilized Ascendant Consciousness puts awareness into the light that is the crown chakra, one can see all those who have mastered human life completely -- all those who departed from this Earth via the Path of the Sages, all those who have attained Unified Consciousness.

They are connected to the Sutra Atman on a higher plane of existence than those still on the Earth; therefore, these two sutras provide the formula for full cognition of the entire range of the Sutra Atman (This entire range is known as the liṅgam.), the entire range of Creation from the lowest level of insentience to the highest degree of Heaven. Everyone is already positioned somewhere on this Infinite, Eternal column of light; these two sutras open one to full cognition of one's position. From this platform of achievement, everyone else, before or after, can be seen and known ("vision," darśanam, can also be translated, "understanding"). All of creation is open to direct perception; so is everyone in it, at any time, past, present or future.

Pada III. Sutra 34

प्रातिभाद्वा सर्वम् ॥३४॥

Prātibhād vā sarvam

Or by saṃyamaḥ on intuition, all.

All that there is to be known can be known by intuition. This is the sutra that eliminates the need for all the others. By mastery of intuition, the perfection of all other practices is had. Just as when you befriend the emperor, all the empire desires to serve you, just so, all the perfected aspects of consciousness bow to one who has perfect intuition.

The prime function of the crown chakra is omniscience or all-knowingness; the formula revealed in this sutra fully opens that.

It is truly shocking, once one understands the full potential of the human in enlightenment, how practically everybody on the Earth lives such limited existences of pain, suffering, illness, and unending trouble. All power and all knowledge await those who can renounce their belief in separation and limitation and rejoin with their Creator in perfect Unified Consciousness. This is not hard to do, nor does it require years of arduous practice, nor is this possible only for a chosen few. Anyone can accomplish this, for the Ascendant exists fully inside everyone. All the qualities of the Absolute exist fully inside everyone; anyone can at any time open to this perfection and the old world will instantly fall away.[34]

---

[34] -- Certain modern religious sects are frightened by this and other similar sutras, for they maintain that only God and Christ are perfect, the human is therefore forever lesser, separate and inherently evil. This fear-based thinking proves their incomprehension of the omnipresence of God and also proves they know neither the Son nor the Father.

(continued...)

Pada III. Sutra 35

हृदये चित्तसंवित् ॥३५॥

Hṛdaye chitta saṃvit

By saṃyamaḥ on the heart, full knowledge of consciousness.

This sutra contrasts with III.19, in which saṃyamaḥ on thought led to knowledge of, but not Union with, the highest value of consciousness. *Full* knowledge of consciousness, however, means Union with consciousness, and therefore fulfills the requirement of III.20.

The heart is the fourth chakra, the primary seat in the human of the soul. The altar to God exists in the heart; it is the most important energy center in the body because just here is the strongest connection to the Infinite.

In the modern world, many think that consciousness is an artifact of the body. These think that the nerve cells in our brains magically produce our awareness. Nothing could be less likely than several billion cells joining together to produce consciousness. This misunderstanding is based on a fundamental confusion about exactly what consciousness *is.* Consciousness is the fundamental reality of everything; it shines through everything. In its pure form, consciousness *is* the Ascendant. Through limiting belief and experience, consciousness identifies with boundaries; this obscures the

---

(...continued)

The titles and beliefs of such may seem very different from the scribes and pharisees of Jerusalem at the beginning of the Christian era, but their limited beliefs and understandings demonstrate their direct spiritual lineage to those who were supposed to maintain the Truth but instead twisted it into a belief system of fear and ignorance and found their only safety in murdering any God-realized prophet that happened to wander their way. See Appendix 1.

experience of consciousness by itself, pristine, pure. But through Ascension, one gradually learns to identify less and less with the boundaries and more and more with the Absolute Reality of the Ascendant. When this happens, one learns on the basis of direct experience that consciousness precedes the body -- precedes and will continue indefinitely after the destruction of the component cells that structure the nervous system.

Pada III. Sutra 36

सत्त्वपुरुषयोरत्यन्तासंकीर्णयोः प्रत्ययाविशेषो भोगः परार्थात्
स्वार्थसंयमात्पुरुषज्ञानम् ॥३६॥

Sattva puruśayor atyanta asaṃkīrṇayoḥ pratyaya
aviśeṣaḥ bhogaḥ para arthāt svārtha saṃyamāt puruṣa jñānam

Experience comes from thoughts that are not extraordinary and wonderful.
Sattva and the Ascendant are eternally distinct.
By saṃyamaḥ on the purpose of sattva and the purpose of the Ascendant comes knowledge of the Ascendant.

"Experience" means the experience as in II.18 -- that which leads to relative enjoyment, not that which leads to enlightenment. As long as thoughts continue to move in their old grooves, experience will continue not to be particularly fascinating or rewarding. Most thoughts one can think fall into this category. What, then, leads to liberation? Only extraordinary and wonderful thoughts. What are these? Thoughts which give true knowledge of the Ascendant. From the last sutra, it is clear that this can be gained by saṃyamaḥ on the heart chakra. But this is not the only technique.

Why have more than one technique? Simply because of the tenacity of the old beliefs and behavior patterns. Most of life has been deeply committed to the field of relative experience and enjoyment. The mind is very used to variety and change for stimulation. By introducing more than one Ascension Attitude, the mind becomes stuck less often. A coarse mind will tend to coarsen anything, will tend to force new experience into the old grooves, the grooves of the familiar. To avert this, an effective Teaching needs more than one channel into the Ascendant.

This is why Patañjali introduces more than one technique; this is why in the teaching of Ascension, we use twenty-seven Ascension Attitudes. It may well be that any given individual will not need all the twenty-seven to gain Unified Consciousness. It may even be that any given individual might need no more than one or two to gain the highest degree of enlightenment. But practically speaking, most individuals will require most or all of the Ascension Attitudes, simply because the life-long habits of strain, limitation and suffering are so deeply ingrained. Will twenty-seven always be enough? Absolutely, yes, if they are practiced consistently.

Sattva is the fundamental force of Nature that is responsible for all evolution, purity, clarity and light. From the standpoint of the Waking State of Consciousness, the brilliant, all-but-Infinite light of sattva may seem the same as the Ascendant. But the Ascendant lies forever beyond all boundaries, even those that are most like it in nature. So by saṃyamaḥ on the difference between the purpose of sattva and the purpose of the Ascendant comes clear knowledge of the Ascendant.

This technique (indeed, all the techniques of the third chapter), will obviously not work very well (or at all) without the clear experience of Ascendant Consciousness. Without that, one could think at great length about these concepts, but there would be no special or extraordinary or wonderful result but only further experience. A thought of Truth is not the same as the experience of Truth. Thinking about the distinction between any two things will not give the experience of either, although it might inspire one to try the experience. You could tell a child a thousand times that although mud does *look* like chocolate, it tastes nothing like chocolate. But let him taste mud only once, then he *knows.* Saṃyamaḥ is a tool for direct experience, it is not an instruction to think about anything.

The highest purpose of relative existence, regardless how pure, regardless how aligned with sattva, is still distinct from the absolute purity of the Ascendant. By understanding the distinction between these two, one gains perfection in knowledge of the Ascendant.

One name for the Ascendant is Sat, which means "Eternal" or "Truth" or "Absolute." Sattva adds tva to sat. What is this tva? Tva means "you" or "other" or "many." By adding the faintest impulse of individuality to the absolute purity of the Ascendant is created the first impulse of duality, sattva. Sattva is still and forever intimately connected to the Ascendant: Sat is still visible inside it. The other two guṇas, rajas and tamas, are much different in form. Only sattva maintains the strength and integrity and clarity of the Ascendant. And yet it also contains duality in the form of otherness; it contains multiplicity; it contains the possibility of a second. The Ascendant is forever non-dual, stable in its perfect Silence, in its Absolute, Eternal Perfection. Sattva is similar to it in form, but it moves in the relative Universe, and therefore contains within it the seed of duality. As in the yin-yang symbol, each of the fundamental forces contains within it a dot -- the faintest impulse of other, of multiplicity.

Pada III. Sutra 37

ततः प्रातिभश्रावणवेदनादर्शास्वादवार्ता जायन्ते ॥३७॥

Tataḥ prātibha śrāvaṇa vedana ādarśa āsvāda vārtā jāyante

From that is gained intuition, higher hearing, touch, sight, taste and smell.[35]

From full knowledge of the Ascendant comes full use of intuition, in which anything desired to be known can be known (see III.34, commentary). The higher uses of the senses also naturally develop. This is a hallmark of the Sixth State of consciousness, Exalted Consciousness. The ability to perceive the subtler levels of reality develops when one is freed from bondage to the guṇas. Once one is fully aware that one *is* the Absolute, then the senses are freed from the dominance by the relative forces of Nature, and therefore their limits are removed. The Ascendant is everywhere, inside all beings, inside all things. The ability to move one's Ascendant Consciousness into the domain of the guṇas -- into the relative Universe of three dimensions, of name and form -- is inherent within the Ascendant. One can hear, touch, see, taste, smell anywhere at any level of existence when one is fully cognizant of the Ascendant. This is complete freedom of the senses from the bondage of the body.

---

[35] -- This order of the development of the senses follows the order of manifestation of matter from the Ascendant: hearing from the Unified Field of all the Laws of Nature (sattva), touch from the subtle form of air (gaseous matter, sattva + rajas mixed), sight from the subtle form of fire (energy, rajas), taste from the subtle form of water (the liquid form of matter, rajas and tamas mixed), smell from the subtle form of earth (the solid form of matter, tamas). (see III. 42, commentary).

Pada III. Sutra 38

ते समाधावुपसर्गा व्युत्थाने सिद्धयः ॥३८॥

Te samādhāv upasargā vyutthāne siddhayaḥ

These by-products of Ascendant Consciousness are perfections to the outward-directed.

As long as the mind remains oriented outward, so long will intuition and the higher sense perceptions be regarded as useful acquisitions. Only when one is perfectly established in the highest degree of enlightenment do they become irrelevant. Once one *owns* the bank, the dollar bill in the wallet does not seem very significant. But if one is familiar only with abject poverty, even a single dollar can appear as a great boon. It is all a matter of perspective, based entirely on one's level of consciousness.

It can also be that the glorious wonder of celestial perception can hinder one's growth to Unified Consciousness. It is possible to remain in the Sixth State, Exalted Consciousness, for quite a long time, following the Lunar Path, the Path of the Gods. Everything is so beautiful, so glorious, so wonderful, so extraordinary, it is hard to imagine or even desire more. But any duality, even the slightest, is not the ultimate reality of Unified Consciousness.

Regardless how stimulating and utterly delightful the Sixth State is, it is not the ultimate perfection of the Ascendant. True knowledge and the association with the fully enlightened are two ways to avoid this. Knowledge can inspire one to continue on past the wonder of the celestial; those living in Unified Consciousness can gently remind one that Exalted Consciousness is not, after all, the final goal of human evolution.

To develop these perfections before Perpetual Consciousness is gained is possible but is not in any way desirable, for one can be completely overshadowed by the wonder of the celestial and not reach the Ascendant at all. This is why the development of consciousness, to be effective in the highest degree, proceeds first to the Fourth State of Ascendant Consciousness, then to the Fifth State of Perpetual Consciousness, then and only then to the celestial experience of Exalted Consciousness.

Pada III. Sutra 39

बन्धकारणशैथिल्यात्प्रचारसंवेदनाच्च चित्तस्य परशरीरावेशः ॥३९॥

Bandha kāraṇa śaithilyāt prachāra saṃvedanāch cha
chittasya para śarīrāveśaḥ

From loosening the cause of bondage and from full knowledge of the subtle movements of the mind, consciousness enters the body of the Ascendant.

The cause of bondage is the identification of the Self with the not-self. When this decreases due to the full knowledge that the Self is, in fact, Absolute and not the boundaries, attachment to the objects of perception weakens and eventually ceases. This is the result of Perpetual Consciousness, but Perpetual Consciousness does not automatically give full knowledge of the movements of the mind; this is a by-product of intimate familiarity with the subtlest level of mental activity, which develops in Exalted Consciousness.

In other words, it is perfectly possible to experience the Absolute (the Fourth State) and even live the Absolute permanently (the Fifth State) without knowing much or anything about the mechanics of how and why thought moves through the mind. But because one establishes full witnessing in Perpetual Consciousness, the ability to learn about these movements is born there.

"Full knowledge," saṃveda, means that one has complete and perfect understanding of every phase of the development of thought. Thought is, in the Waking State, typically experienced only on the most surface level. But there are deeper levels to every thought, as described in I.17. When one has completely mastered these, the mind is also fully expanded to the Ascendant; it knows that it is everywhere, that is perceives everything, that it *is* everything. Knowing this, one knows all that is to be known.

What is "the body of the Ascendant?" Since the Ascendant is omnipresent and universal, the body of the Ascendant *is* the Universe and everything and everyone that is in the Universe. So through mastery of the movements of the mind, one recognizes that one is inside of everyone and everything, automatically. There are no limits to this -- one can look out of anyone's eyes, hear with anyone's ears, know what anyone knows, as a by-product of one's completion of consciousness. One is no longer chained to a limited physical existence.

In Reality, one never was, no one ever is, but from habit of belief in the Waking State, we *believe* that we are so limited. This leads to the bizarre beliefs in life and death, illness and old age, suffering and unhappiness that characterize what is typically considered normal human life in the Waking State. Normal human life! What a tragic travesty. Born an immortal to walk among the stars and laugh with the gods, friable man instead crawls among the worms for seventy autumns and cries alone or with the dogs before decaying back into dust.

Pada III. Sutra 40

उदानजयाज्जलपङ्ककण्टकादिष्वसङ्ग उत्क्रान्तिश्च ॥४०॥

Udāna jayāt jala paṅka kaṇṭaka ādiṣu asaṅga utkrāntiḥ cha

From mastery of the life-breath known as udāna comes non-entanglement in water, mud, thorns and the like as well as physical Ascension.

This explains the most important subtle movement of the mind that must be mastered to be able to leave the body at will. "Physical Ascension" means that one can depart from the body at any time.

The life-breath or prāṇa is that which connects the soul to the body. In the body, prāṇa divides into a five-fold functioning: prāṇa, vyāna, samāna, apāna and udāna. The prāna is the inward and outward breathing that brings in oxygen and breathes out carbon dioxide; the vyāna carries the oxygen throughout the arterial network and capillaries and carries away the carbon dioxide via the veins; the samāna is the breath involved with the digestive function in the stomach and small intestine; the apāna is the downward passing of gas through the small and large intestine; and the udāna is the upward-directed ultimately subtle breath that rises from the heart.

The most important upward channel or naḍi that the udāna must traverse is the suṣumna. When one's consciousness firmly masters this upward-rising breath in the suṣumna, one's relation with the physical Universe dramatically changes. One is no longer bound to the material; one avoids entanglements of all kinds, both subtle and gross. And one gains the ability to leave the body along the Solar Path, the Path of the Sages, *at will.* This is descriptive of one who stands on the very threshold of Unified Consciousness. Mastery of the subtlest movements of the life-breath brings freedom throughout the structure of creation, for one is re-aligned with the omnipresent Source of all that is.

Pada III. Sutra 41

समानजयाज्ज्वलनम् ॥४१॥

Samāna jayāt jvalanam

By mastery of the life-breath known as samāna comes blazing radiance.

The samāna is the division of the life-breath that is responsible for digestion (see the previous sutra). The digestive fire is often not particularly efficient in the Waking State. This is in part due to the quality and quantity of food ingested, in part due to stresses lodged in the walls of the small and large intestine, in part due to conflicting demands from the mind on the digestive system. One cannot well digest if one is emotionally or psychologically upset.

The modern human is often the victim of an environment that does not mesh well with the natural physical state of the human body. Whenever fearful or angry emotional states are turned on, the digestive system is ordered to shut down and blood pressure is told to rise to prepare for fight or flight. This archaic response to stress is completely natural and is very valuable at the appropriate place and time -- faced by a drunken man holding a knife in a dark alley, for example. But in the modern world, fight-or-flight is turned on often and repeatedly, so much so that the digestive system shuts down and stays shut down and the blood pressure goes up and stays up.

As stress decreases and is removed from the nervous system, the conflicting demands from the mind change; this alters enzymatic production to allow for maximum effect from digestion. Also as stress decreases, the mind starts functioning more clearly to inspire one to eat better quality foods in better quantity and balance. And the stress dissolves from the body, the impacted deposits in the intestines are dislodged. For all these reasons, digestion starts to function more and more efficiently. When this happens, the products created by digestion begin to change.

There are three specific digestive products that dramatically change life -- these are known as soma, ojas, and amṛta. Amṛta is that which bequeaths physical immortality. Every cell can regenerate indefinitely and perfectly; the amṛta is the physical cause of perfect cell replication indefinitely.

Ojas is that which causes "blazing radiance." Even in the first days of Ascension, it is common for new practitioners to appear much brighter and clearer. This is in part due to the decrease in fatigue and stress, in part due to the increase in ojas. Ojas is like a cleaner oil burning in a lamp -- it burns without smoke, without residue. Ojas soothes or coats every joint with superfluidity; the skin becomes softer, younger, more supple; the internal organs become healthier and more youthful.

Soma is the essential building block out of which ojas and amṛta are created. It is also the physical counterpart of the abilities and experiences of all higher states of consciousness. Soma is known as "the glue of the Universe." It unites everything; most importantly, it unites the Ascendant to everything else. Soma consists of S + OM + A. OM is the ultimate vibration that underlies and causes all of creation (see I.27 & I.28 commentaries). S represents Union with the Ascendant. A stands for the unmanifest fullness of the three guṇas, those fundamental forces of Nature which create all the material Universe. So Soma unites the Ascendant with the full range of creation; development of this locks one into full and perfect experience of the celestial (Exalted Consciousness) and full awareness of Unified Consciousness. This is *the* product of digestion that is indispensable for the growth of consciousness.

Pada III. Sutra 42

श्रोत्राकाशयोः संबन्धसंयमाद्दिव्यं श्रोत्रम् ॥४२॥

Śrotra akāśayoḥ saṃbandha saṃyamād divyaṃ śrotram

By saṃyamaḥ on the connection of hearing to space comes divine hearing.

The other supernormal powers of sensation develop through saṃyamaḥ on the connection of the surface style of functioning of the senses with the appropriate state of matter: touch with the gaseous state, sight with the energy state, taste with the liquid state and smell with the solid state.

Some of these are apparent, given our current state of understanding of sensual processes, and some are not. Smell, for example, recognizes solid particles; taste recognizes liquid particles; sight functions because of electromagnetic phenomena. But touch being rooted in the gaseous state is not immediately obvious, nor is hearing with space. Hearing would seem more logically related to the gaseous, for we don't normally consider hearing to consist of anything other than air molecules banging together and colliding with the eardrum which vibrates the inner ear, stimulating the cochlea to send signals to the brain, where these nerve impulses are interpreted as sound.

This roughly describes the physical mechanics of hearing, but does nothing to explain what hearing *is*. Just as consciousness is not the product of the neurons in the brain, just so hearing exists without the physical structure that hearing uses to hear. Sound waves strike the eardrum continually but we often don't hear them, either because we are asleep or distracted. It takes awareness to use the machinery.

What is the connection of the senses to consciousness? They flow through the channels of the five states of matter. Hearing flows through space, which is the ground state of quantum mechanics, the Unified Field of all the Laws of Nature. Space is the vacuum itself, with no matter left in it at all. Modern physics has realized that so-called empty space is not truly empty -- it fluctuates continually with vast energy. This fluctuation has been thought to have little observable impact on the physical Universe, except in the regions where space is so intensely curved back onto itself that these fluctuations flutter into reality. For example, in the region of a superplasmic body (a black hole), gravity is so very strong that the continually created fluctuations of energy can be pulled apart -- one half of a virtual matched particle pair spirals into the black hole, the other is released to enter the three-dimensional Universe. In this way, a black hole gradually shrinks.

Space or akāśa is not nothing. It vibrates with Infinite energy. Scientists tell us that this entire Universe came out of a region of "empty space," some 10^{-43} centimeters in size, some ten to sixteen billion years ago. Science also declares there is enough energy in every cubic millimeter of space to create a nearly infinite number of similar Universes.

Divine Hearing does not require air molecules, nor any physical machinery of the body. It is, rather, a pure extension of consciousness through the subtle state of the five elements. All the Natural Laws that structure creation dance in the purity of space. By knowing this state, the full power of hearing naturally results.

Pada III. Sutra 43

कायाकाशयोः संबन्धसंयमाल्लघुतूल समापत्तेश्चाकाशगमनम् ॥४३॥

Kāya akāśayoḥ saṃbandha saṃyamāt laghu tūla samāpatte cha ākāśa gamanam

By saṃyamaḥ on the connection of the body to space is acquired lightness like a tuft of cotton and free motion through space.

The connection of the body of anything to the external world is quite curious -- wherever the boundaries of an object are, there the rest of the Universe seems to begin. But this ancient view of the three-dimensional isolation and integrity of objects is being more and more fundamentally questioned. With every breath, for example, we breathe in 10^{23} atoms -- a thousand-trillion-trillion atoms -- which join us to become part of us; we breathe out a similar number of molecules that were a moment before part of our bodies. Our body is in a constant state of transformation, exchanging life and matter with the rest of the Universe continually.

Furthermore, every atom of every cell in the body is primarily just empty space. 99.999% of all matter is empty. Take any atom and expand it to the size of a Superdome and what do you have? In the center, a small beebee of solidity -- this is the atom's nucleus -- and a handful of infinitesimal ghosts fluttering around the bleachers at enormous speed -- these are the electrons -- and there is nothing else at all, except for the seething motion of almost-energy, almost-matter that fills up all of empty space.

So what exactly is the relation of a physical, three-dimensional body of name and form to this empty space, this ākāśa? The body is primarily nothing other than this empty space. Matter, then, is largely an artifact of sensual experience; as consciousness becomes firmly established in the Absolute, one naturally gains full use of the senses; the celestial opens fully to us. When this happens, it becomes very easy to change the rules which before seemed absolute. Natural Law is inviolable only so long as one is not familiar with the Source of Natural Law. Once this happens, one can rewrite any of the script that creates this Universe at will. Levitation is thus a by-product of intimate familiarity with the Ascendant.

There is more to be gained from this sutra. What ages a body? Heaviness of thought. Gravity takes and pulls life back into the ground. It is the attachment to the things of this world that causes life to become heavier and heavier until the body bends and sags and eventually falls into dust. Light thoughts tend to activate the Natural Laws that stand in opposition to gravity, those of levitation. The fact that levitation is rare in the modern world does not invalidate these laws. The fact that few have even the foggiest notion or even belief in the higher laws is not a proof that they do not exist. Reality has a certain wonderful disdain for the thought structures of belief created in the Waking State of Consciousness.

"Connection," saṃbandha, in this and the previous sutra, means literally, "union with bondage." We touch here on the very structure of ignorance. The will of the enlightened breaks all boundaries, even those that appear inviolable in the Waking State.

Pada III. Sutra 44

बहिरकल्पिता वृत्तिर्महाविदेहा ततः प्रकाशावरणक्षयः ॥४४॥

Bahir akalpitā vṛttir mahā videhā tataḥ prakāśa āvaraṇa kṣayaḥ

When the movements of the Absolute are actually experienced outside, without the body, then the obstruction of illumination is destroyed.

The second part of this sutra is a perfect repetition of II.52. There are many routes that lead to the perfection of consciousness, but they are truly only one. II.52 described this from the perspective of the breath, and described this as a breathless state. In I.19, the activity of the body stilled because thought aligned with Being. This was descriptive of the movement to Perpetual Consciousness. In this sutra, the cause is Absolute movements of awareness being experienced outside of the body. When consciousness has sufficiently developed so that one can maintain the experience of the Absolute moving without the body functioning at all, one has come very close to full Realization. In I.19, awareness was experiencing pure Being as the body stilled, but here there are Absolute movements of awareness without the body.

Movements of Infinity may seem very improbable from the perspective of the Waking State, but this is a very real experience as Perpetual Consciousness grows into Unified Consciousness. It is precisely the Infinite moving from the inside to the outside that structures awareness of the Infinite on the outside. This sutra, then, is descriptive of a very refined level of Exalted Consciousness, one beginning to merge into Unified Consciousness.

"Actually experienced" means not in imagination, but truly. One could perhaps imagine that waves of Absoluteness were flowing all around and through one, but it would not be real. The acid test for expansion of consciousness is the complete cessation of bodily activity. If one continues to experience the movement of the Unformed *and* the body is utterly still, it cannot be a by-product of aberrant mental functioning but must be the experience of Ultimate Reality.

One does not have to have such an experience for long in order for the obstructions to illumination to fall away. Indeed, one having such an experience clearly even once would be sufficient to remove the barriers to full enlightenment. There is not far to go when one can experience the waves of Infinity without the body functioning at all.

Pada III. Sutra 45

स्थूलस्वरूपसूक्ष्मान्वयार्थवत्त्वसंयमाद्भूतजयः ॥४५॥

Sthūla svarūpa sūkṣma anvaya arthavattva saṃyamād bhūta jayaḥ

By saṃyamaḥ on the purpose of the connection of the Absolute Self to the gross and the subtle, comes mastery of the elements.

"Purpose," artha, also means "cause, meaning, reward. wealth, object" (see I.28). "The gross" means the physical structure of the Universe; "the subtle" means the Natural Laws which underlie and motivate all the transformations in the Universe. The "connection of the Absolute Self to the gross and the subtle" is the physical body. By holding these three in continual focus while experiencing the Absolute comes full mastery over the external Universe, which will be explained in the following sutra.

There are no limits to the human other than those which are artificially imposed by belief in separation and isolation. The true state of the human is to be absolutely free, everywhere, always. This does not come from changing beliefs but from changing experience. Belief can stop or remove experience, but only new experience can change old beliefs, rewrite them with a new script made from granite.

Pada III. Sutra 46

ततोऽणिमादिप्रादुर्भावः कायसंपत्तद्धर्मानभिघातश्च ॥४६॥

Tataḥ aṇima ādi prādurbhāvaḥ kāya saṃpat tat dharma anabhighātaḥ cha

From that comes perfection of the body, aṇima and the other physical masteries; further, Natural Law ceases to have a noxious effect.

Perfection of the body will be explained in the next sutra. It comes from the portion of the saṃyamaḥ in the previous sutra that deals with the body; i.e., the *connection* of the Absolute Self to the gross and the subtle.

Natural Law ceasing to have a noxious effect comes from the portion of the saṃyamaḥ that connects the Ascendant Self to *the subtle*. In the Waking State, the mind is continually creating mutually contradictory desires. Natural Law does what it can to support all desires, but when the desires mutually contradict each other, what can Nature do? The noxious effect of Natural Laws comes from their functioning in opposition to each other (see II.47 & II.48, commentaries).

The physical masteries result from the portion of the saṃyamaḥ that connects the Ascendant Self to *the gross*. These are: aṇima, mahima, laghima, garima, prākāmya, prāpti, īśatvam, vaśitva and yatra kamavasayitva.

Aṇima means that the body can shrink to any size by readjusting the size of space inside its constituent atoms. Mahima is the opposite -- the body can expand to any desired size. Laghima is another version of III.43 -- the body becomes perfectly light at will. Garima is the opposite -- the body becomes heavy at will.

Prākāmya is the power of fulfilling all desires instantly. Prāpti is the power of manifesting any physical object. Īśatvam is the mastery of creation, maintenance and destruction; i.e., mastery of the three fundamental forces of nature, the guṇas. Vaśitva is command over all; i.e., invincibility. And yatra kamavasayitva is the ability to go anywhere in the Universe instantly. This is also a by-product of III.43.

Pada III. Sutra 47

रूपलावण्यबलवज्रसंहननत्वानि कायसंपत् ॥४७॥

Rūpa lāvaṇya bala vajra saṃhananatvāni kāya saṃpat

Perfection of the body consists of beauty of form, grace, strength and adamantine endurance.

"Grace," lāvaṇya, means perfect co-ordination.

"Adamantine endurance," saṃhananatvāni, implies freedom from all injury, destruction, hurt, affliction, disease and even death itself.

These two sutras indicate that most if not all of the physical problems in life come from a confusion of the purpose of the body. When the mind misunderstands what the body is for, it issues conflicting demands. The body is a wondrous pharmacy, capable of creating any drug in response to thought and feeling. When the mind is out of control, misunderstanding its True, Absolute Nature, it is as if at the mercy of external events. This leads to conflicting thoughts and feelings which place conflicting demands on the body.

Conflicting demands on the body decrease coordination and endurance and increase weakness. Our habitual thoughts also structure our body's size and form and mold our faces in response to their imperious demands. As the mind becomes more orderly and peaceful, diet is no longer abused; therefore meager body size naturally increases and excess body size naturally decreases. As the mind becomes more simple and linear in functioning, the body straightens and becomes perfect in posture. And as one's thoughts become softer and sweeter, the hard lines etched in the face from bitter experiences in life melt away and are replaced by the suppleness and innocence of untarnished youth.

Enlightenment is thus the key to physical rejuvenation. But one need not wait until enlightenment is complete for this process to begin. Those who Ascend regularly are biologically younger than their peers who do not. The average is some seven years younger after a year of regular Ascension and fifteen years after three years. The boundaries and limits we normally impose upon life are entirely a product of our beliefs.

Pada III. Sutra 48

ग्रहणस्वरूपास्मितान्वयार्थवत्त्वसंयमादिन्द्रियजयः ॥४८॥

Grahaṇa svarūpa asmitā anvaya arthavattva saṃyamāt indriya jayaḥ

By saṃyamaḥ on the purpose of the connection of the Absolute Self to perceiving and to the ego comes mastery of the senses.

This parallels III.45, only here the focus is on the inner Universe: the senses, mind, intellect and ego. The mind and intellect are the connecting link between the Absolute Self and the process of perception and the ego.

Full mastery of the senses will be explained in the following sutra.

In the Waking State, there is unending confusion about what motivates the functioning of the internal machinery of consciousness -- the senses, mind, intellect and ego. This saṃyamaḥ clarifies these. They are all intermingled and confused in ignorance, leading to subjection to the vagrant motions of the mind and the senses. The senses act like wild stallions, violently pulling the chariot of the mind in opposing directions. Why? Because the charioteer is unknown. The person believes that the ego is in charge. But the ego is an illusion merely. Without full knowledge of the Absolute Self, there can be no consistent or permanent control of the mind or the senses.

Pada III. Sutra 49

ततो मनोजवित्वं विकरणभावः प्रधानजयश्च ॥४९॥

Tato mano javitvaṃ vikaraṇa bhāvaḥ pradhāna jayaś cha

From that comes the speed of the mind, use of the senses without the body, and mastery of the Primordial Cause.

This sutra parallels III.46. There the result of saṃyamaḥ on the three elements of the external Universe are described; here the result of saṃyamaḥ on the three primary constituents of the inner Universe are described.

"The speed of the mind" comes from that portion of the saṃyamaḥ in the previous sutra that deals with the *connection* of the Absolute Self to perceiving and to the ego; i.e., the mind. The speed of the mind means that the senses can travel throughout creation as quickly as the mind thinks. The speed limit of light does not apply to the mind, when the purpose of this connection is fully known. The senses' speed is released from the confines of relative laws.

"Use of the senses without the body" comes from the portion of the saṃyamaḥ that connects the Ascendant Self to *perceiving*. Complete freedom from the physical structure of the organs comes as a result of mastering the purpose of the mind, that which controls the senses, that which is the connection between the Absolute Self and the organs of perception.

"Mastery of the Primordial Cause" results from the portion of the saṃyamaḥ that connects the Ascendant Self to *the ego*. The Primordial Cause is that which gives rise to all other causes and effects. What is that? It is simply the belief in separation; this is all that fuels the life of the ego. The ego is the illusory structure created by the soul in its effort to maintain the boundaries of its belief.

From the perspective of the Waking State, it may sound surprising that it is the belief in limited individuality that is responsible for the creation of all the boundaries of the internal and external Universe. Nevertheless, this is the experience in enlightenment. Anyone rising to Perpetual Consciousness and beyond finds that the structure of the Universe is radically different from that supposed to be true in the Waking State.

In Perpetual Consciousness, all of the external world continues on, competely separate from the Absolute Self within. In Exalted Consciousness, one perceives that all external activity proceeds from the fundamental forces of Natural Law, the guṇas. And in Unified Consciousness, the guṇas are perceived as being illusory manifestations of the belief in duality -- which is another name for the ego. The train is going to all the stations, choose a destination, buy a ticket and get on board.

So full mastery of the knowledge of the purpose of the connection of the Absolute Self to the ego results in full development of Unified Consciousness, for one has completely cognized the illusory nature of the Primordial Cause.

Pada III. Sutra 50

सत्त्वपुरुषान्यताख्यातिमात्रस्य सर्वभावाधिष्ठातृत्वं सर्वज्ञातृत्वं च ॥५०॥

Sattva puruṣa anyatā khyāti mātrasya sarva bhāva

adhi ṣṭhātṛtvaṃ sarva jñātṛtvaṃ cha

From full awareness of the difference between sattva and the Ascendant comes the highest authority over all existence and all-knowingness.

These are the eighth and ninth results of the development of knowledge of the difference between sattva and the Ascendant (see III.36 & III.37). When this development is perfected, the highest power and knowledge naturally result.

"Highest authority," adhi ṣṭhātṛtvaṃ, can also be translated "unwavering witnessing." All of creation is perceived as separate from the Absolute Self. From this complete separation, in time all knowledge of creation naturally develops. So this phrase includes both the goal and the path to the goal.

Sattva is the highest power in the relative Universe. When one fully cognizes this primal force, one gains all authority over all that exists, for sattva already possesses that. And sattva also contains all knowledge. So full awareness of sattva bequeaths that as well.

Pada III. Sutra 51

तद्वैराग्यादपि दोषबीजक्षये कैवल्यम् ॥५१॥

Tat vairāgyād api doṣa bīja kṣaye kaivalyam

Detachment even from those destroys the source of ignorance. That is Unified Consciousness.

The ultimate growth of consciousness results from the detachment from even the highest powers and abilities in the created Universe. Once one can withdraw even from full mastery of sattva, the source of all afflictions in life is destroyed. This naturally gives rise to the highest development of human consciousness, Unified Consciousness.

The word here translated "ignorance," doṣa, is one of those truly wonderful words in Saṇskrit that has dozens of interlocked meanings. For example, it also means, "defect, blemish, failing, taint, bad quality, fault, crime, sin, guilt, vice, damage, injury, evil, bad consequence, morbid affection" and so forth. In short, doṣa means all that constitutes the discomforts and limitations of life. Being free from all that hurts and binds means that life is lived in fulfillment, in joy, in perfection, in the absolute completion of life in harmony with the Ascendant.

Pada III. Sutra 52

स्थान्युपनिमन्त्रणे सङ्गस्मयाकरणं पुनरनिष्टप्रसङ्गात् ॥५२॥

Sthānya upanimantraṇe saṅga smaya akaraṇaṃ

punar aniṣṭa prasaṅgāt

When invited by the highest powers, do not smile with arrogance or have contact with them, for this leads again to addiction and undesirable results.

"Do not smile with arrogance," smaya akaraṇaṃ, can also be translated, "it is natural to be astonished."

"Contact," saṅga, can also be translated, "attachment, desire, obstruction." These are also ways of describing the source of renewed addiction to the relative boundaries of ignorance.

"Undesirable," aniṣṭa, also means "displeasing, unlucky, evil, calamitous."

"Addiction," prasaṅgāt, is the extreme form of "contact," saṅga -- it is the same word with the prefix, pra, attached. Pra means "in the highest degree, ultimate limit, exceedingly, greatly." The ultimate limit of contact is addiction. One should not wish to be re-attached to the boundaries of ignorance. If one cracks the door even slightly, it will burst back open with a host of undesirable consequences. It is natural, perhaps, to be attracted to union with the Supreme Forces in Nature, but the "last temptation" before the dawn of Unified Consciousness can lead one to spiral back again into Exalted Consciousness or even further into the depths of attachment.

Why should the Highest Powers and Principalities in the Universe attempt to derail one from attaining the ultimate destination of Unified Consciousness? Every level of creation has its corresponding level of happiness. All beings everywhere in creation naturally assume, therefore, that their existence is the best. Would a cat prefer to be a human? Or a deer? Similarly, the Highest Powers of Nature are quite assured of the importance and vital necessity of their roles. Is this bad? No, but for a human aspiring to the highest realization, the Path of the Gods is a lesser destiny by far than the Path of the Sages.

Testing is not a bad thing -- it enables us to identify and root out those final tendencies which would otherwise keep us in ignorance. One gains in strength by overcoming obstacles. Testing, then, actually serves as a boon in our growth.

Pada III. Sutra 53

क्षणतत्क्रमयोः संयमाद्विवेकजं ज्ञानम् ॥५३॥

Kṣaṇa tat kramayoḥ saṃyamād vivekajaṃ jñānam

By saṃyamaḥ on the apparent succession of the joyful moment of Eternity is born discriminative knowledge.

There is only one time and that is Now (see I.1, commentary). And yet, the Universe seems to continue to change. This is the root of the power of māyā, the illusion that maintains the integrity of everything, everywhere, always. When one has mastered the full appreciation of the difference between the Eternal Now and the changing manifestations of time, one rises to discriminative knowledge in Unified Consciousness -- one learns to distinguish in all places and times between the temporal and the Eternal, between the finite and the Infinite. This is the ultimate discrimination in regard to time. The next sutra extends this to all physical characteristics.

Pada III. Sutra 54

जातिलक्षणादेशैरन्यतानवच्छेदात् तुल्ययोस्ततः प्रतिपत्तिः ॥५४॥

Jāti lakṣaṇa deśaiḥ anyatā anavachchhedāt tulyayos tataḥ pratipattiḥ

The truly united appear different because of separate existence, outward appearances and spatial position. From discriminative knowledge comes the perception of Eternity shining equally through them all.

As Unified Consciousness develops, one realizes more and more clearly that one Self shines through all beings, in all places and times, regardless of outer appearances to the contrary. One ceases to judge anyone or anything by its external appearance; instead one looks within to the perfection of the Ascendant shining clearly inside them all.

In other words, the final steps of the growth of consciousness are spurred by intellectual discrimination. The intellect learns to recognize the difference between the Self and the not-self in all places and all times. When one can perceive the subtlest level of reality, the level in which all Natural Laws are forever operating, one small step further takes one into continual appreciation of the Ascendant underlying those Natural Laws.

The following sutra takes this description to the ultimate limit of experience.

Pada III. Sutra 55

तारकं सर्वविषयं सर्वथाविषयमक्रमं चेति विवेकजं ज्ञानम् ॥५५॥

Tārakaṃ sarva viṣayaṃ sarvathā viṣayam akramaṃ cha
iti vivekajaṃ jñānam

When discriminative knowledge simultaneously experiences the Eternal Now in all of creation and every part of creation, that is Deliverance.

What is the limit of the growth of consciousness? The experience of Eternity in all things everywhere at all times simultaneously. This is the ultimate development of Unified Consciousness, called here Deliverance or Liberation, called in other texts, Brahman.

Brahman is a further refinement of Unified Consciousness. In Unified Consciousness, one perceives the Infinite in the external world, but only in one object at a time. One has unified the Ascendant Self on the inside with the Ascendant perceived everywhere outside, but the perception is of only one object at a time. In this sutra, discriminative knowledge takes the evolving soul one step further, the final step a human living on Earth can accomplish. Not only is the primary focus experienced as Infinite, everything of creation and every aspect of creation is simultaneously experienced as Infinite.

The growth to this ultimate refinement of Unified Consciousness is absolutely natural and spontaneous -- the primary focus of Infinite Awareness gradually expands to take in the secondary objects of perception and then the tertiary objects of perception and then continues until the entire creation with all its myriad parts has been absorbed by the Ascendant. This is why Brahman is called "the Devourer" in the Upanishads -- it eats all the boundaries, eventually producing the pure experience of the Ascendant in everything, everywhere, always, simultaneously.

Such is Deliverance. Such is Liberation. Such is the ultimate development of consciousness in Unified Consciousness. And the truly good news is that every human already has the potential to live this ultimate state built into the human nervous system. It is only sad belief built upon the shaky foundation of misinterpreted experience that keeps life bound to the dismal limits of ignorance. It is not just that any belief *can* change with new experience, any belief *will* necessarily change if it does not fit into the new experiential network.

Pada III. Sutra 56

सत्त्वपुरुषयोः शुद्धिसाम्ये कैवल्यम् ॥५६॥

Sattva puruṣayoḥ śuddhi sāmye kaivalyam

When purity is equal to the purity of the Ascendant, that is Unified Consciousness.

Discriminative knowledge is not an absolute requirement for gaining Unified Consciousness. This most refined state of consciousness can also develop from refinement of purity. This theme will be further developed in the next chapter, the final chapter on Unified Consciousness. As one gradually becomes more and more filled with the purity of sattva, one gradually rises into the perfection of Unified Consciousness. It could be said that sattva is eternally established in Unified Consciousness; when an individual rises to the plateau of perfect identity with sattva in every thought, word and deed, throughout the entire structure of the body in all its parts, Unified Consciousness automatically results.

It might be worthwhile to observe that the growth of consciousness through absolute purity is a more difficult path, particularly in the modern world with its myriads of toxins in the air, food and water and with its constant sensual stimulation that is anything but pure. Even so, if it is possible to be absolutely pure, the goal will be reached.

Lest anyone conclude that there is any requirement for Unified Consciousness other than to function in life as the mind and body were designed to function, Patañjali adds this sutra at the end of his chapter on Splendor. All the perfections are sattvic in nature; one need do nothing but become ever more sattvic and the highest human consciousness will automatically dawn.

Thus ends the Third Quarter of the Science of Yoga: SPLENDOR

FOURTH QUARTER:
UNIFIED CONSCIOUSNESS

Pada IV. Sutra 1

जन्मौषधिमन्त्रतपःसमाधिजाः सिद्धयः ॥१॥

Janma auṣadhi mantra tapaḥ samādhijāḥ siddhayaḥ

Birth, diet, Ascension, austerity and Absolute Awareness give birth to perfection.

This extends the thought of the last sutra. Purity can come through many different means. Those who are very fortunate are born with very pure nervous systems. These can attain perfection with their very first breath. Many who consider themselves (or are considered by others) to be divine incarnations are such fortunate souls -- they never have to experience ignorance.

Such births are very rare and becoming even more rare in the modern world as the level of impurity, stress and toxins in the environment and in the parents' nervous systems inexorably rises. Even so, from time-to-time, it can happen. Krishnamurti is one example. Mother Meera is another. Without ever experiencing ignorance, they have very little or no ability to raise others to enlightenment, but this does not diminish the Reality of their own Self-realization.

Birth also means rebirth. A new birth occurs every time one experiences the Absolute. When one drops all the accumulated mental debris even for an instant and experiences the Ascendant, the entire structure of the belief system is shaken. This *is* rebirth; as this happens, life dramatically moves in the direction of purity. Many people have completely reorganized their lives on the basis of a single experience of higher Reality -- they adopt extensive belief systems or abandon extensive belief systems, based on one glimpse behind the veil of the senses.

It is also possible to dramatically change the life through transformation of diet and introduction of different herbs. This procedure can be extraordinarily effective for eliminating stress, given appropriate guidance. Without enlightened counsel, however, such an approach will not prove very effective. Nor indeed will Ascension learned from an unrealized source be very likely to transform life much. Any tool for self-development is only going to be effective if it is properly used; such instructions are difficult to come by if the source is defective. Without immediate feedback from an enlightened source, how would one ever know if he/she was Ascending correctly or not? One *might* be, but then again, one might not. Years could go by without any significant progress toward the goal.

Similarly for austerity. What value austerity without appropriate guidance? And yet, with guidance, austerity, Ascension, diet and rebirth all align as natural by-products of the experience of the Ascendant. One naturally desires to give up that which does not serve one on the basis of expanded levels of experience -- that is true austerity; one naturally desires to focus ever more earnestly and consistently on expansion after one has tasted the Absolute -- that is true Ascension; one naturally desires to reform every aspect of what the body and senses ingest once one has discovered the Infinite hiding within -- that is true diet; and one is automatically reborn to higher and higher levels of existence with every experience of Ascendant Consciousness -- that is true birth.

This sutra is also describing the various components of the growth of perfection in the life from the most gross to the most subtle. Birth is the transformation of the physical state, diet is the transformation of the senses, Ascension is the transformation of the mind, austerity is transformation of the intellect (deciding for higher and ever higher true pleasure is the function of the intellect) and Absolute Awareness is the transformation of the spirit or the ego to completion in the Infinite. All aspects of the personality thus join together to create perfection.

Pada IV. Sutra 2

जात्यन्तरपरिणामः प्रकृत्यापूरात् ॥२॥

Jāti antara pariṇāmaḥ prakṛti āpūrāt

The transformations of inner birth flood through because of Nature.

Nature is omnipotent in the created Universe. This sutra affirms that all evolution is under the control of Nature. The individual gradually rises higher and higher over a long period of time due to the upward-directed powers of Nature -- the three guṇas operate in perfect harmony to lift life systematically to ever-higher stages.

But humans with their free will can step off the up escalator and even reverse the normal flow. This is called becoming demonic. Life in a cycle of increasing restriction is painful for those on such a path; Nature does not support their desires very much, because the natural current of life flows in quite the other direction. Attempting to swim against the stream of evolution is difficult, tiring and often quite painful.

Reverse again for even an instant to harmony with the upward-directed forces in the Universe and life, bliss, health and peace flood through the soul, bringing about faster and faster rebirth into higher and higher phases of existence. Nature pushes continually for life in accord with the upward current; when an individual reverses demonic, self-destructive tendencies and adopts the divine current of Ascending life instead, the whole structure of creation reverberates with bliss and enthusiasm. Superabundance of satisfaction and fulfillment rush through the soul; life transforms at once to full realization.

Pada IV. Sutra 3

निमित्तमप्रयोजकं प्रकृतीनां वरणभेदस्तु ततः क्षेत्रिकवत् ॥३॥

Nimittam aprayojakaṃ prakṛtīnāṃ varaṇa bhedas tu tataḥ kṣetrikavat

Individual actions do not cause Nature to flood transformations, but they do remove the obstacles just as a farmer (removes the barrier in an irrigation ditch).

This sutra explains that individual actions (such as the diet, Ascension and austerity of the first sutra) do not *make* Nature transform life. Nature wishes to transform life all the time anyway. All the individual can do is remove the self-imposed blocks to the Infinite light. And then the Absolute floods through the soul, drying every tear, brightening every dark and sad corner with its wonderful radiance. This is certain, once one stops holding closed the door to the entry of the Ascendant. How does one remove the self-created obstacles? In any way that will work!

Three lesser translations of "remove the obstacles," varaṅa bhedas, make this sutra deeper and richer in meaning: "woo and seduce" is one, "blossoming of the magical tree" is another and "winning over the concealed as an ally" is the third. A farmer seduces and woos Nature to produce a plentiful harvest. Just so, the sincere aspirant can do much by modifying thought and behavior to entice Nature to flow more abundantly. And if one can succeed in so doing, Nature does indeed become a magical wishing-tree, from which every desire is met abundantly and even in advance of the recognized need. This is the role of a great friend and ally. All of life becomes supremely fulfilling and absolutely effortless when the secret processes of Nature serve one's every desire.

"Remove," bhedas, can also be translated, "break, divide, shatter, pierce, perforate, cleave, interrupt, separate," etc. Sometimes ruthlessness also plays its part in evolution -- but only when it is directed against the false creations that keep life bound in ignorance.[36]

---

[36] -- This is exactly the function of the Black Ishayas. They are utterly committed to destroying the ignorance of the world. They consider this true compassion. See Second Thunder for a description of the Black Ishayas in the world.

Pada IV. Sutra 4

निर्माणचित्तान्यस्मितामात्रात् ॥४॥

Nirmāṇa chittāni asmitā mātrāt

The distortions of consciousness are all from the ego.

Distortions are those created works that do not proceed from Nature. Their mother is not evolution but illusion. These artificial structures are the likes and dislikes, the attachments and aversions which keep consciousness bound to the Waking State. Consciousness undistorted is clear and experiences exactly what it is -- Infinite, Absolute, non-changing. Consciousness distorted fluctuates and trembles, breaking the purity of Absolute Silence into multiplicity. These distortions are precisely the obstacles that must be removed for healing life to flood through the body and mind.

What is the source of these distortions? Simply the belief in separation that *is* the ego. All creations of consciousness that lead to suffering are the work of this one erroneous belief, the belief that it is possible to be separate from the Ascendant.

Pada IV. Sutra 5

प्रवृत्तिभेदे प्रयोजकं चित्तमेकमनेकेषाम् ॥५॥

Pravṛtti bhede prayojakaṃ chittam ekam anekeṣām

The shattering of higher thought causes one consciousness to appear as many.

"Shattering," bhede, can also be translated, "removing, breaking, dividing, bursting, seducing, interrupting," etc (see IV.3). The primary result of the ego-created distortions of consciousness is that the upward-directed thoughts inspired by Nature become distorted, broken, twisted into illusions of multiplicity. Just as a handful of pebbles dropped into a still pool shatters the calm reflection of the single Moon into a myriad of broken shards, just so the distorted tendencies arising from the ego make the simplicity of Unified Consciousness appear as duality.

Higher thoughts are those that are caused by Nature; these are the thoughts that are intimately related to the flood of evolutionary transformation, those that lead to Unified Consciousness. Just as the intelligent actions of the first sutra cause the flood of positive actions of the second sutra, just so the illusory distortions of the fourth sutra cause the illusory dividing of Unified Consciousness into many of this sutra.

This dividing *is* illusion only; that which is eternally One can *never* be divided. But the belief in this dividing results when the upward-directed thoughts are over-shadowed by distorted thinking. Upward-directed thoughts, since pure, are strong and supported by all the Laws of Nature. Distorted thoughts, since marred by illusions, are weak and supported by nothing save the false constructs of the ego. The howling wind of desire can *seem* to shatter the perfect stillness of the Eternal Ocean of Bliss, but such is fantasy merely. Let the soul stop supporting the ego's mad rush toward self-destruction, even for an instant, and the ocean returns to absolute Stillness and peace.

Pada IV. Sutra 6

तत्र ध्यानजमनाशयम् ॥६॥

Tatra dhyāna jam anāśayam

Of these many, only those born from Resonance are free from deep stress.

Typically, when consciousness divides into many, there is the creation of deep stresses that give rise to further thoughts and desires. But in an Ascending mind, the Resonance of individual consciousness with Universality does not produce stress. Why is this? Simply because a mind resonating with the One is in perfect harmony with Nature, with the fundamental structure of the Universe, functioning as it was designed to function. Since this is so, no further stress is created. And, therefore, the thoughts born from Resonance give no support to the old way of thinking and desiring that upholds the boundaries of the Waking State. Only the thoughts that vibrate in perfect harmony with Natural Law give freedom from the continuance of self-destructive tendencies. With no deep stress being created, no future afflicting thought and action will result; this frees life to progress upward back into Unified Consciousness. In other words, of the myriads of thoughts a mind can think, only Ascending thoughts free life from bondage and ignorance.

Pada IV. Sutra 7

कर्माशुक्लाकृष्णं योगिनस्त्रिविधमितरेषाम् ॥७॥

Karma aśukla akṛṣṇam yoginaḥ trividham itareṣām

The action of those established in Union is neither bright nor dark. Others create three kinds.

Dark action is that which leads to bondage and suffering. It comes as a result of excessive dominance of tamas guṇa, the fundamental force of Nature that causes destruction, stillness, death, darkness, inertia. Bright action is that which leads to liberation and joy. It comes from the dominance of sattva guṇa, the fundamental force of Nature that causes creation, evolution, life, light, progress.

The three guṇas born of Nature do not touch those established in Unified Consciousness, for they have realized their absolute Oneness with the Ascendant. This sutra takes the assertion of the previous to its logical conclusion -- not only does Resonance not create deep stress, it creates no impression of any kind. For those moving in frictionless flow with the Ascendant in every thought, word and deed, there is no result of action, for there is no independent action. One is completely separate from the functioning of the three guṇas, therefore there is no action that is sticking to the doer. All is being done by the guṇas.

The third kind of action is that born from the dominance of rajas guṇa, the fundamental Natural Law that provides all energy and passion. When this guṇa predominates, life moves, but the motion may be creative or destructive, depending on whether it inclines toward sattva or tamas. In the lives of those who are not racing onward with the experience of Union, they cycle from dominance by sattva to dominance by rajas to dominance by tamas. Not established in freedom from the three guṇas, they are caught again and again by the distortions of consciousness that fracture Unified Awareness into multiplicity.

Pada IV. Sutra 8

ततस्तद्विपाकानुगुणानामेवाभिव्यक्तिर्वासनानाम् ॥८॥

Tataḥ tat vipāka anuguṇānām eva abhivyaktiḥ vāsanānām

The fruition of these creates the suitable conditions to manifest unfulfilled desires.

The three kinds of unenlightened action have several results, none of them desirable. The most significant result of unenlightened action is the continuing bondage to the wheel of experience. Actions create impressions in the Waking State; these lead to future desires. If the impressions continue to exist, they will continue to affect every area of life. In order to fulfill past desires, Nature will organize the guṇas to create the necessary environment.

Action leads to impression which leads to desire which leads to action which leads to impression which leads to desire -- there is no escape from the wheel thus set revolving as long as one is still bound to the three kinds of action. Where, then, is there escape? Only through the fourth kind of action -- the action of one established in Unified Consciousness is not bright, not dark, not mixed. And how does one maintain Unified Consciousness? From Resonance in the Absolute.

There is no freedom from the consequences of the three kinds of action without permanently established Unified Consciousness, for the guṇas will continue to create the necessary environment to fulfill all desires. Once the impulse of thought has been created, it continues bouncing around creation forever, producing effects, creating worlds and Universes in response to its original intent. For the Sons and Daughters of the One God are like unto their Creator in this: anything they create is as Eternal as are they; anything they create is nothing other than an extension of their Infinite minds. The next sutra elaborates on this theme.

Pada IV. Sutra 9

जातिदेशकालव्यवहितानामप्यानन्तर्यं
स्मृतिसंस्कारयोरेकरूपत्वात् ॥९॥

Jāti deśa kāla vyavahitānām api ānantaryaṃ smṛti saṃskārayoḥ eka rūpatvāt

Although hidden by time, space or re-birth, there is an uninterrupted succession of desire because memory and impressions are of one form.

"Hidden," vyavahitānām, can also be translated, "carried away, invisible, obstructed, separated from." These are all descriptive of the interrupting effect of the changes of time, space and circumstances that seem to break the continuity of life.

Have you ever been carried completely into your past simply by smelling a specific scent? The olfactory nerves are deeply connected in the brain with those areas that store memory. You may be a completely different person, with all new beliefs, living in quite another world thirty years later, but instantly you are back home in your mother's kitchen, with the coffee percolating in the old pot on the counter and the bacon frying on the stove. What provides this continuity? Memory -- or impressions. They mean very much the same thing, as this sutra observes.

During the past few years, there has been a great deal of challenge in the scientific and medical community to the old belief that memory is somehow stored in the physical structure of the body. Rather than being a storage mechanism, the fifteen billion neurons of the brain are a tuning device to contact the morphogenic field of memory. If the tuning device is damaged, the translation from the non-changing field of memory into the field of activity will be damaged. If the damage is too great, there is no possibility of expression on the outside. But the memories remain intact, awaiting the appropriate conditions to manifest.

You may be a mature adult with unlimited responsibilities and power, but simply re-enter your childhood environment, and see how quickly the cloaks fall away and are replaced with a smile of purest joy and innocence. Or if the childhood was painful, step back into that world and feel again the frustration of impotent anguish of a lonely, abused child.

The point is that the continuity of an individual life-stream is assured, for the impressions that give rise to desire and life-state are intimately connected with the non-changing field of perfect memory. Why should desire continue, virtually without a break? Simply because it is our desires that are our creations, and it is precisely our creations that are the tools we have made to climb to our individual fulfillment. Any desire, if unfulfilled, continues to resonate the subtle material of the cosmos, endlessly seeking its resolution. We are made in the image of Divinity; our creations, our desires, are there to bring us more and more happiness. Nature does not judge and say, "This desire is good, that one is bad." The dignity of the Sons and Daughters of God is that all their desires are holy -- only humans judge life and desire as being positive or negative.

This does not mean, of course, that one should not be intelligent about desiring -- obviously, some desires serve life, health, progress and joy and others don't. Part of the evolution of consciousness is based on the ability to discriminate between what is and what is not useful. But from the standpoint of the Ascendant, all motions look about the same. Nature, in other words, will work to fulfill any human's desire about anything whatsoever, and moreover will continually and indefinitely keep the individual connected to the desire stream through the mechanics of impression and memory without interruption. This, then, is Nature's role and purpose -- to fulfill the desires of the human. It is the human's role and purpose to desire intelligently, to create those desires and thoughts that serve evolution to complete consciousness.

Pada IV. Sutra 10

तासामनादित्वं चाशिषोनित्यत्वात् ॥१०॥

Tāsām anāditvaṃ cha aśiṣaḥ nityatvāt

These are beginningless and abide forever.

The questions naturally come to those who are sincerely desiring to understand Reality, "What is the Source of me? How long will I live? How long will my creations continue?" Patañjali here says that memory and impressions are as old as time and will continue as long as the Universe exists. Memory is ingrained in the subtle matrix of the Universe. Anything that happens anywhere at any time is recorded in the subtle, in the akaśa.

For anyone with sufficient clarity of consciousness, this beginningless and endless record can be tapped. But even without that clarity, the individual is intimately conjoined with this universal field of memory and impression; it will continue to function indefinitely to connect the individual to his/her desires and their effects. There is no escape from the wheel of desire-action-impression without Ascending it.

Pada IV. Sutra 11

हेतुफलाश्रयालम्बनैः संगृहीतत्वादेषामभावे तदभावः ॥११॥

Hetu phala aśraya ālambanaiḥ saṃgṛhītatvād eṣām abhāve tad abhāvaḥ

Since the cause is attached to its fruits and bears them as their foundation, if the cause ceases to exist, the effects will also cease to exist.

Evolution is not a hopeless struggle against immeasurable odds. Rather, it is a simple and direct upward movement into the light. The consequences of the last sutra might lead one to despair about the difficulty of ever breaking the connection to the deep-rooted stresses that cause self-destructive behavior patterns. How to change behavior? Change desires. How to change desires? By removing their source. But if impressions are beginningless and endless, as the last sutra clearly declared, how is it possible to end the cause?

How to end the cause will be more deeply explained in IV.27 & IV.28, but the general principle is clear. If it is possible in any way to be free from the cause, the effects will cease. If the root is cut, the fruit will wither on the vine. If the foundation is destroyed, the walls will fall. This is the epitome of common sense. If an effect is undesirable and very difficult to change, modify it on a subtle level. It is much simpler to handle a tree when it is still an acorn than after it has become a mighty oak. This is the principle of skill in action. It is also vastly more efficient than attempting to heal manifest effects. Easier, quicker and much more effective.

Pada IV. Sutra 12

अतीतानागतं स्वरूपतोस्त्यध्वभेदाद्धर्माणाम् ॥१२॥

Atīta anāgataṃ svarūpataḥ asti adhva bhedāt dharmāṇām

Throughout the past and the future, the Absolute Self always exists. Regardless how tortured the path, the invincible forces of Natural Law do not fail to uphold life.

Here lies the master key to freedom from all stress, from all self-destructive tendencies, from all desires that do not serve life. Throughout time, there has always existed an alternative to the incessant demands of past impressions. Beyond the confines of the relative, beyond all the limits of space and time from the grossest to the subtlest lies the Infinite Ascendant.

Regardless how far one believes he/she is removed from the Ultimate, the connecting links from the manifest to the unmanifest -- the invincible forces of Natural Law -- have not ceased to support life. And therefore the ability to reconnect to the Source consciously has never been lost. Regardless how shrouded the belief in the innate Unity of life, regardless how shattered life is in terms of habit, experience, ill health and suffering, still the Ascendant lies inside each one of us and supports everyone of us. The Ascendant lives eternally inside everyone; the forces of Natural Law connect us both now and forever with our Source. Therein lies the simple solution to the bondage of ignorance. Freedom from desires and past impressions has always been and always will be possible: it is the natural outcome of realizing our Eternal connection with the Source.

Pada IV. Sutra 13

ते व्यक्तसूक्ष्मा गुणात्मानः ॥१३॥

Te vyakta sūkṣmā guṇātmānaḥ

All paths, whether clear or obscure, are of the nature of the guṇas.

"Clear," vyakta, also means, "manifest, evident, distinct." It means that one is marching straight to the goal. Obscure here means devious or twisted; i.e., not simple. There is nothing in the created Universe that exists apart from the fundamental forces of Natural Law. This is why it is always possible to return to the Source, for the guṇas are the instruments of the Source, they exist in, from and because of the Source. Some paths lead back toward the Ascendant, some paths seemingly lead away from the Ascendant, but all paths are built of nothing other than the fundamental forces of Nature. Therefore, from any point in Creation, it is a very short step back to the omnipresent Source. It takes no effort or time to re-open to the Reality of life; nothing need be done but turn back to the Ascendant Source.

ॐ

Pada IV. Sutra 14

परिणामैकत्वाद्वस्तुतत्त्वम् ॥१४॥

Pariṇāma ekatvāt vastu tattvam

The True Nature of all objects is the Unity underlying transformations.

Another valid translation is, "The True Nature of Unity dawns through all transformations."

"True Nature," tattvam, can also be called, "very essence, Truth, Reality."

Beneath the surface transformations caused by the guṇas, the Absolute continues on, ever the same, never changing. The surface flux may seem very dominant; it may seem impossible ever to bring peace, stability or order to the individual thrashing about through life, but underlying whatever the surface may show is the eternally silent ocean of Ascendant Consciousness and bliss. Therefore the ability to be free from the transformations of the guṇas is inherent in the very structure of life. There is no one anywhere at any time that cannot still the wandering chaos of choppy random thoughts and experience the perfect orderliness and clarity of the Silence of the Ascendant. Life, therefore, is simple, direct and clear -- it is only necessary to step back one small step to the underlying Unity, and all transformations will line up directly with the upward currents of creation.

Pada IV. Sutra 15

वस्तुसाम्ये चित्तभेदात्तयोर्विभक्तः पन्थाः ॥१५॥

Vastu sāmye chitta bhedāt tayoḥ vibhaktaḥ panthāḥ

Since Consciousness perceives the Unity of objects as divided, the paths are different.

What is the source of different paths? The shattering of consciousness into the illusion of many. It is the consciousness of the knower that determines the experiences of life. If one is straight and clear inside, the path is straight and clear. This is not dependant on the external world, it is entirely dependant on the internal. In the Waking State, it is common to feel that life is happening *to* us, that we are the recipients of whatever comes to us, be it for good or ill. We feel that we are the victims of our environments, of our families, or of a harsh and judgmental God.

Contrast this with any of the stages of enlightenment: we *know* we are the Source of our light. Rather, we know that the Source of our Good is the omnipresent Ascendant Consciousness which we live continually; we recognize also that all that returns to us that is not desirable is the result of our past, unenlightened action. Who is there to blame? No one, for all is our own creation, none others.

The paths we follow through life may seem divided, but the Reality underlying all of them is the same. All objects, all of everything, everywhere, always, have at their root the One Unchanging. Only if we perceive separation in the Primal Unity will we necessarily have to follow separate paths to arrive at our goal.

Pada IV. Sutra 16

न चैकचित्ततन्त्रं वस्तु तदप्रमाणकं तदा किं स्यात् ॥१६॥

Na cha eka chitta tantraṃ vastu tad apramāṇakaṃ tadā kiṃ syāt

But the Reality of the Unity of objects is not dependent on the consciousness of their Unity, for if objects were incorrectly known, then what would become of them?

This sutra observes that all objects are united to the Ascendant independently of our knowing them to be or not. Regardless of everyone's or even anyone's belief, the fundamental Reality of life is not likely to change. Not so very long ago, practically everyone believed the world to be flat, and the Sun rotated around it. Practically everyone believed this, but very little change in the orbits of the Earth and our companion star was observed as a result of that!

Today, practically everyone believes that waking, dreaming and sleeping are all the states of consciousness that there are, that there is no reality of higher consciousness, that enlightenment is either a myth or valid for only a chosen few, or the exclusive property of the monks of antiquity. But these beliefs do not change the Reality of the fact that anyone anywhere at any time can break through the clouds of limiting belief and experience and live the complete knowledge of the One that underlies everything. Reality continues on, quite independently of our belief.

This is a great blessing, for if Reality *were* dependent on our conscious knowledge of Unity, the world would be a hopelessly chaotic place for the vast majority of humanity. It would, in fact, be indistinguishable from the dream state, which has no direct connection to Reality. So there exists independent Reality. The tree falling in the forest makes a crashing sound, if any conscious mind is aware of it or not.

Pada IV. Sutra 17

तदुपरागापेक्षित्वाच्चित्तस्य वस्तु ज्ञाताज्ञातम् ॥१७॥

Tad uparāga apekṣitvāt chittasya vastu jñāta ajñātam

Objects are correctly known or not, depending on the intention of consciousness to be colored by them.

The external world has its own independent reality, but all we know of it is how it affects us. Consciousness is like a mirror; it reflects whatever is placed in front of it. As it reflects, it changes. Not in its essential nature, but in what it believes itself to be.

"Colored," uparāga, can also be translated "darkened" or "eclipsed." Consciousness is darkened by its contact with objects; its knowledge of the Ascendant is eclipsed. How much this occurs is dependent on the intention of individual consciousness. When Consciousness is clear, i.e., free from the belief in limitation and separation, then objects are known as they really are. They are known fully; their essential Unity is also fully understood. This is Unified Consciousness.

On the other hand, if the consciousness is slightly less clear, if there is still some faint projection of old beliefs, then there will be the experience of the subtle in all objects, but the full knowledge of their essential Unity with the Ascendant will not be there; this describes Exalted Consciousness and Perpetual Consciousness. And if the consciousness is not clear at all, then the objects' essential reality will be almost entirely unknown; this is known as the Waking State.

The world is as we believe it to be. Belief is not being used here in any superficial sense. Belief here means that level of consciousness that determines our experience of everything. If we wear red glasses, everything appears red to us. If we wear blue glasses, everything appears blue. Only if we take off the glasses will we see clearly. Only by dropping our limiting beliefs will we be able to use our senses of perception as they were designed to be used.

The level of our consciousness determines our intention. Our intention determines what we perceive. As intention becomes clearer and clearer, the ability to perceive what *is* rather than what we *project* naturally develops. But if we still seek validation or meaning from the environment, our consciousness will be colored by that desire; the objects of perception will not be seen clearly.

The world is as we are. What we are inside reveals entirely what we live on the outside. The inner is primary, the external is secondary. Always. Always.

Pada IV. Sutra 18

सदा ज्ञाताश्चित्तवृत्तयस्तत्प्रभोः पुरुषस्यापरिणामित्वात् ॥१८॥

Sadā jñātāḥ chitta vṛttayas tat prabhoḥ puruṣasya apariṇāmitvāt

The movements of consciousness are always known by their Master, the never-changing Ascendant.

The root or Source of all that is, the Eternal Ascendant, is fully conscious of all that was, all that is, all that will ever be. This sutra clarifies the last, for one might think that if consciousness can be eclipsed or colored by varying experience of objects, then consciousness has no state of all-knowingness. It is only consciousness out of the Ascendant that does not know -- when consciousness returns to full awareness of its True Nature, all the outer stages and manifestations are fully known to it.

This sutra may seem confusing, for how can that which never changes know anything? And yet, what does know? What is consciousness, once all the self-defeating beliefs and limitations are removed? Consciousness without motion *is* the Ascendant.

Is Pure Consciousness conscious? Of course, for how else could awareness exist at all? Awareness *is* the Ascendant; all that is required to know it is to still the movements of consciousness. Even if over-shadowed by the movements of thought or the experiences of objects, consciousness never loses its essential nature. Re-awakening to that, one does not cease to be conscious of the movements; in fact, one becomes more aware of them, for one is aware of them in their totality, rather than colored by previous beliefs, judgments and limitations.

Pada IV. Sutra 19

न तत्स्वाभासं दृश्यत्वात् ॥१९॥

Na tat sva abhāsaṃ dṛśyatvāt

They are not self-luminous, they are observed.

The movements of consciousness are not conscious in and of themselves. They are observed by consciousness, but they are not self-luminous. We perhaps don't often think of our thoughts as being objects of our perception, for we are completely overshadowed by them -- we have no knowledge of the Inner Knower but believe that we are our thoughts. In the Waking State, it is assumed that our experiences, our memories, our beliefs, makes us what we are. Or perhaps our definition of who we are rests in the environment -- our club, our family, our home, our car, our job, our friends, our bank account, our possessions -- the list is endless -- but the definition does not include the tenuous, largely or even completely unknown Absolute Inner Self.

Only from the perspective of higher consciousness does it become possible to see clearly what consciousness is and what it is not. Only from the standpoint of Perpetual Consciousness do we clearly witness the thoughts and experiences of life as separate from the Reality of the knower. Withdraw the light of the Inner Self, and what continuance do the movements of thought have? It is not that there are many conscious beings inside -- consciousness is One; its manifestations are many. This will become clearer with the next few sutras.

Pada IV. Sutra 20

एकसमये चोभयानवधारणम् ॥२०॥

Eka samaye cha ubhaya anava dhāraṇam

Everything is joined together in the One; duality is no restriction.

All that is, is united in the Ascendant. Everything comes together in the One, all movements of thought, all objects, all variations in duality have at their root the unchanging sameness of the Absolute. The duality of creation is no hindrance to this ultimate fact. All are unified, regardless how apparently different they may seem on the surface. All of life meets in the perfect Unity of the Ascendant; there is nothing in creation not joined to That.

Some believe that they are so very far removed from peace, joy and light that they never will be able to return. But the Reality is quite other. No one can ever be apart from the Source. There is no "sin" or action that can take one away from the Ascendant, but one can certainly *believe* there is no way home again. Yet, it is belief merely. One taste of Reality is sufficient to restore the full knowledge of the universality of the One. Everyone is always at home, regardless of belief.

"Duality is no help to Focus" is another valid translation of the second half of this sutra. If the mind is divided, it will find it difficult to focus the attention on one thing. This is of course the only valid way to succeed in *any* endeavor -- if life is divided, progress will always be sporadic and weak.

Pada IV. Sutra 21

चित्तान्तरदृश्ये बुद्धिबुद्धेरतिप्रसङ्गः स्मृतिसंकरश्च ॥२१॥

Chitta antara dṛśye buddhi buddheḥ atiprasaṇgaḥ smṛti saṃkaraḥ cha

If consciousness were observed within consciousness, the internal structure of the mind would divide endlessly and memory would be confused.

The sutra observes why duality is not and cannot be the Ultimate Reality. If separate consciousness existed within consciousness, the internal structure of the mind and intellect would also be divided; there would be an infinite regression -- like one sees in a hall of mirrors. There would be no stable application of the internal machinery of consciousness. Furthermore, memory would be inconstant and confused. Memory would cease functioning validly; therefore the subtlest movement of the mind would be distorted. The structure of Natural Law itself would function erratically if the Universe were thus divided. Consciousness is One, therefore the integrity of the personality and the mind is assured. Only those who are imbalanced do not have a stable internal focus; such a state of imbalance makes life ineffective.

Some techniques of meditation advocate trying to remember the Self in the midst of activity. This is actually quite common in India, as also among some Christian sects. The problem with this is that it decreases the power of the mind. By trying to look at two things at the same time, life becomes weaker and diffused. This is a case of confusing the goal for the path to the goal. The pure witnessing of Perpetual Consciousness never comes from such artificially created efforts at duality. This kind of behavior does not lead to enlightenment, but it certainly will lead to greater stress in the nervous system.

Pada IV. Sutra 22

चित्तेरप्रतिसंक्रमायास्तदाकारापत्तौ स्वबुद्धिसंवेदनम् ॥२२॥

Chitteḥ aprati saṃkramāyāḥ tad ākārāpattau sva buddhi saṃvedanaṃ

Consciousness, although unchanging, is the Lord of appearances and has full knowledge of the internal structure of the mind.

"Unchanging," aprati saṃkramāyāḥ, can also be translated "undivided" or "unmoving."

"Appearances," ākārā, can also be translated "shapes, figures, expressions." Consciousness, without ever moving, pervades all its manifestations, expressions and appearances, including full knowledge of the structure of the mind. There is nothing in the personality that is not permeated by consciousness; there is nothing anywhere at any time that is not permeated by consciousness. Consciousness, undivided, unchanging, contains complete knowledge, self-awareness and perfect mastery of all change.

Pada IV. Sutra 23

द्रष्टृदृश्योपरक्तं चित्तं सर्वार्थम् ॥२३॥

Draṣṭṛ dṛśya uparaktaṃ chittaṃ sarva artham

Consciousness, colored by the Seer and the Seen, has all purposes.

Consciousness can be anything. It can look into multiplicity and, forgetting its oneness with what Is, become the object it sees. Losing its inherent purpose and meaning, it adopts the purpose and meaning of the environment. (The reward of that is limited to its own sphere; i.e., whatever is its wealth is its own reward.)

Consciousness can also be colored by the Seer; it can look back onto itself and know the Self. Knowing the Self, consciousness knows the purpose of the Ascendant. The range of potential of the human is from complete bondage, complete identification with the objects of perception to complete freedom, complete identification with the Knower. This is the extent of the possibilities of life -- from absolute absorption in the Universe to absolute mastery of the Universe. It is all based on free will. The human can choose for either -- and *will* choose for whichever seems more charming.

ॐ

Pada IV. Sutra 24

तदसंख्येयवासनाभिश्चित्तमपिपरार्थं संहत्यकारित्वात् ॥२४॥

Tat asaṃkhyeya vāsanābhiḥ chittam api para arthaṃ saṃhatya kāritvāt

Consciousness is filled with innumerable unfulfilled desires, but it also has the purpose of the Ascendant, which is inseparably united to it and causes its actions.

This sutra extends the last and continues the theme of desires, begun in the eighth sutra of this chapter. Consciousness can look toward the manifest creation, identify with the Seen, and be continually overshadowed by unending desires. If that were all that was available to consciousness, there would be little room for change. Human life would then be virtually identical with the life of the animals.

But there is another side to consciousness, that which forever faces its Source. The Ascendant is permanently united to consciousness; indeed, consciousness is nothing other than the Ascendant when it is not colored by the external world. Consciousness, indeed, can be called the purpose or object of the Ascendant, for consciousness is not only of the nature of the Ascendant in its pure state, it is also the primary tool of the Ascendant in the Universe to fulfill itself. The Divine sees through our eyes, thinks with our minds, feels with our hearts, laughs with our mouths, breathes with our breath.

We can live, think and act in perfect harmony with the Ascendant, or we can attempt to act in isolation and separation. The limited desires of the ego pull us away from the realization of who we are, shroud our minds and hearts with pain and suffering, bring us ill health, early aging and death, make us miserable and unhappy and small in our lives. The unlimited desires of the Ascendant bequeath us the realization of our essential nature, free our minds and hearts from pain and suffering, bring us health, longevity and life, make us joyful and happy and large in our existence. It is a very simple change, actually, a very simple choice, either to choose for identification with the Seen or for identification with the Seer. The simplicity of this stems from the fact that the Ascendant is inseparably united to consciousness. We are co-Creators with God, if we remember this fact or not.

The Ascendant causes all actions of consciousness, even those that seemingly lead away from the Ascendant, for the Ascendant is omnipresent. The simple fact is that none of us can in reality ever go away from the Ascendant, because it is not different from what we are. It is only human interpretations based on limited perspectives that some actions are "good" and others are "bad." All are good in the eyes of the Ascendant, even those that *seem* to take us away from it.

This is a subtle understanding and one that could be abused by an ignorant mind, which is probably why Patañjali mentions it only here, quite near the end of his sutras. Someone, for example, could rob a bank and say, "Well, all action is caused by the Ascendant, I didn't do anything." One must continue to be intelligent about one's own self-development. A day will soon dawn in which everyone will see that all life is inevitably leading to the Ascendant; but until that fortunate season, it is necessary to do anything and everything possible to move from the confusion of divided desires back to the simplicity of the Unity of the Ascendant.

Pada IV. Sutra 25

विशेषदर्शिन आत्मभावभावना विनिवृत्तिः ॥२५॥

Viśeṣa darśina ātma bhāvabhāvanā vinivṛttiḥ

For the Seer who perceives this extraordinary and wonderful distinction, the Self is established in Being and the movements of thought utterly cease.

Recognition of the essential nature of the mind is at once extraordinary -- very few ever do this -- and also wonderful in the extreme -- it is Absolute Bliss. The Self established in Being means the Self recognizes that it is the Absolute Ascendant. When this happens fully and completely, all movements of consciousness are reabsorbed in Being. The whole of the Universe of becoming is seen as an expression of Being; this is Unified Consciousness.

This sutra has validity in each of the higher states of consciousness -- in the Fourth State, all thought stills as the Self floats in the Ascendant. In the Fifth State, the Self is established permanently in Being, and one is completely separate from all movements of consciousness, so in this sense the movements of thought have utterly ceased. In the Sixth State, one cognizes the ultimate wonderful and extraordinary result of evolution, the Supreme Being (see I.24); here, too, one is completely separate from all movements of consciousness. In the Seventh State, one perceives the Infinite underlying everything; therefore all separate movements are eternally still, for all movements are perceived as being nothing other than the fluctuations of Silence.

Pada IV. Sutra 26

तदा हि विवेकनिम्नं कैवल्यप्राग्भारं चित्तम् ॥२६॥

Tadā hi viveka nimnaṃ kaivalya prāg bhāraṃ chittam

Then, verily, consciousness at its deepest level develops discrimination and praises the dawn of Unified Consciousness.

Praise is the primary response of an evolving soul to the glory and wonder of the perfection of the Universe. Praise is also the primary means of rising beyond the Waking State. With Praise alone, one can completely erase all self-destructive beliefs and internal programs. With Praise alone, one can rise to Perpetual Consciousness, Exalted Consciousness and Unified Consciousness. Praise is like magic, it washes the soul with Gratitude and Love. Praise, being the most active of the Ascension Emotions, is the easiest to develop simply by deciding to appreciate rather than criticize or condemn. Life is easy to change. It only requires a single decision, to use the mind in an upward direction instead of downward.

Discriminative knowledge is the function of the intellect; it is the intellect that completes the transformation from Exalted Consciousness to Unified Consciousness. What is the ultimate use of the intellect? To decide to appreciate rather than condemn. The last step is also the first. At any and every moment, one can choose to focus upward instead of downward, to focus on the eternally new joy of the Ascendant instead of on the confusion of the boundaries; this leads in time to the ability to discriminate between the changing and the Unchanging.

Evolution may sound like a series of discrete stages, but it is in reality a seamless whole, a natural flow of life from boundaries to the Boundless. And Praise stands everywhere on the One Path, forever bringing light and joy.

Pada IV. Sutra 27

तच्छिद्रेषु प्रत्ययान्तराणि संस्कारेभ्यः ॥२७॥

Tat chhidreṣu pratyaya antarāṇi saṃskāre bhyaḥ

If there are gaps in that, thoughts still arise within due to previous impressions.

"Gaps," chhidreṣu, also means, "leaks, perforations, defects, failings, weak points." Anything that breaks the Absolute Reality of Unified Consciousness is a stress. Through the imperfections in Unified Consciousness, previous impressions inspire thoughts to arise, thereby opening the door to potential injury and suffering. Until Unified Consciousness is permanently established, one is not utterly free from thought (as in IV.25).

What to do? How can one be free from self-destructive desire? By eliminating the thoughts of desire. And how is this accomplished? By eliminating the impressions that give rise to the desires. And how are impressions removed? By going back onto the Self as described in II.10.

ॐ

Pada IV. Sutra 28

हानमेषां क्लेशवदुक्तम् ॥२८॥

Hānam eṣāṃ kleśavat uktam

Removal of these is accomplished in the same way as fundamental tendencies are removed, as previously described.

This sutra says that the mechanics of developing Unified Consciousness is the same as the mechanics of developing Perpetual Consciousness. The same process of Ascending, continued for a long enough time, naturally develops the highest degree of enlightenment.

"Removal," hānam, also means, "leaving, abandonment, cessation." The impressions stored in the nervous system cease to exist for us, are abandoned and run away from us when we turn back onto the Self (see II.10, commentary). As the impressions of the Absolute become deeper and clearer, the other impressions of stress and limitation are overshadowed and replaced (see I.50, commentary). The subtle recording mechanics of the nervous system are intimately responsive to our desire, thought and experience; as we focus more and more consistently on Reality, on the Absolute, the impression born of that erases all other impressions, for it is an impression-less impression (see IV.6, commentary). This is how the nervous system was designed to be used.

It is as if we have a magical machine, capable of granting any desire, if we only give it the proper fuel. But not knowing what the proper fuel is, we try various substances and find that the machine does not work very well. The deposits left by these improper fuels begin to clog the internal structure of the machinery so that it works less and less efficiently. If the proper fuel starts being used, the machine will begin to work better and better, but the internal machinery may still be quite clogged. When these internal deposits are dislodged, the machine may run roughly at those times. Just so, the mind, through being fed improper beliefs and desires, functions very inefficiently; this leads to a great deal of internal pollution.

Physical stress and mental impressions of lack and insufficiency are the same thing, seen from two different perspectives. With the experience of the Ascendant, the mind and body work as they were designed to work; this naturally results in the dissolution of the internal physical deposits of stress and heals the fatigued and over-weakened areas in the nervous system as a by-product of the experience of the Absolute. The deep impressions of stress and limitation are erased as they are abandoned. They cease to function for us as we remove our attention from them. The breaks or gaps in the permanence of Unified Consciousness rapidly close as the impressions dissolve.

Pada IV. Sutra 29

प्रसंख्यानेप्यकुसीदस्य सर्वथा विवेकख्यातेर्धर्ममेघः समाधिः ॥२९॥

Prasaṃ khyāne api akusīdasya sarvathā viveka
khyāte dharma meghaḥ samādhiḥ

By loosing even the last vestiges of selfish interest in the highest consciousness, complete discriminative awareness produces from Ascendant Consciousness support of Nature like a raining cloud.

Interestingly enough, "the highest consciousness," prasaṃ khyāne, can also be validly translated, "the final addictions of consciousness." *Any* movement of consciousness is not Absolute Pure Consciousness. Even the highest, graceful, delightful, pleasing, soothing, propitious, bright (also valid translations of prasaṃ) experience of consciousness is not the same as Absolute Pure Consciousness. By losing the final traces of limited individuality even in that, the full power of discriminative knowledge dawns. When this occurs, Natural Law not only ceases to have a noxious effect (III.46), it pours out its support in a flood.

When one is established in the home of all the Laws of Nature, one is automatically supported by all the Laws of Nature. The Laws of Nature exist to serve their Maker. In Unified Consciousness, one has re-established complete identity with the Source; when this happens, the entire structure of creation stands ready to serve. All of the Natural Laws are already working constantly to support the intention of the Ascendant. When one has realized the permanent connection with the Absolute, the first stage of manifestation of the Ascendant, the cloud-like fullness of Natural Law, supports in every conceivable way. Not only is one protected from the undesirable, one is possessed of the splendor of complete mastery. This is a description of Absolute Perfection. One in Unified Consciousness, having lost all contact with the limited desires of the ego, is naturally established in Perfect Wisdom, in Absolute Clarity. All the Laws of Nature serve, fulfilling every need in advance of the recognition of lack or desire.

The highest desire of the best servants is to fulfill their master's intention even before the master recognizes she wishes for something. The Natural Laws are very, very good at fulfilling the desires of the Ascendant. For one who has fully recognized identity with the Ascendant, there is no necessity to desire. Individual desire exists only so long as separation exists, as long as there are gaps or breaks in Unified Awareness. Isolated individual desire quite effectively blocks the instantaneous fulfillment of desire, for even the faintest vestiges of individuality resonates with the Ascendant to produce less effect, less support, less than omnipotent power. But when individuality has opened permanently to the Ascendant, all desire *is* Cosmic Desire and therefore is fulfilled automatically, naturally and gracefully. Life is perfect in its simplicity and grace; effortless achievement is the norm.

It should be emphasized again; this state is actually normal human life. This is how life functions when freed from stress, freed from the beliefs in limitation and separation that are the whole of the life of the ego. This is not a far-off or an ideal state. This lies within every thought, every experience, every desire, every dream -- the Ascendant underlies everything that is, was or will be. Since this is so, it is not now, never was and never will be difficult to experience That. It is only necessary to stop that which is separating and dividing life away from the Reality, and the Truth shines through clearly. It is always there, regardless how shrouded the mind is with sad beliefs of frustration, illness and despair.

Pada IV. Sutra 30

ततः क्लेशकर्मनिवृत्तिः ॥३०॥

Tataḥ kleśa karma nivṛttiḥ

From that, all movements of fundamental tendencies and even all effect of action cease.

From the perfection of Unified Consciousness, there are no longer gaps or breaks through which previous impressions can give rise to self-destructive tendencies. The slate has been washed clean; the experience of the One has stilled all vagrant movements. Just as a single pebble dropped into a quiet pond produces perfectly coherent ripples and a handful dropped produces chaos, just so, the single experience of the Ascendant produces perfect coherence in the life, replacing the chaos of the 50,000 thoughts a day of the Waking State. This produces serenity, health, peace, deep rest and joy.

In the state of perfected Unified Consciousness, all the effects of returning action are automatically averted. There is no inevitability about the future. Life can be anything we wish it to be. We commonly believe this when we are young but learn to disbelieve it when we experience that life does not always bring us what we think we want. And the older we become, the more rigidly we believe our way of thinking and living is the only way. The more of our lives we have devoted to one way of believing, the harder it is to change ourselves; the harder it is even to think favorably of our peers or offspring who live a very different lifestyle from ours.

This rigidity is the root of aging. This rigidity keeps us from bending in adverse weather -- the old, rigid oak breaks in the hurricane; the supple young willow bends to stand another day. When we become infinitely flexible by fully and permanently establishing our Awareness in the Ascendant, all the slings and arrows of outrageous fortune do not strike us; we bend around them, wind past them and are *free.* Having no hard knots of stress inside, there is no response to the blows from our returning action; they pass through us and, finding no fertile field in which to grow, they pass on. Finding no resonance in us, they do not stick to us or find any responding echo in us. Therefore Unified Consciousness is called Absolute Freedom. Nothing any more touches, nothing anymore binds. One moves freely through all experience, untouched, free, unrestricted everywhere.

Pada IV. Sutra 31

तदा सर्वावरणमलापेतस्य ज्ञानस्यानन्त्याज्ज्ञेयमल्पम् ॥३१॥

Tadā sarva avaraṇa mala apetasya jñānasya anantyāt jñeyam alpam

Then all veils of impurity vanish, knowledge becomes Infinite and what remains to be learned is insignificant.

Complete support from all the Laws of Nature shrivels all impurities just as a fire burns all moths. The glass of the nervous system is completely cleansed; therefore, it reflects the Ascendant perfectly.

One characteristic of the Ascendant is Infinite Knowledge. What blocks all-knowingness? Simply the impurities in the nervous system. Anything can be directly known to those who have removed all stress from their nervous system. That which "remains to be learned is insignificant" does not mean that there is nothing left to be known or experienced, it means that compared to the Infinite majesty of the Ascendant, there is little of relative value. Standing in full sunlight, the light of a small candle seems insignificant. Life continues to gain experience and grow in the known, but this gain and growth has little value or meaning compared to the Infinite Knowledge of the Ascendant.

ॐ

Pada IV. Sutra 32

ततः कृतार्थानां परिणामक्रमसमाप्तिर्गुणानाम् ॥३२॥

Tataḥ kṛta arthānāṃ pariṇāma krama samāptir guṇānām

Then, their purpose fulfilled, the transformations and apparent succession of the guṇas end.

What is the purpose of the guṇas? Enjoyment and liberation (see II.18). The guṇas continue to transform until full enlightenment is attained, after which their ultimate meaning has been attained. As long as the individual has not attained completion of consciousness, the incentive for continuing action exists.

The guṇas continue to change in dominance until they are no longer needed. Rajas is dominant in waking, tamas in sleep, sattva in dreaming. As our habits change, the dominance of the guṇas change in our lives. A healthier, purer life becomes increasingly sattvic; a sickening, impure life becomes increasingly tamasic. Life revolves from dominance by one guṇa to dominance by another, bringing experience and enjoyment, as they do their best to fulfill all desires until the day of perfect Union with the Source arrives. And then they stop.

ॐ

Pada IV. Sutra 33

क्षणप्रतियोगी परिणामापरान्तनिर्ग्राह्यः क्रमः ॥३३॥

Kṣaṇa pratiyogī pariṇāma aparānta nirgrāhyaḥ kramaḥ

Even though indissolubly linked with the joyful moment of Eternity, unless one grasps the extreme end of transformations, succession of the guṇas continues.

There is no succession of moments in Reality -- there is only the Eternal Now. But as long as one does not know this fact completely, then transformations continue on, and therefore the apparent succession of change continues. Only by complete and permanent stabilization of Unified Consciousness is the apparent succession replaced by permanent cognition of Eternity.

Shining between every transformation, in the gap between the end of one and the beginning of the next, is the Infinite. Shining in the gap between all the states of consciousness is the Infinite. Shining between every particle of matter, every moment of time, is the Infinite. But one does not often (or ever) perceive this, because attention is caught by the illusory succession of change. By familiarity and continual focus on change, one forgets the unchanging Eternity of Now.

What, in the final analysis, is the apparent succession of time and change? It is nothing other than the Eternal Now. At the end of all change, the Eternal remains. And between all apparent changes, the Eternal shines through. Every gap between transformations reveals the Eternal, for those with the eyes to see. And at every moment of change, in Reality there is nothing other than Now.

Succession seems to demonstrate that Eternity is not Eternal. It seems to be the opponent or adversary of the joyful moment of Eternity. But this is illusion merely. When all transformations end, what becomes of the apparent succession? All that remains is the permanence of Eternity.

The apparent moving succession of the guṇas is nothing other than time. Our belief in and perception of time continues until we are fully aware of the Eternity that permeates and underlies every moment of time and every particle of space. This is complete knowledge.

Pada IV. Sutra 34

पुरुषार्थशून्यानां गुणानां प्रतिप्रसवः कैवल्यं स्वरूपप्रतिष्ठा
वा चितिशक्तिरिति ॥३४॥

Puruṣa artha śūnyānāṃ guṇānāṃ pratiprasavaḥ kaivalyaṃ
svarūpa pratiṣṭhā vā chiti śaktiḥ iti

Unified Consciousness results when the guṇas return back inward
because the Ascendant's purpose is fulfilled, or when
the Absolute Self is permanently stabilized in
the Divine Power of Pure Consciousness.
Thus.

The Ascendant's purpose is for the Absolute to be known. Once one identifies utterly with the ultimate purpose of the Ascendant, the need for transformation of the guṇas is over; this ends time for the individual established in Eternity. The guṇas, having fulfilled their purpose, become completely quiescent.

Another way of saying this is that the experience of Ascendant Consciousness is itself turned back onto itself until it is permanently established, eyes open, eyes closed, at every moment, during every experience, permeating all the manifestations of creation flowing from Pure Consciousness.

"Pure Consciousness" is the same consciousness (chitti) mentioned many times throughout these sutras, but here Mahārṣi Patañjali leaves off one "t" -- chiti -- implying that this is the Ultimate Limit of Consciousness open to itself.

The "Divine Power" translates śaktiḥ, which is the word in Sanskrit that represents the omnipotent power of Mother Nature. All forces of the Universe from the Supreme Being down to the humblest sub-atomic particle have the Power of Life, śaktiḥ, intimately associated with them. Without the Divine Power of God, nothing would be. This is the end of Yoga, the end of the Science of Union, the end of all development of consciousness, the end of all separation. In Unified Consciousness, the Absolute flows throughout all of creation, perceived in every manifestation of space and time, contained in every moment, in every particle of space from the smallest to the largest.

The guṇas returning back to their Source might make Unified Consciousness seem a flat or pointless state, but the second half of this sutra points out the unlimited wonder and joy of the ultimate state of human consciousness. All of creation is perceived as part and parcel of the Absolute Self, all of space and time is permeated with the power and bliss of the perfection of God.

This is full enlightenment. *This is full enlightenment!*

Thus ends the Fourth Quarter
of the Science of Yoga:
UNIFIED CONSCIOUSNESS.

APPENDIX 1: A NOTE TO OUR CHRISTIAN BRETHREN

It has become an unfortunate habit in much of the Christian world to condemn Teachings from other lands, cultures and ages. This is highly unfortunate, for Truth is Universal; it can therefore be apprehended by anyone, anywhere at any time.

There is also a deep confusion in our modern world about the distinction between the self and the Self. Yoga, meditation and the Yoga Sutras are condemned by some because they are directed towards the self -- hence, they say, Satanic. Yoga, true meditation, and the Yoga Sutras *are*, in fact, *Self*-directed: they lead anyone practicing them correctly deeper and deeper into awareness of the Self. But they are not at all *self*-directed -- they, in fact, lead in quite the opposite direction from the self. The self is a false construct created by the ego. It is a belief in the limitation of the individual soul, containing most often a belief in suffering and death and a fundamental attachment to ignorance -- ignoring the Reality that is everywhere.

The Self, on the other hand, is the individual spark of God within everyone. By the undeniable Reality of the Omnipresence of God, it follows that God exists inside every human heart (as well as everywhere else!). This is the Self that the Yoga Sutras teach us how to contact. Enlightenment is nothing other than living in continual communion with this divinity within. This continual contact is what is meant by "praying without ceasing"[37] -- it is most assuredly *not* trying to hold some verbal formula or mental image in the mind.

---

[37] -- "Pray without ceasing." I THESSALONIANS 5:17 Cf. LUKE 11:8, 18:1, 21:36

What, then, is self-worship? Small "s" self-worship, also known as Satanism or idolatry, is the bondage of the individual life to the creations of the ego -- to the world of opposites, to suffering and death. Whenever one's attention is primarily on that which will pass away instead of on the Eternal Unchanging, one is increasing the hold of the ego on the life and committing idolatry.

Thus the Waking State of Consciousness is the prime playground of Satan. And anything that takes us away from this illusory construct of the ego back into the Reality of our Infinite Inner Light must of necessity be the work of Christ and the Holy Spirit. The fruits of the individual moving toward the Divinity within are peace, love, health, joy and life. The fruits of the individual moving outward toward the ego-created illusions are disharmony, hatred, sickness, misery and death. Therefore the Yoga Sutras of Patañjali are a prime tool for creating Christians of the spirit rather than those of the letter of the law.[38] Whosoever realizes his or her identity with the Christ within will recognize his or her ability to manipulate Natural Law in the same manner as did Christ.

These are not "miracles," not any more than plugging in your radio so it can entertain you with music is a miracle. To the uninitiated, technological advance produces miraculous results. To the uninitiated, directly manipulating Natural Law with the mind produces miraculous results. But to those who understand the underlying principles of consciousness, nothing Christ did was impossible to understand or to replicate.

---

[38] -- "Who also hath made us able ministers of the new testament; not of the letter, but of the spirit: for the letter killeth, but the spirit giventh life." II CORINTHIANS 3:6.

Christ obviously knew this perfectly well (as does anyone with His degree of understanding of the universality of Infinity); this is why He said that those who would come after Him would do greater works than He did.[39] And this is why He also said that you would recognize His true followers by their works,[40] for He knew that only those in constant contact with the Infinite could consistently perform such actions. And this also explains why He cautioned against those who taught in their name only[41] -- for this implies that they are teaching from their egos -- the true Teachers will always speak as mouthpieces for the Infinite. Even two thousand years of mistranslation and editing has not been able to obscure these basic truths entirely.

The world has not changed so very much in two thousand years. Scribes and pharisees may be names from the past, but their spiritual heirs are with us everywhere still. Any religious leader that reads but does not understand, or speaks only what he/she has been taught without directly experiencing the underlying Reality of the omnipresence of Divinity, has absolutely no business teaching about God, Christ, or the Holy Spirit.

---

[39] -- "Verily, verily, I say unto you, He that believeth on me, the works that I do shall he do also; and greater works than these shall he do; because I go unto my father." JOHN 14:12. Cf. MATTHEW 21:21&22.

[40] -- "And these signs shall follow them that believe; In my name shall they cast out devils; they shall speak with new tongues; They shall take up serpents; and if they drink any deadly thing, it shall not hurt them; they shall lay hands on the sick, and they shall recover." MARK 16:17&18

[41] -- "But I know you, that ye have not the love of God in you. I am come in my Father's name and ye receive me not: if another shall come in his own name, him ye will receive." JOHN 5:43 Cf. JOHN 12:42&43

This is an impoverished age. We worship our doctors as gods, yet they do not heal. We worship our politicians as gods, but they do not lead. We worship our houses, our cars, our bank accounts, our lawyers, our insurance policies, our TVs, our VCRs, anything and everything that we value more than the living experience of the Infinite. We have made an extraordinarily superficial world out of paradise.

Even those expressly charged with custodianship of the Infinite, our temples, churches and synagogues, our ministers, priests and rabbis, do not lead us to God. They do often lead us to greater confusion and fear. God is not to be found in the future, after death, in some heavenly after-life state. God is Here and God is Now. This is *not* a tenet of faith, it *is* a matter of direct personal experience.

If you have the living experience, twenty-four hours a day, of the Infinite Christ within, then you are a Christian -- otherwise, you have not been truly reborn to the Spirit. You are an aspirant, perhaps, but to be established in the Infinite is a permanent experience. Therefore the Yoga Sutras, far from being a Satanic work, are a tool for making true Christians. Since they are systematic and lead directly to permanent contact with the Infinite, they could well be described as one of the most important tools for becoming a true Christian -- which, from our perspective as Teachers of Ascension, means exactly the same thing as Yoga, enlightenment and Self-realization.

It is interesting to note that according to the tradition maintained by the Ishayas, the Apostle John, enjoined by Christ, established the teaching of Ascension and ordered the Ishayas to keep it hidden from the world until now. They also maintain that Christ and his cousin, John the Baptist, travelled to India before they taught in Galilee and learned the techniques of Ascension from direct-line descendants of Patañjali. There is only one True Teaching on the Earth. It appears different from waking state perspective but it is in Reality Eternally one. Regardless how seemingly opposed the outer manifestations, Truth is one.

-MSI

ॐ

APPENDIX 2: THE CHAKRAS

The chakras (literally and in the west, "wheels of fire") are the seven subtle energy centers located along the spine. Their location in the body corresponds with the location of the spine's major nerve ganglia. In the West, the memory of the chakras is retained in the image of the caduceus, the traditional symbol for the healing arts:

The open eagle wings represent fully developed consciousness, the highest degree of enlightenment, in the crown chakra. The staff represents the suṣumna (literally "very gracious"), the central channel in the spine through which the energy of life rises to bring enlightenment. The two serpents represent the two subtle channels that run alongside the suṣumna, the iḍa and the piṅgala. The chakras are located where the iḍa and the piṅgala cross. The iḍa and the piṅgala originate in the base chakra and terminate in the sixth chakra. The piṅgala is white and carries solar energy and the forces of the day. This energy moves our consciousness upward toward the rational. The iḍa is black and carries lunar energy and the forces of the night. Its downward movement takes us into the unconscious, the source of regeneration, creativity and intuition. In the average person, life energy flows primarily along the iḍa and the piṅgala, supplying energy to the sense organs and faculties of awareness that maintain the illusion of the world. It is only with the awakening of enlightenment that the energy flows fully and completely up the central channel, the suṣumna.

When this happens, the chakras reverse their orientation from downward and outward to upward and inward.

The chakras connect our consciousness with our bodies. In the Waking State, the mind experiences chaos: at least 50,000 incoherent thoughts a day race through everyone's mind, many of them mutually contradictory, many of them desiring the useless or the impossible. The physical body attempts to respond to these chaotic thought patterns; the impossibility of doing this results in sickness, failure of the organs, aging and eventually death. Most of our mental energy is literally thrown away every day in this self-destructive manner. Once the mind is freed from the source of these 50,000 thoughts -- the defenses, complexes and addictive compulsions of our habitual beliefs and judgments -- the energy of complete consciousness rises up the spine, enlivening each of the seven chakras, resulting in permanent inner silence, perfect awareness of the Ascendant and complete bliss.

Śiva and Śakti

In the ancient Sanskrit language of the fully enlightened, this process of growth of consciousness is described as the ecstatic union of Kuṇḍalinī Śakti with her divine lover, Śiva. Śakti sleeps in the first chakra at the base of the spine; Śiva lives alone in the crown. When enlightenment dawns, Śakti rises from the base and marries Śiva in the crown; they then move together to dwell forever in the heart. Their merging expresses the experience of Ascending: subject/object duality is abandoned for Infinite bliss, Eternal love.

Kuṇḍalin means "coiled" or "spiral" and refers to the spiral patterns of energy found throughout the natural world, from the DNA molecule to the shape of sunflowers, from Earth's orbit around our sun to galaxies. With an "ī" added on the end, Kuṇḍalinī, it becomes a feminine noun which also means snake. A serpent rests in a coil and releases its energy when it straightens and strikes. Kuṇḍalinī is therefore symbolic of the primordial essence of nature, pre-rational, pre-verbal, capable of inflicting death if misused and yet also capable of giving complete healing if properly channeled. It is a symbol of the regenerative powers of the deepest levels of the personality, the source of creativity, intuition, miracle-power.

The Ascendant is often personified as Śiva, which means "kind, friendly, gracious, pleasant, auspicious, prosperous, happy." Śiva rules the Ānanda (bliss) quality of the Ascendant. The physical structure of the Universe is Śiva's lover, Śakti: "ability, capacity, power, strength, skill". Śakti represents the Holy Spirit in Christian terminology, the Power of God manifest in the created Universe, Mother Nature. When giving form to the formless, She is called Māyā Śakti. Māyā means illusion; it comes from ma, "that not" & ya, "which": "that which is not," or from ma -- "to measure, to form, to display" : "that which displays or forms" . From Her divine imagination, Māyā Śakti conjures up the great illusion of the Universe by veiling the Ascendant in matter. The True Nature of life is hidden from our obscured minds because of Māyā's power.

Śakti is also considered the Revealer of Truth and the Great Liberator. All she brings into temporary existence will someday return to its original essence in the Ascendant. This function is personified as either Kuṇḍalinī or the awe-inspiring Kali (literally "time, strife, dissension"). To the ego-centered person attached to the material world, Kali is a wrathful and horrifying goddess of destruction. But to those in search of liberation from the illusion of suffering and ego-identification, she is a saviouress.

The imagery of Śiva and Śakti as lovers points toward their interdependence. Although apparently separate, they are in truth two complementary aspects of a single Unity; one does not exist without the other. The double-sexed Supreme Deity is thus both temporal and Infinite. Śiva is the unlimited whole, Śakti is the ongoing convergence of parts that make up the whole; Śiva is transcendent and changeless, Śakti is phenomenal and mutable. Śiva is the Lord of the Ascendant; Śakti is Mother Nature, creating the appearance of duality on the surface of perfect unity.

The seventh chakra, at the top of the head, is related to the original transcendental union of Śiva and Śakti. In the sixth chakra, in the center of the head, Śakti separates from Śiva and creates the mind and the intellect. The five remaining chakras, located from the neck to the pelvis, represent the five stages of progressive crystallization of the Ascendant into matter: ether, air, fire, water and earth. Each stage is denser as it contracts out of the previous element, until the ultimate limit of solidity is formed in earth.

Śakti is often pictured as dancing, wearing a tinkling anklet. As the rhythms of her dance increase in complexity and passion, the fabric of the Universe is woven in seven layers of increasing density. Thus the seven chakras of the microcosm in the human are the reflections of this seven-fold division of the macrocosm.

After Māyā Śakti creates the world, she as if hibernates in the depths of the material Universe -- in the root chakra at the base of the spine, in the earth element. While Kuṇḍalinī Śakti sleeps, our lives are dominated by the blind forces of the instincts, desires and concepts of the ego. The purpose of Yoga is to withdraw this divine energy from the ego's belief systems and direct it back up the central channel in the spine, the suṣumna. When this happens, Śakti manifests in each of the chakras and reveals higher and higher levels of consciousness. Ultimately our awareness is released from the limitations of the ego and partakes in the divine pleasure of Śiva and Śakti's ecstatic union: individuality rises consciously back to its source in Universality.

I. Mūladhara: The Survival Chakra

The root chakra lies at the base of the spine. It corresponds with the archetypal theme of the primal womb, a symbol of the original wholeness from which life developed. The ego in Mūladhara has not yet separated the world into duality, into the Knowledge of Good and Evil. Mūladhara literally means, "the support of the root" or "the bearer of the foundation" or "the keeper of the beginning." It is the source of the energy of life: Kuṇḍalinī lies coiled here, ready to manifest and awaken us to our true Selves. Mūladhara connects us to the most primitive realms of life, instinctual rapport with Mother Nature.

Mūladhara is often represented by a lotus with four red petals, symbolizing the other four elements contained within the earth element. Inside these four is frequently placed a yellow box which represents the earth element; inside that is an elephant with seven trunks, representing the supporting function of Mūladhara for the seven chakras. Elephants are symbols for earthly abundance and good fortune and are sacred to Indra, that aspect of Nature that rules the Natural Laws of Earth. Mūladhara is closely associated with returning karma, for it is on the earth that our karma is played out. It is the domain of form, rigidity and the inertia of tamas guṇa. In the terminology of Ayur Veda, it is the prime manifestation of Kapha in the body.

The root chakra translates the life force into survival, the root instinct. Confidence, trust and feeling safe are therefore functions of Mūladhara. Prenatal, birth and early life experiences create the stresses that lodge in Mūladhara. These early factors largely determine our orientation toward the world in all our subsequent years. If our early environment was safe and protective, filled with love and security, then trust in the world is usually well established. If, on the other hand, the environment of the womb and early life were disruptive or emotionally cold, than the stresses in the first chakra tend to make us see the world and other humans as frightening.

Being grounded and at one with life indicates a properly functioning first chakra. Sympathetic resonance with the electromagnetic frequency of the earth (7.8 Hz) is a function of Mūladhara; this is interrupted not only by stress but by air, water, food, and electromagnetic pollution. Being out of tune with the natural vibration of the earth leads to greater stress and eventually results in degeneration of tissues and organs and death.

II. Svādhiṣṭhāna: The Pleasure Chakra

Svādhiṣṭhāna means literally, "one's own place" or "one's sweetest abode." It is associated with the sexual organs. Symbolically, it is represented by a lotus with six saffron petals, symbolizing its secret connection with the Sixth State of Consciousness. Inside the flower is often a crescent moon, representing the water element, or the sea monster Makara (Leviathan in the West) symbolic of the mysterious powers hiding within the unconscious. Makara is sacred to Varuṇa, that aspect of Nature that rules the Natural Laws of the Ocean. The fragile ego may shrink in fear at confronting the awesome forces of the unconscious: Makara crashes its tiny island of belief with the omnipotence of tidal waves.

Svādhiṣṭhāna relates to the pre-rational Dream State of Consciousness. This chakra is the beginning of awakening to consciousness of feelings, both our own and others. Stress in Svādhiṣṭhāna frequently results from the early years in which we learned to differentiate ourselves from our mother and environment; stress here causes defenses or projected idealism to avoid being vulnerable to feelings. Because the second chakra is often quite blocked in the Waking State, the conscious mind is often uncomfortable with painful or powerful feelings. As Kuṇḍalinī rises from the first chakra, it may activate the stress in the second; this may cause us to seek union with another at any cost, using our lovers to fulfill our deep longing to unite with the other half of our soul. The phantom lover can appear as an incredibly seductive image projected from the unconscious depths of our personality; this can be a particularly painful distraction from the growth of consciousness.

As the second chakra is opened, the ability to feel both pleasure and pain increases. This ambivalence can make it a courageous task to move beyond defenses and regain the feeling self with its capacity for true intimacy. To heal the second chakra, it is necessary to let go of past fears, disillusionments and disappointed romantic expectations. Celibacy is useless if the old scars have not been healed. Attempting to force feelings to our rigid control can develop over-protectiveness, clinging, anger, jealousy, unawareness of feelings, inability to receive love, or addiction to approval. When properly developed, Svādhiṣṭhāna produces the energy necessary to unite with another soul and fuels the growth of consciousness to enlightenment. Wholeness in the second chakra establishes a positive emotional identity: we know we are loved and lovable; we accept our feelings and realize that others accept our feelings; we can give emotional support without condition.

III. Maṇipura: The Power Chakra

Maṇipura means "shining like a pearl" or the "fortress (citadel) of the jewel." It is a lotus of ten yellow petals, frequently containing within it a red inverted triangle that symbolizes Agni, Lord of the Natural Laws that rule Fire. Maṇipura is the fullest embodiment of rajas guna in the body and is often pictured containing a ram, symbolic of Aries, fire, passion and the Ayur Vedic Pitta.

Located at the navel, the third chakra is the gathering point of the streams of subtle energy called naḍis that control all functions of the body. It regulates the flow of vital energies throughout the body. Patañjali says that through mastery of Maṇipura full knowledge and mastery of the body is attained (see III. 30, commentary).

It is here in the third chakra that we learn to assimilate the contents of the unconscious mind. As we do so, more spiritual energy becomes available to us; with this, our relationship with our body and with our world is healed. An undeveloped third chakra leads to power trips and the attempt to control others by forcing them to the ego's will. Arrogance stems from an undeveloped third; on the other hand, charm, warmth, generosity and a sunny disposition radiate from an open third.

IV. Anāhata:
The Love Chakra

The fourth chakra is located in the heart. Anāhata means, "new" or "not struck," which is a reference to the nature of the subtlest level of vibration, the universal sound of OM which is the first stage of manifestation of creation. Anāhata has twelve bright green petals; inside of which are two overlapping triangles, representative of the ability of the individual to evolve upward or devolve downward, depending on how this chakra is used. Anāhata represents the air element; and Vāyu, the Lord of the Natural Laws that rule the Wind.

Anāhata is the primary seat of the Ascendant in the body and therefore represents the union of individuality with Universality. This is the source of the Spiritual Fire, the purging fire of God's Love, the Sacred Fire of devotion and spiritual inspiration. This fire transforms our personal identity. Like the phoenix, the ego is consumed and transformed by the opening of the heart chakra. When Anāhata opens, a strong desire naturally comes for all beings to share in the love and peace of Infinite Awareness. In the Buddhist tradition, this urge is expressed by the Bodhisattva vow: "I will not leave the Earth until all beings gain enlightenment." This is pure expression of Compassion, one of the most important qualities of enlightenment.

All forms of romantic love are motivated by the search for union with the Source of Love. The highest form and fulfillment of romantic love comes when we learn to love unconditionally, to accept with complete understanding the other's feelings. This perfect openness and sincere surrender creates what is called a Holy Relationship. In time this spreads from the Ideal Couple to all beings, for energy flowing through the heart chakra transforms and neutralizes negative energy everywhere.

Many New Age teachings advocate developing the heart chakra. But if this attempt is made without first releasing the ego drives of the lower three chakras -- such as anger, depression, arrogance, desperation, emotional insecurity -- love cannot flow freely. Attempting to force love is not the same thing as a spontaneous outpouring of love; this can lead to highly undesirable results.

The conquest of a dragon or a monster by a hero in order to free a maiden is a common archetypal theme in mythology. Some examples: Theseus kills the Minotaur to save Ariadne from the labyrinth in Crete; Perseus cuts off Medusa's head to overcome the dragon holding Andromeda prisoner; St. George slays the dragon to save the fair princess. Monsters and dragons cannot enjoy the maiden or the wealth they horde; they keep these treasures simply to possess them. The dragon represents the ego out of control; the romance between the freed maiden and the rescuing hero symbolizes the union of the fruitful, intuitive and mystical aspects of the subconscious and the evolving soul. This is the archetypal image behind all romantic love. But we don't often recognize this as the source of our desire for the knight in shining armor or for the chaste princess. Each person can recognize his or her innate wholeness and the unconditional love in that which has been projected onto the beloved. The Holy Relationship then serves as an external vehicle for translating this inner experience to the world. Every act of sincere love enlivens our environment.

Through nourishing others with divine love, we are automatically transported beyond the limitations of personal, self-oriented reality. Fully evolved Beings such as Christ or Buddha (Buddha means "enlightened one") are windows into the spiritual depths in us all. The radiance that shines through them awakens us from our worldly ego-dreams into compassion and unconditional love. The Buddhists tell a story about a monk so ugly and deformed no one would give him alms. He often felt rejected and alone. Buddha observed the plight of this monk and manifested himself in a body that was even more grotesque. When the monk saw this wretched creature coming through the forest, he was filled with perfect compassion. The depth of his emotion was so great that he automatically gained full enlightenment.

V. Viśuddha: The Chakra of Miracles

Viśuddha means "purified," "simplified," "sanctified," "freed from doubt." The fifth chakra, located at the base of the throat, opens when Perpetual Consciousness is established, and therefore marks the complete passage of consciousness beyond the instinctive, reactive and habitual realm of the ego into the Eternal Freedom of Divine Consciousness -- into the perfect choice of life lived in the Now. Its element is ākaśa -- the ether -- the Unified Field of all the Laws of Nature out of which the four grosser elements come. Its lotus consists of sixteen blue petals and often includes a white circle, symbolizing the ether and the completion of Perpetual Consciousness, an inverted triangle, symbolizing the feminine powers of Nature, and often a white elephant, holding one of its seven trunks up into the air, symbolizing the victory over the instinctive forces of the lower chakras.

As the manifestation of ākaśa in the body, Viśuddha represents the origin of all sounds and vibrations. Mastery of the fifth chakra creates the ability to hear all sounds and understand all languages including those far removed (e.g., clairaudience; mental telepathy), those of the birds and animals and those which are celestial or inner (e.g., the gods, devas and elementals). From the sounds or vibrations of Nature come the specific attributes of everything; hence all forms of knowledge are contained within the sound of all objects in creation. Mastery of Viśuddha implies the ability to do anything desired: manifest any desired situation or alter any physical form. For example, it is said that those who have mastered Satya, truthfulness of speech, can speak anything and have it come true. Viśuddha is thus a primary tool in Healing.

We are all already continually creating our world with our desires, thoughts, beliefs, prejudices. The more we evolve in consciousness, the more our individual reality is aligned and unified with the whole of existence. It is not that we become better at creating reality; every human being is already perfect at that. But we do become better at changing our viewpoint to a wholly positive, evolutionary and Cosmic perspective. And this means that the whole of Nature supports our every desire, for our every desire is the same as God's desire.

Any voice has the power to transform a person's life, but this power is not often appropriately or consistently used. The voice contains complete information about the speaker. To a skilled listener, every voice reveals full knowledge of the speaker's emotions and mental orientation. One certain way to become more effective in life is to communicate more clearly. Often the voice is revealing double messages. When something is being requested, the underlying message is often, "I don't deserve this," or "It will never work out," or "They'll never do this for me." The secret of true communication is in saying only one thing at a time. This comes from mastering listening. When we begin to listen to the personal subconscious, we can sort out the programming and desires that are inappropriate. Erasing these old programs and replacing them with growth-enhancing patterns gives us greater access to the Ascendant, to health and to life.

A current example of the misuse of the power of speech and of Viśuddha is in an imbalanced use of affirmations. There are a number of different teachings today that encourage a constant repetition of positive or idealized statements. One unfortunate effect of this is a polarization between conscious ideals and the unconscious belief systems of the destructive internal programming. If we fail to recognize, accept and change unconscious emotional and psychological imprints, these forceful tactics of the ego will only serve to create tension and resistance in the personality and can lead to a dangerous split between the conscious and unconscious minds.

The highest use of Viśuddha is prayer. Most today think of prayer as a request (or a demand) for God to fulfill desires. Prayer in its true sense, however, is a form of communication between the soul and the Higher Powers in Nature. Prayers are thought forms that can filled with information from deeper levels of the personality, from spiritual beings on the higher planes or from the Ascendant itself. Prayer can be considered a way of asking for what is best from the perspective of the higher or highest levels in Creation. It is a way of opening to Truth, to create the necessary conditions to be receptive to the Rain of Grace descending from the spiritual dimensions. Prayer is a way of orienting the limited self to the Universal Self. The positive results of prayer are in no way related to our beliefs about God; what is important is that we address ourselves to our conception of the Highest Force for Good, whatever we may call It or whatever we may believe about It. Thus true prayer *is* Ascension and Ascension *is* true prayer.

VI. Ājñā:
The Third Eye

Ājñā means "servant" or "ordered from above" or "not ignorant." It consists of two petals, often represented as connected to a disc of the moon. This chakra is the reservoir for Soma. As such, the sixth chakra is referred to as the ocean of nectar. Inside the lunar disc is often an inverted triangle, symbolic of the feminine power of Śakti; frequently a liṅgam (symbolic of Śiva) is inside that. This same configuration is also often found in the root and heart chakras; it is in these three that the conjoined power of Śiva and Śakti is the strongest. The root is the seat of the physical body; the heart is the seat of the emotional body; the sixth is the seat of the mental body.

Ājñā is called the third eye because of its potential for celestial perception, clairvoyance, the ability to perceive the subtle energies of non-physical realms, and fully established Exalted Consciousness. Seeing auras, knowing the future, remembering past lives, communicating with celestial beings are some of the abilities that are available to any human with an awakened sixth.

Ājñā is located in the center of the head. Its two petals are associated with the left and right hemispheres of the cortex. The left hemisphere is predominately analytical, logical, mathematical and linear. It is masculine or yang and controls the right side of the body. The right hemisphere is primarily spatial, artistic, musical, intuitive, holistic and is considered receptive, yin, feminine. It controls the left side of the body. The forward facing petal of Ājñā (nearer the forehead) is associated with the rational qualities of consciousness. The rear petal near the center of the skull is more intuitive.

In our modern world, over-emphasis on left-brain activity has upset the balance of the sixth chakra. We often misuse the power inherent in awareness. We desire to understand what is happening in our world to gain control over it or protect ourselves from it. By watching life in order to manipulate it, control it or criticize it, we place ourselves out of touch with and opposed to reality. This is like finding ourselves in a rushing river and holding onto the bank because we are afraid to let go. Will we be swept away and drowned? Will we be crushed by the raging torrent? Who knows! Until we let go and flow, we will never find out where the River of Life is trying to take us. Maybe it will carry us to paradise!

If the sixth chakra is intensely blocked, we may desire not to see at all. This can result in intense rebellion against our parents or our society, or, in extreme cases, to weak vision or even to blindness or deafness. It is not *what* we see but *how* we see that determines our experience. If we see a rope lying on the ground and mistake it for a snake, our hearts may stop from fear of something that was never there. Our experience of reality is based on projection of our beliefs and judgments. When Caucasians first came to the Sandwich Islands and fired their cannons, the natives did not hear the violent noise, because such things were impossible in their world. We tend to laugh at their ignorance, but everyone in the Waking State is equally caught by the incessant demands of the ego and its view of the Universe.

When both the petals of Ājñā are in balance, the individual is open and receptive to the world, to emotions and to intuition. Instead of manipulating life, the inherent nature of the Universe is directly understood; life is lived in harmony with Natural Law. Intellect and intuition complement and complete each other. Latent intuitive abilities open new vistas; we perceive our essential unity with all that is. Celestial perception is the norm. Leaving through Ājñā at the time of death is the Lunar Path, the Path of the Gods.

VII. Sahasrara:
The Crown

Sahasrara means, "granting victory" or "producing might" or "possessing one thousand." Sahasrara is represented by a thousand-petalled lotus, with each of the fifty letters of the Sanskrit alphabet written on it twenty times. Inside the lotus is often a crescent moon representing Soma; an inverted triangle, representing the three parts of OM; and rays indicating the light of immortality that radiates from Sahasrara. The thousand-petalled lotus is centered in the anterior fontanel -- the soft spot on babies' heads. When the soft spot hardens, beginning at about six months, the infant's Infinite Awareness is shrouded. The ego with its dreams of separation and limitation comes back to life at this time. If one leaves through Sahasrara at the time of death, one is freed from the cycle of death and involuntary rebirth. This is called the Solar Path, the Path of the Sages. Radiating from its perfect whiteness is the amṛta, the nectar of immortality. Omniscient Wisdom is seated in the crown.

If the seventh chakra is closed, the accumulated wisdom and purpose of the soul through its many births remains unconscious. On the other hand, an open seventh becomes a channel of communication to the higher soul, Cosmic Mind. The soul is often compared to the Sun; its various incarnations are like the planets. From the perspective of a planet, all the other planets are either ahead of it or behind it in their orbits. But when the soul remembers its True Nature, these other lifetimes can be experienced simultaneously from its other-dimensional perspective. During the final stages of the soul's journey on the Earth, then, all its lifetimes are brought clearly into focus for the purpose of gaining complete wisdom.

We have been conditioned by our beliefs about reality, but eventually we relinquish our attachment to the dramas that have composed our world views. Through myriad incarnations, we discover more and more of our innate wisdom. After numerous experiments, we gradually unfold our True Nature -- Sat-Chit-Ānanda, Absolute Bliss Consciousness. We remember that we are indivisible rays of the One Unchanging.

Beyond form, beyond thought, beyond concepts of being or non-being, our individual consciousness plunges into the fathomless sea of the Clear Light of the Ascendant through the Golden Doors of Being in the crown chakra. As we integrate this ultimate experience, we begin to identify with the whole living through its myriad parts. The individual body-mind recognizes that it is a conscious hologram of the entire Universe. There is nothing left to do but Be, allowing the flow of creation to pass through us unobstructed. This is the doorway to immortality, for the individual has become an incarnate expression of All-That-Is. A life of service and cooperation with Cosmic Forces begins and continues forever.

Jai Īśam Īśvaram

INDEX

ALSO BY MSI:

First Thunder, An Adventure of Discovery

This is the story of the first Westerner to visit a secret Order of monks called the Ishayas. The Order was founded by the Apostle John after he wrote the Apocalypse. What the Ishayas preserved in their monastery was a series of techniques for tapping into the subtlest energy of who we are. These techniques are called Ascension. First Thunder is written like an adventure novel – it is a great introduction to what the Ishayas are teaching and at the same time is a wonderful story. First Thunder is the ideal book to introduce people to the experiential techniques taught by the Ishayas. $12.95.

ASCENSION! An Analysis of the Art of Ascension as Taught by the Ishayas

This book clearly explains the ancient teachings of the Ishayas, an ancient order of monks who were entrusted by the Apostle John to preserve the original teachings of Christ until the third millennium. The Ishayas hold that the original teachings of Jesus were not a belief system at all, rather a mechanical series of techniques to transform human life into a constant perception of the perfection within the human heart. Real expansion of consciousness occurs only through direct, personal experience. Ascension! is an invitation to awaken to the innermost Reality of your wonderful, exalted soul. This text also includes a description of the Ishayas' 27 Ascension Attitudes. $11.95.

SECOND THUNDER Seeking the Black Ishayas

This and the subsequent volumes of the Thunder series are visionary works. They are expressions of where we've come from and where we're going; they are a report on the human condition; they are statements of Universal Consciousness. Second Thunder shares a Visionary Truth, an expression of the highest aspirations of our souls. $17.95.

About the Author MSI

"In an instant of frozen time, no longer than the gap between two heartbeats, a being fully and permanently in contact with the Source Universe shared his vision with me. This was a free gift, a wordless joining of his infinite mind with mine.

In the years that have passed since that magical, suspended instant, I have only begun to appreciate what this means to my life, to remember that which I long ago knew fully well but then forgot. I am an Unbounded Being. Living in a human body, I experience the Ascendant continually, twenty-four hours a day. The Thunder books are an attempt to explain this state of consciousness, to describe the Reality of the wonder of this experience." – from MSI's Introduction to <u>Second Thunder</u>

MSI personally trains teachers of the Seven Spheres described in his books. He presently resides at the Society for Ascension's Academy in the Great Smoky Mountains in North Carolina.

Instruction in the Ishaya's Ascension is available only through personal instruction from a qualified teacher. For more information about the Seven Spheres, courses of instruction, or in-residence teaching training, please write or call:

Society for Ascension
130 Biodome Drive
Waynesville, NC 28786
(704) 926-7853

Any of the books may be ordered from the same address. Please include \$3.00 shipping and handling. Quantity discounts are available on bulk purchases. **Attention Book stores and distributors:** Call SFA Publications at (704)926-7853 for wholesale ordering.